MORDENKAINEN'S MAGNIFICENT EMPORIUM

ROLEPLAYING GAME SUPPLEMENT

Jeremy Crawford ✦ Stephen Schubert ✦ Matt Sernett

CREDITS

Design
Tavis Allison, Scott Fitzgerald Gray,
Robert J. Schwalb, Matt Sernett, Jeff Tidball

Additional Design
Richard Baker, Eytan Bernstein, Greg Bilsland,
Logan Bonner, Mike Mearls, Claudio Pozas,
Chris Sims, James Wyatt

Development
Jeremy Crawford (lead), Stephen Schubert

Editing
Cal Moore (lead), Tanis O'Connor

Managing Editor
Kim Mohan

D&D R&D Senior Producer
Christopher Perkins

D&D R&D Group Manager
Mike Mearls

Playtesters
Aaron Brosman, Angela Amburn, Brittani-Pearl Macfadden,
Bryan Amburn, Cliff Thrasher, Douglas Kilpatrick, Galen
Mullins, Greg Hartman, Ian Ramsey, James Auwaerter,
Jeffrey Barnes, John Stanford, Jonathan D'Silva, Jordan
Conrad, Keith Richmond, Kevin Lawson, Krishna Simonse,
Lori Anderson, Matthew Fuchs, Nicholas Wolfanger,
Patrick Neal, Sarah LaValle, Shawn Merwin, Todd Keck,
Tom Dale, Tony Lawrence

D&D Senior Creative Art Director
Jon Schindehette

Art Director
Kate Irwin

Cover Illustration
William O'Connor

Graphic Designer
Yasuyo Dunnett

Interior Illustrations
Vincent Dutrait, Emrah Elmasli, Wayne England, Brian
Hagan, Jeff Himmelman, Tyler Jacobson, Michael Komarck,
Howard Lyon, Warren Mahy, David Martin, Jim Nelson,
William O'Connor, Hector Ortiz, Marc Sasso, Chris
Seaman, Cynthia Sheppard, John Stanko, Beth Trott, Franz
Vohwinkel, Eva Widermann, Ben Wootten

Publishing Production Specialist
Erin Dorries

Prepress Manager
Jefferson Dunlap

Imaging Technician
Carmen Cheung

Production Manager
Cynda Callaway

Game rules based on the original DUNGEONS & DRAGONS® rules
created by **E. Gary Gygax** and **Dave Arneson**, and the later
editions by **David "Zeb" Cook** (2nd Edition); **Jonathan Tweet,
Monte Cook, Skip Williams, Richard Baker,** and **Peter
Adkison** (3rd Edition); and **Rob Heinsoo, Andy Collins,** and
James Wyatt (4th Edition).

620-28069000-001 EN
ISBN: 978-0-7869-5744-6

First Printing:
September 2011
9 8 7 6 5 4 3 2 1

U.S., CANADA, ASIA, PACIFIC,
& LATIN AMERICA
Wizards of the Coast LLC
P.O. Box 707
Renton WA 98057-0707
+1-800-324-6496

EUROPEAN HEADQUARTERS
Hasbro UK Ltd
Caswell Way
Newport, Gwent NP9 0YH
GREAT BRITAIN
Please keep this address for your records

WIZARDS OF THE COAST, BELGIUM
Industrialaan 1
1702 Groot-Bijgaarden
Belgium
+32.070.233.277

Visit our website at DungeonsandDragons.com

CONTENTS

MICHAEL KOMARCK

Introduction

The years die, burned to nothing by time, darkening my memory with their passing—like soot that builds upon a hearth beam. I am Mordenkainen, and although I do not look it, I am old. I have outlived rivals, enemies, and friends. I have lived long enough to see rivals become friends and friends become enemies—and to see enemies returned to the fold of friendship. But for a few dust-mad liches dreaming in their lonely tombs, my friends and I represent the last of the old guard. Who born in the last forty years can measure of themselves an ounce of the worth of Otiluke, Bigby, Tenser, or Robilar—or even Rary or Evard?

Bah! What does it matter? I grow self-pitying as I approach the end of a century. Surely the young fools who test the wards upon my vaults are no younger or more foolish than my companions and I were when we delved into the dungeons of Castle Greyhawk or Maure Castle. They all have their reasons, just as we did long ago.

And what are those reasons? What draws adventurers today to plumb the death-trap depths of the earth and brave the terrors of curse-bound ruins? What called us to do the same in the past—and drives me still?

It all boils down to power: the wealth that can buy it, and the magic that can wrest it from the ether.

Once I sought power for its own sake. Now I seek it to keep it from others. I do not wish to rule the world—only my small part of it. Yet many are the grasping hands of those who would claim control. Some use evil means toward such ends, while others pursue a more virtuous path, but regardless of the manner of its acquisition, power wielded to dictate over all is power used to disastrous effect. Friends will be lost, great works will be cast to ruin, and wars will be fought, but none shall gain the upper hand over all as long as I and the Circle of Eight remain.

We balance the scales.

In some cases, that means a feather's touch: a word or two in the right ear, an heir spirited away from assassins, or a storm to cast a ship off course—simple feats accomplished with a trifling of magic. At other times, circumstances dictate that our hand falls more heavily. Fortunate for us and the world that those times are few.

Too often, our actions hinge upon who possesses some item of power. Those whom we oppose might have dug up some relic of antiquity or simply taken one such from unwitting treasure hunters. To combat that imbalance, we arrange it so that those hunters or other adventurers win their way to the items necessary to destroy the relic. We set events into motion so that a magic shield finds its way onto the arm of a certain warrior. Our enemies give that warrior a sword that corrupts him into a monster for their cause.

Of course, not all magic items represent pieces on the chessboard. Steeped in the power of magic as we of the Circle are, it can be easy to forget that fact.

When you watch a feather drift to the surface of the water and it expands into a boat before your eyes, how can you do anything but marvel? And no matter how many times you pull forth a swatch of cloth and unfold it to reveal its hidden contents, the wonder of that moment never diminishes.

Even those items that present a more obvious threat can be joyful things. The cloak that renders you unseen can be used to great effect by those with ambition, or for thrills by those who are simply curious or mischievous. The sword forged by angels might cut a swath through the orcs, gnolls, and ogres of the world, or it might simply protect a farmer's sheep from wolves.

After all, most magic items—even those made with evil intent—are not themselves evil. They do not of themselves seek dominion over the world. That is a trait particular to their wielders.

Of course, what evil can be wrought by an item in the wrong hands depends much upon the item itself. That is why I seek to know ever more about the magic items of this world—and others.

It might surprise some that I write of other worlds. And no, I do not imply other planes, but other places—places filled with various lands and countries with inhabitants that see themselves as the most important and central to the universe, just as we do.

I care little for them, as I am from this world, this Oerth. Just as these other worlds have similar magic items, I'm sure there are some among them who serve as I and the Circle of Eight do. Let them sort out their own problems; we have enough of our own.

I have recorded the stories for the items I encountered from these other worlds so that they can be known for what they are should they find their way into our own. Often their properties are shockingly similar to items that can be discovered all over Oerth, so the idea of items (and perhaps other travelers like myself) passing between worlds might not be so far-fetched.

By cataloguing what exists—and what is rumored to exist—I hope to be forewarned of the danger of any item when it falls into the wrong hands. Soon I will share this knowledge—if not with the world, then with the Circle of Eight. Surely someone besides myself should be armed with this knowledge.

I suppose, if you are reading this, I have already chosen to share it. In that case, I hope you take what you learn here and put it to sensible use. I would not have this book used as some plunderer's to-do list! Instead, tread lightly, act wisely, be wary, and be well.

—Mordenkainen, from his secret master copy of the *Magnificent Emporium* before he burned its pages and then disintegrated the ash.

Scholar's Note: This excerpt and others to follow were gleaned from the original master text during the production of one of its eight copies. As a former apprentice to Mordenkainen, please understand that I take my life in my hands by disseminating his work without his permission. Please treat this text with the utmost care and secrecy.

—Qort

THE PROMISES OF MAGIC

The crystal sphere glowing upon its pedestal, the jewel-encrusted sword jutting from a heap of gold, the embossed breastplate glittering in the depths of a murky pool, the gloves that slip on like a second skin, the dusty tome laden with inscribed spells, the bottle that holds a swirling blue liquid—these items promise magic, and magic promises power. It might be the power to dominate others, but it might also be the power to do something extraordinary such as walking through a wall, seeing through stone, or taking flight. All kinds of magic await you in the pages of this book. How you use it is up to you.

Making Magic Items Magical

Mordenkainen's Magnificent Emporium supplements your DUNGEONS & DRAGONS game in a new way. Of course, it presents items galore of all types, but this tome also puts a lot of emphasis on the fun elements of an item's history, appearance, or folklore.

The goal of this treatment is to make magic items more magical. Some players see magic items as rules elements to acquire rather than objects of wonder. That's fine if that's how you want to play, but if you're looking for more engaging items and you want to bring a sense of excitement back to their acquisition, *Mordenkainen's Magnificent Emporium* can help.

Many of the items in this book were created by writing their descriptions and story elements first. The rules for how the items work were developed after that. That's the reverse of how magic items have been typically designed.

SELLING MAGIC ITEMS

Each of the magic items in this book has a rarity, either common, uncommon, or rare, that affects how much a seller can expect to receive for it.

Uncommon and rare items, made during an earlier age through methods no longer understood, are so valuable that they cannot normally be purchased—they can be gained only as treasure. Anyone who chooses to sell such an item, assuming a buyer can be found, can expect to receive the full given sale price for a rare item, and 50 percent of the sale price for an uncommon item.

The knowledge of crafting common items still remains in the world, however, and such items can be bought and sold more easily (though they are by no means available on every street corner). Adventurers who want to sell common magic items can expect to receive 20 percent of their sale price, since the demand for such items is relatively low.

This change in how an item is designed puts the inspiring elements about an item front and center instead of its game rule information. Rules elements can be made unique and fun, but without good story elements to support them, they tend to be a little dry. Hopefully, you'll take inspiration from what you find in this book to make your game more fun.

HOW TO USE THIS BOOK

For the Dungeon Master: You can simply use this book as another resource to stock treasure troves, but there are other ways *Mordenkainen's Magnificent Emporium* can enhance your game. Look at the stories about these magic items as an additional resource for you. An Arcana check can tell the players the history of an item, but that aspect of an item can become much more engaging by incorporating it into the history of your world or its current events.

For instance, the ruling line of a kingdom might consider a certain item a part of its regalia of rulership. Once it goes missing, the heroes could become embroiled in the politics of the realm and the history of the item as they seek whomever stole it.

A wizard might discover the means to create some useful item whose power was thought lost to the ages. The characters might seek out this wizard in order to obtain the item, only to discover that many others have had the same idea.

For Players: Common magic items that a character might find for sale are presented throughout this book, and you can use *Mordenkainen's Magnificent Emporium* as a resource for character building. If you're inclined, you can put together a short wish list of rare and uncommon items you'd like your character to find.

Perhaps some item that was a family heirloom for generations has been lost or stolen. Maybe a relative whom your character admires was an adventurer and was lost with the item in some famous dungeon. The item could have been passed down to a rival branch of your family or clan.

You might face the destiny of being saddled with a cursed item when you reach a certain age. Maybe your family rid itself of a curse that had long plagued it, but a seer has predicted its return to your hands.

Alternatively, your character might be fated to claim some great weapon and use it to defeat an equally great evil. Or you could seek an item to prove your claim to a birthright.

Perhaps you belong to a family or a cult dedicated to the eradication of the works of some spellcaster, and you seek several items in order to destroy them before they can be used for evil. The possibilities are limited only by your imagination.

CHAPTER 1

Armor

As a *puissant fighting man, Robilar of course wore armor of all sorts throughout his career, and I owe much of my practical knowledge of the topic to watching him in battle and due to a small amount of his instruction. Of course, I've scoured libraries for information about magical armor, studied the many suits I've discovered in treasure troves or peeled off the smoking remains of my foes, and naturally I have created many such items as part of my own aspirations for protecting myself and those in my employ.*

I find that those who wield swords place a great deal of importance on shields. It's a natural blindness of most melee combatants to emphasize protecting themselves against the kinds of attacks they make with their own weapons. When you see what the edge of a sword does to the bared flesh of an enemy, you cannot help but think of your own body cut and your own blood shed. A suit of shining mail seems a great boon, and if it can be enchanted to ward off arrows or deflect a giant's hammer, so much the better.

I find such thinking is often shortsighted. Does lightning glance away from that breastplate? How will chain links protect you from seeping acid? When does fire not burn skin, and what is leather if not skin? Is it not better to be a swift-stinging wasp or a nigh-invisible gnat than an armored beetle waddling underfoot?

Of course, at times you must play anvil to the hammer's blow. Some threats cannot be avoided. Someone must meet the enemy face on and hurl flesh at foe. And at these times—when steel must stop a dragon's charge—I am grateful to my shortsighted allies for their blind faith in the strength of armor.

Their deaths give me time to complete my spells.

I should perhaps not have written that last sentence, but as a guide to the magic items of this world and others, I think truth should play the paramount role. And the truth is that we wizards cannot always rely upon spells alone. If you spend your time summoning beasts, raising protective fields of force, and warding yourself against unearthly energies, when do you have time to assault your enemy? An armored warrior between you and your target proves both a distraction for your foe and a natural bulwark. And that ally will be more confident in his role (and will last longer) if girded in enchanted armor.

—Mordenkainen, from his master copy of the *Magnificent Emporium*, on a magically hidden page accessible only by those who can cast spells

BEN WOOTTEN

New Armor and Shields

Many kinds of armor and shields are designed to provide a barrier against harm and little else. For most adventurers, protection from a troll's club or a drow's poisoned blade is all that's needed. However, some rarer types of armor provide added benefits and features. This book introduces new, exotic armors that have more to offer than the more common options.

Although these new kinds of armor and shields are useful, they demand specialized training to utilize them. The feats presented on page 11 allow characters to use these items without restriction.

Reading the Armor and Shields Table

An entry on the Armor and Shields table contains the following information.

Armor/Shield: The armor or shield's name.

Armor Bonus: The armor bonus to AC that a creature gains while wearing the armor.

Shield Bonus: The shield bonus to AC and Reflex that a creature gains while using the shield.

Check: The penalty to Strength-, Dexterity-, and Constitution-based skill checks that a creature takes while wearing the armor or using the shield. This penalty is called an armor check penalty. It does not apply to ability checks (such as a Strength check to break down a door or a Dexterity check to determine initiative in combat).

Speed: The penalty to speed that a creature takes while wearing the armor or using the shield.

Price: The item's cost in gold pieces.

Weight: The armor or shield's weight.

Properties: An item's properties. See below for new definitions.

Base Type: A suit of armor or a shield counts as the indicated type for the purpose of determining what magical properties it can gain.

Armor and Shield Properties

Barbed: A suit of barbed armor or a barbed shield is covered with spikes and hooks designed to injure creatures foolish enough to grab at it.

While you wear barbed armor or wield a barbed shield, a creature takes damage equal to 2 + one-half your level when you escape that creature's grab on your turn or when that creature escapes your grab. If you wear barbed armor and carry a barbed shield at the same time, the creature takes this damage only once.

Durable: A suit of durable armor gives added protection by absorbing some of the force from attacks. However, in doing so, the armor takes damage.

The first time you take damage during an encounter, reduce that damage by an amount equal to the armor's durability rating (for instance, 2 for ring mail). The armor then loses this property until you repair it during a short rest or an extended rest.

Durable armor provides greater damage absorption when it is enchanted. Add the enhancement bonus of the armor to the durability rating of light armor, and add twice the enhancement bonus to the durability rating of heavy armor.

Tough: Tough armor is reinforced with additional plates designed to protect vulnerable areas.

The first time in each encounter a critical hit is scored against your AC while you're wearing tough armor, the critical hit becomes a normal hit.

ARMOR AND SHIELDS

Armor	Armor Bonus	Check	Speed	Price (gp)	Weight	Properties	Base Type
Studded leather (light)	+3	–	–	35	28 lb.	Tough	Leather
Ring mail (light)	+3	-1	–	40	30 lb.	Durable 2	Chainmail
Banded mail (heavy)	+6	-1	-1	55	35 lb.	Tough	Chainmail
Splint mail (heavy)	+7	-2	-1	50	55 lb.	Durable 3	Scale
Spiked plate (heavy)	+8	-3	-1	55	60 lb.	Barbed	Plate
Full plate (heavy)	+8	-1	-1	65	60 lb.	Tough	Plate

Shield	Shield Bonus	Check	Speed	Price (gp)	Weight	Properties	Base Type
Barbed shield	+2	-3	–	20	18 lb.	Barbed	Heavy

Ring mail

Spiked plate

Studded leather

Banded mail

Some warriors care more about what their armor looks like than the protection it offers. Others wear mismatched motleys of plates and leather like some sort of badge of honor. Personally, if you're relying on bits of leather and metal for fashion or protection, I think you're in trouble.

Splint mail

WAYNE ENGLAND

Armor and Shield Descriptions

Banded Mail: Banded mail consists of a suit of chainmail reinforced with layers of metal plates arranged in strips along the suit's midsection. Banded mail offers the same level of protection as chainmail while proving lighter and more flexible. A warrior in banded mail moves as quickly as one in leather armor.

Barbed Shield: Although a shield is usually a defensive item, a barbed shield turns the tables on attackers because of the long spikes and blades attached to it. While too awkward to use as a weapon, a barbed shield provides added protection against enemies that attempt to grab you, because the spikes and barbs built into it cut into them.

Barbed shield

Full Plate: Though the dwarves are loath to admit it, human smiths crafted the first suits of full plate for the use of mounted knights. Of course, the dwarves are quick to add, they did perfect those initial, flawed designs. Among all the kinds of heavy armor, full plate offers unmatched protection and flexibility.

Ring Mail: This flexible but sturdy armor consists of a typical suit of leather armor with a series of metal rings sewn onto its surface. The rings enhance the armor's sturdiness, improving its protective qualities while still offering the maneuverability of lightweight armor.

Spiked Plate: A dwarven innovation, spiked plate is a suit of plate mail studded with sharp, metal spikes. The dwarves developed this armor to deal with subterranean beasts such as hook horrors and umber hulks that grasp and crush their prey.

Splint Mail: First developed by the dwarves, splint mail consists of vertical strips of metal bound to a thick layer of leather and chainmail. Because it is so heavy and ponderous, few other than dwarves wear it in battle. While it lacks the protective elements of plate, it is scale armor's equal. More important, its rigid construction allows it to absorb some portion of an enemy's blows.

Studded Leather: Studded leather is leather armor reinforced with metal studs. It provides a middle ground between hide armor and ring mail. It is more flexible than either, while its reinforced construction gives it a slight edge over hide.

Magic Armor Bonuses

Of course, magic armor provides an armor bonus to AC just as nonmagical armor does. But magic armor works a little differently, because its armor bonus often increases at higher levels rather than remaining a static value. As a set of armor receives more powerful magical enchantments, the armor improves due to a combination of rare materials and advanced techniques needed to allow it to hold the more powerful enchantments.

Consult the tables here to find out the total bonus to AC for a suit of armor based on its enhancement bonus and its armor bonus.

MAGIC RING MAIL

Level	Enhancement Bonus	Armor Bonus	Total Bonus to AC
1-5	+1	+3	+4
6-10	+2	+3	+5
11-15	+3	+3	+6
16-20	+4	+4	+8
21-25	+5	+4	+9
26-30	+6	+5	+11

MAGIC STUDDED LEATHER

Level	Enhancement Bonus	Armor Bonus	Total Bonus to AC
1-5	+1	+3	+4
6-10	+2	+3	+5
11-15	+3	+3	+6
16-20	+4	+4	+8
21-25	+5	+4	+9
26-30	+6	+5	+11

MAGIC BANDED MAIL

Level	Enhancement Bonus	Armor Bonus	Total Bonus to AC
1-5	+1	+6	+7
6-10	+2	+7	+9
11-15	+3	+8	+11
16-20	+4	+9	+13
21-25	+5	+10	+15
26-30	+6	+12	+18

MAGIC SPLINT MAIL

Level	Enhancement Bonus	Armor Bonus	Total Bonus to AC
1-5	+1	+7	+8
6-10	+2	+8	+10
11-15	+3	+9	+12
16-20	+4	+10	+14
21-25	+5	+11	+16
26-30	+6	+13	+19

MAGIC SPIKED PLATE AND FULL PLATE

Level	Enhancement Bonus	Armor Bonus	Total Bonus to AC
1-5	+1	+8	+9
6-10	+2	+9	+11
11-15	+3	+10	+13
16-20	+4	+11	+15
21-25	+5	+12	+17
26-30	+6	+14	+20

I encountered a certain thief wearing armor of escape. He proved quite troublesome when placed in both conventional and magical restraints. Once I determined that the armor was enchanted, I attempted to remove it. Of course, I failed—at least initially. Oddly, I found the application of sovereign glue to be the key to separating the thief from his protection. I simply adhered the suit to a boulder and pushed him down a well. I suppose he could thank the properties of the armor for his swift egress from the suit and return to the surface. That's a lesson about magic all would do well to mark: Beware overconfidence in an enchantment's intent, and be ready to use it in ways not intended.

ARMOR TRAINING FEATS

With new gear come new techniques and tactics for using it. The following feats are designed to interact with the armor and shields introduced in this book. All these feats are in the armor training category.

Armor Proficiency: Banded Mail

Prerequisite: Proficiency with chainmail
Benefit: You gain proficiency with banded mail.

Armor Proficiency: Full Plate

Prerequisite: Proficiency with plate armor
Benefit: You gain proficiency with full plate.

Armor Proficiency: Ring Mail

Prerequisite: Proficiency with hide armor or chainmail
Benefit: You gain proficiency with ring mail.

Armor Proficiency: Spiked Plate

Prerequisite: Proficiency with plate armor
Benefit: You gain proficiency with spiked plate.

Armor Proficiency: Splint Mail

Prerequisite: Proficiency with scale armor
Benefit: You gain proficiency with splint mail.

Armor Proficiency: Studded Leather

Prerequisite: Proficiency with hide armor
Benefit: You gain proficiency with studded leather armor.

Shield Proficiency: Barbed Shield

Prerequisite: Proficiency with heavy shields
Benefit: You gain proficiency with barbed shields.

Magic Armor

Whether crafted from metals carved from astral domains, forged in the first embers stoked by Moradin, or formed from the scales of a sea creature, magic armor provides unmatched protection.

Some suits of armor come with histories, rumors, and stories. A suit of magic plate recovered from an ancient tomb might have once belonged to a great emperor. Alternatively, the leather armor taken from a famous outlaw might be a red flag to any of that outlaw's allies and friends, making whoever wears it a prime target for assassination.

Armor of Dogged Grit

It has been suggested that a suit of armor of this sort—which is invariably dented, scarred, and worn, not to mention mismatched after decades of having demolished greaves, gauntlets, and buckles swapped in and out—gains its power by absorbing the endurance of those who have worn it over the ages. Such assertions are untrue but impossible to squelch; the truth is that the enchantments put on these suits can be imbued only in armor that has been well used and even abused.

An adventurer who wears *armor of dogged grit* is able to keep fighting through nearly any battle, no matter how many of the enemy's blows he or she must endure. The armor appears little better than a run-of-the-mill version of its kind at turning blows, but the one wearing it can fight on, even after suffering grievous harm, until the battle is won.

Armor of Dogged Grit			Level 7+ Uncommon		
While in this armor, you continue to fight on with grim determination, even though you absorb blows that would fell most combatants.					
Lvl 7	+2	2,600 gp	Lvl 22	+5	325,000 gp
Lvl 12	+3	13,000 gp	Lvl 27	+6	1,625,000 gp
Lvl 17	+4	65,000 gp			
Armor: Chain, scale, or plate					
Enhancement Bonus: AC					
Property					

Whenever you take 20 or more damage from an attack, you gain 5 temporary hit points at the end of the current turn.
> Level 12 or 17: Whenever you take 30 or more damage from an attack, you gain 10 temporary hit points at the end of the current turn.
> Level 22 or 27: Whenever you take 40 or more damage from an attack, you gain 15 temporary hit points at the end of the current turn.

Armor of Escape

No matter what shackles or bindings are used on the wearer of this armor, they are less effective at holding their prey. The obvious way to circumvent this armor—forcibly removing it—is impossible without the wearer's consent (or death).

Stories are still told in Hammerfast's taverns about one famous rogue from recent memory who escaped from the trade guild's dungeon thanks to her *armor of escape*. After being caught infiltrating the guild's treasury, she bluffed the guards into thinking that she was a spy sent by Mayor Goldspinner to test the treasury's defenses. Before they tried to remove her armor and gear, she convinced the guards to check her story with their captain. By the time they returned, now knowing her lie for what it was, she had made her exit.

Armor of Escape			Level 2+ Common		
Thanks to this armor, you shrug off shackles and bindings as easily as you would remove a pair of breeches.					
Lvl 2	+1	520 gp	Lvl 17	+4	65,000 gp
Lvl 7	+2	2,600 gp	Lvl 22	+5	325,000 gp
Lvl 12	+3	13,000 gp	Lvl 27	+6	1,625,000 gp
Armor: Any					
Enhancement Bonus: AC					
Property					

You gain an item bonus to escape attempts equal to 2 + the armor's enhancement bonus. In addition, this armor cannot be removed without your consent while you're living.

Armor of Scintillating Colors

This armor was created by an archmage indentured to an ancient king who sought to bedazzle even the gods with the splendor of his personage. It is said that the kingly armor the archmage created for his liege shone as brightly as the sun, and all who saw its brilliance were overcome by the wearer's majesty. The archmage assured his liege that the armor's magic would affect even those of immortal—perhaps even deific—power. However, the fact that neither the ancient monarch nor his *armor of scintillating colors* exists in any other stories suggests that either the enchanter's capabilities were not as great as he believed, or the archmage deliberately overstated the armor's power to rid himself of the megalomaniacal king. Whatever the case, a few powerful archmages have attempted to recreate this armor throughout the centuries, with limited success.

Armor of Scintillating Colors			Level 9+ Uncommon		
The majesty imbued upon you by this vibrant armor compels enemies in your presence to stand down.					
Lvl 9	+2	4,200 gp	Lvl 24	+5	525,000 gp
Lvl 14	+3	21,000 gp	Lvl 29	+6	2,625,000 gp
Lvl 19	+4	105,000 gp			
Armor: Cloth, leather, hide, or chain					
Enhancement Bonus: AC					
Property					

You gain an item bonus to Diplomacy checks and Intimidate checks equal to the armor's enhancement bonus.

☼ **Utility Power** (Aura, Charm) ✦ **Daily** (Minor Action)
> *Effect:* You activate an aura 2 that lasts until you attack, until the armor is removed, or until the end of the encounter. Whenever an enemy in the aura targets you with a melee or a ranged attack, it must first succeed on a saving throw to make the attack against you.

Blending armor

Armor of the Charging Wind

Warriors of the Feywild rely on speed and cunning as much as brute force. Where a dwarf warrior shrugs off attacks with his or her plate armor and hews an orc in half with an axe blow, an eladrin fighter dashes among his or her foes, dodging blows and making quick, sharp attacks at enemies' vulnerable areas. *Armor of the charging wind* embodies the latter fighting style by drawing on the power of elemental air and fey illusion magic to make its wearer as invisible as the rushing wind.

Armor of the Charging Wind				Level 5+ Uncommon	
This elegantly crafted armor allows you to rush unseen across the battlefield, moving like the wind.					
Lvl 5	+1	1,000 gp	Lvl 20	+4	125,000 gp
Lvl 10	+2	5,000 gp	Lvl 25	+5	625,000 gp
Lvl 15	+3	25,000 gp	Lvl 30	+6	3,125,000 gp
Armor: Cloth, leather, or hide					
Enhancement Bonus: AC					
Utility Power (Illusion) ✦ Encounter (Free Action)					
Trigger: You start a charge.					
Effect: You are invisible until the end of the current turn.					

Blending Armor

One ancient tale speaks of an entire army that moved over the land as if it were leaves blown by the wind, appearing suddenly upon the breeze. If the soldiers of such an army were all clad in *blending armor*, it is easy to understand the origin of that story. The colors and textures of *blending armor* continually blend and swirl to match its surroundings, erupting into a wild cacophony of movement when its wearer is in action and settling into a stable pattern when he or she is at rest. Whether worn by everyone in an army or by an individual, this armor makes it easy for its wearer to move stealthily and remain unnoticed.

Blending Armor				Level 9+ Uncommon	
When you move, this armor erupts into swirling colors whose palette is taken from the surrounding environment, obscuring your exact position.					
Lvl 9	+2	4,200 gp	Lvl 24	+5	525,000 gp
Lvl 14	+3	21,000 gp	Lvl 29	+6	2,625,000 gp
Lvl 19	+4	105,000 gp			
Armor: Cloth, leather, or hide					
Enhancement Bonus: AC					
Property					
You gain an item bonus to Stealth checks equal to the armor's enhancement bonus.					
Utility Power (Illusion) ✦ Encounter (Move Action)					
Effect: You gain a +2 power bonus to all defenses until the end of this turn, and you shift up to 3 squares.					

HOWARD LYON

Blessed Armor of Kord

It is said that *blessed armor of Kord* was worn by the deity himself during the war against the primordials. Over time, shards of that suit were scattered to the corners of the planes. A few of the armor's constituent pieces have been discovered in the millennia since those battles of antiquity—a greave, a vambrace, the gorget. Other parts of the original *blessed armor of Kord* no doubt still rest in ancient tombs and treasure hoards, waiting to be rediscovered. Suits of armor fashioned in recent times sometimes incorporate recovered scraps of the original. Such suits are also referred to as *blessed armor of Kord*, though they are but pale imitations of the original.

When any component of this suit is incorporated into a suit of ordinary armor, the whole becomes charged with the power of Kord, and its wearer can release discharges of lightning and thunder upon his or her enemies. It is thought that bringing several of the pieces of Kord's original armor together would increase these benefits exponentially, but this act has never been accomplished; some believe that the dissolution of the armor is Kord's will, and that to reunite the pieces would invite the god's disfavor.

Blessed Armor of Kord			Level 18+ Rare		
Charged with divine power, this armor lets you unleash Kord's mighty wrath on enemies who dare attack you.					
Lvl 18	+4	85,000 gp	Lvl 28	+6	2,125,000 gp
Lvl 23	+5	425,000 gp			
Armor: Chain, scale, or plate					
Enhancement Bonus: AC					

⚔ **Attack Power** (Lightning, Thunder) ✦ **Encounter** (Immediate Reaction)

Trigger: An enemy adjacent to you hits you.

Effect: Melee 1 (the enemy that hit you). The target takes 15 lightning and thunder damage.

Level 23 or 28: 20 lightning and thunder damage.

⚔ **Attack Power** (Lightning) ✦ **Daily** (Minor Action)

Effect: Close burst 2 (enemies in the burst). Each target takes 10 lightning damage.

Level 23 or 28: 15 lightning damage.

Doppelganger Armor

This strange armor has been mentioned in many tomes containing lore about enchanted items. Although every account describes each suit of *doppelganger armor* as having similar capabilities, no two of these accounts agree on the armor's physical characteristics.

Doppelganger armor's strange power is its ability to take on the protective properties of the armor being worn by its wearer's opponent. It can absorb and exhibit the qualities of plate mail, a shield, or even the magical protections placed on enchanted armor. All scholarly sources agree, however, that each wearer can claim the protective benefits of an opponent's defenses only while that opponent lives and fights, since the armor's magic draws upon the foe's skill and abilities as well as its defenses.

Doppelganger Armor			Level 5+ Uncommon		
As you focus on a nearby enemy, this armor flares with magical energy, changing itself to match the defenses of your foe.					
Lvl 5	+1	1,000 gp	Lvl 20	+4	125,000 gp
Lvl 10	+2	5,000 gp	Lvl 25	+5	625,000 gp
Lvl 15	+3	25,000 gp	Lvl 30	+6	3,125,000 gp
Armor: Any					
Enhancement Bonus: AC					

Utility Power ✦ **Daily** (Minor Action)

Effect: Choose one enemy within 5 squares of you. You gain a +2 power bonus to the defense that is the enemy's highest until the end of the encounter or until that enemy drops below 1 hit point.

Despite its name, doppelganger armor does not give one the shape-shifting capability of those loathsome creatures, nor does it allow one to take on the appearance of an enemy's armor of clothes. Rather, it has the curious property of granting one protection while an enemy is alive. While useful when attempting to slay or negotiate with a single opponent, it seems a hard property to use when many foes dog you. Can you risk not swinging your sword at one in order to protect yourself from many?

Ebon Armor

The armor worn by the living dead slowly becomes imbued with shadow magic. When a death knight, a wight, or some similar horror is defeated, a skilled wizard can preserve the magic bound within the armor before it dissipates. Imbued with the power of the grave, *ebon armor* allows its wearer to siphon life energy from dying foes.

Ebon Armor			Level 3+ Uncommon		
This black armor's breastplate is detailed with small skulls at its joints and breastplate, as if it had been crafted for an undead warrior.					
Lvl 3	+1	680 gp	Lvl 18	+4	85,000 gp
Lvl 8	+2	3,400 gp	Lvl 23	+5	425,000 gp
Lvl 13	+3	17,000 gp	Lvl 28	+6	2,125,000 gp
Armor: Chain, scale, or plate					
Enhancement Bonus: AC					
Properties					

✦ You gain necrotic resistance equal to 3 + twice this armor's enhancement bonus.

✦ When an enemy adjacent to you dies, you gain temporary hit points equal to 3 + this armor's enhancement bonus.

Fishscale Armor

The original *fishscale armor* was made for the leading captain of a seagoing fleet belonging to a rich merchant house. The armor's singular capability is derived from the virtues of the fish scales from which it is painstakingly crafted. The armor's wearer can swim through water as freely and swiftly as a fish can.

Naturally, the original captain's counterparts from other merchant houses soon commissioned the construction of similar armor, and the pirates who opposed those fleets commissioned or stole their own copies, making this armor commonplace for a time—among the extremely wealthy, at least.

Fishscale Armor		Level 8+ Common	
While wearing this armor, you slide through the water like a great fish.			
Lvl 8	+2	3,400 gp	
Lvl 13	+3	17,000 gp	
Lvl 18	+4	85,000 gp	
Lvl 23	+5	425,000 gp	
Lvl 28	+6	2,125,000 gp	
Armor: Hide or scale			
Enhancement Bonus: AC			
Property			
You gain a swim speed equal to 3 + the armor's enhancement bonus.			

Gloaming Armor

Gloaming armor is designed to make its wearer invisible with a simple command. Some suits are also enchanted to dampen sounds the wearer makes, and at least one rumor tells of a suit of this armor that can project a silence effect out a short distance to those around it. Although some sages think it's possible to create *gloaming armor* out of sturdier materials, the only known examples of the enchantment have been placed on less noisy types of armor such as cloth, leather, and hide.

Gloaming Armor		Level 5+ Rare	
You fade from view even as the noise of your footfalls recedes.			
Lvl 5	+1	1,000 gp	
Lvl 10	+2	5,000 gp	
Lvl 15	+3	25,000 gp	
Lvl 20	+4	125,000 gp	
Lvl 25	+5	625,000 gp	
Lvl 30	+6	3,125,000 gp	
Armor: Cloth, leather, or hide			
Enhancement Bonus: AC			
Property			
You gain an item bonus to Stealth checks equal to the armor's enhancement bonus.			
Utility Power (Illusion) ✦ Encounter (Standard Action)			
Effect: You become invisible until you attack or until the end of the encounter. You can end this effect as a minor action.			
Level 15, 20, 25, or 30: While you are invisible, allies within 5 squares of you gain an item bonus to Stealth checks equal to the armor's enhancement bonus.			

Fishscale armor

Greater Armor of Eyes

Many believe that a paranoid crafter enchanted the first suit of *greater armor of eyes*. The armor's effect is simple: It allows the one wearing it to see in all directions at once. It is impossible to gain any advantage against someone wearing this armor by attacking him or her from behind or from an unnoticed position, and avoiding the wearer's notice is difficult. There are dangers to such protection, however, because it is thought that the paranoiac who enchanted the original armor died in a particularly poetic fashion from the gaze of a basilisk.

Greater Armor of Eyes		Level 14+ Rare	
While you wear this armor, your visual senses expand in every direction, enabling you to avoid unseen attacks.			
Lvl 14	+3	21,000 gp	
Lvl 19	+4	105,000 gp	
Lvl 24	+5	525,000 gp	
Lvl 29	+6	2,625,000 gp	
Armor: Any			
Enhancement Bonus: AC			
Properties			
✦ You gain an item bonus to Perception checks equal to the armor's enhancement bonus.			
✦ You cannot be blinded.			
✦ You gain darkvision.			
✦ *Level 24 or 29:* You don't grant combat advantage for being flanked.			

Hide of Worms

The material that makes up this strange suit of armor seems normal at first glance. Closer inspection reveals that the armor's weave is crafted from thousands of inch-long worm castings, pressed and woven together. The nature of the maggot-sized worms used in this way has been lost to history, but they must not have been mundane creatures; else why use such minute elements to construct a suit of armor?

Someone wearing *hide of worms* armor can pass safely through soil and dirt, carrying along anything else worn or held. The chronicles of a certain notorious bandit king of antiquity whose signature accoutrement was his *hide of worms* are rife with accounts of him enticing enemies to follow him beneath the ground, eventually submerging them entirely and leaving them to die, buried alive. Such tales are probably overstated.

Hide of Worms			Level 12+ Uncommon	
You press your body to the ground and pass freely into it, burrowing through the dirt easily.				
Lvl 12	+3	13,000 gp	Lvl 22 +5	325,000 gp
Lvl 17	+4	65,000 gp	Lvl 27 +6	1,625,000 gp
Armor: Leather or hide				
Enhancement Bonus: AC				
Utility Power ✦ Daily (Minor Action)				
Effect: You gain a burrow speed of 3 until the end of the encounter, but you cannot use this speed to move through solid stone.				

Plate Mail of Etherealness

Nonmagical plate mail is a damage barrier of the highest order, but at great cost to the wearer's mobility. *Plate mail of etherealness* offers nearly flawless magical protection and grants its wearer superior mobility on the battlefield. The armor's wearer can travel between the dimensions that define the planes, making walls and similar barriers no more hindering than a gentle breeze.

Most of the burnished surfaces of *plate mail of etherealness* shine with a misty silver light, like the flashing sun seen through a thin fog.

Plate Mail of Etherealness			Level 17+ Uncommon	
You surprise your enemies by using this armor to move through a hindering obstacle to get behind them.				
Lvl 17	+4	65,000 gp	Lvl 27 +6	1,625,000 gp
Lvl 22	+5	325,000 gp		
Armor: Plate				
Enhancement Bonus: AC				
Utility Power ✦ Encounter (Standard Action)				
Effect: You are phasing until the end of your next turn.				

Robe of the Archmage

A multitude of legends talk about archmages and their exploits. Even though each story varies considerably, one common element often exists: Each archmage wore a protective item of tremendous power known as a *robe of the archmage*. Some such robes are said to provide nigh-invulnerable physical protection to their wearers, while others offer equal defense against other kinds of attacks, whether magical or psionic. Other tales tell of robes that are reputed to amplify the raw power of the magic commanded by their wearers, or that allow their wearers to channel spells normally beyond the grasp of mortals. A few dark rumors even claim that some robes instantly slay anyone but their owner who dons them.

Robe of the Archmage		Level 20+ Rare	
You can tap this robe's power to broaden your magical ability, but at a cost, since your body acts as a conduit for that force.			
Lvl 20 +4	125,000 gp	Lvl 30 +6	3,125,000 gp
Lvl 25 +5	625,000 gp		
Armor: Cloth			
Enhancement Bonus: AC			
Properties			
✦ You gain a +1 item bonus to Fortitude and Will. *Level 25 or 30:* The bonus increases to +2.			
✦ After each extended rest, you can prepare one additional utility power of your level or lower from your spellbook. You must have a spellbook to use this benefit, and the additional power can be the same level as another utility power you prepare.			
Utility Power ✦ Daily (Minor Action)			
Effect: You take damage equal to your bloodied value that can't be reduced in any way. The next damage roll you make with an arcane attack power before the end of the turn has all of its damage dice maximized.			

Curse the wizard that created the first robe of the archmage! Now any whelp of a hedge conjurer or witless apprentice that finds one considers himself an archmage. Then these fools seek magic far above their station or grasp at power as if donning a robe made them royalty. What a blasted nuisance. I hesitate to count the number of "archmages" I've reduced to dust. Still, I've found that for wizards worthy of the title, a robe of the archmage can be a useful item.

Robe of Useful Items

Those capable of scaling the greatest heights of intellect are often saddled with the inability to give proper thought to the mundane and unexceptional. For this reason, a transcendent genius of ancient times labored for a year and a day to craft this extraordinary robe, rather than simply remembering to pack his traveling pouches before departing on a journey.

A *robe of useful items* is exactly what its name suggests: a garment whose pockets, pouches, and sleeves hold utensils, tools, and implements that its wearer can bring forth on command. Corkscrews, rope, mirrors, candles, fishhooks—a *robe of useful items* can produce nearly anything portable and mundane.

Robe of Useful Items			Level 2+ Common		
No matter what simple item you need, you can find it in one of this robe's many pockets.					
Lvl 2	+1	520 gp	Lvl 17	+4	65,000 gp
Lvl 7	+2	2,600 gp	Lvl 22	+5	325,000 gp
Lvl 12	+3	13,000 gp	Lvl 27	+6	1,625,000 gp
Armor: Cloth					
Enhancement Bonus: AC					
Utility Power ✦ Daily (Minor Action)					

Effect: You procure one nonmagical item worth up to 10 gp (with the DM's approval) from the robe. The item is generic (a torch or a rope, for instance), not a specific item (the key to a particular chest). The item lasts for 1 hour. When it disappears, you regain the use of this power.

I find it's handy to simply wear a robe of useful items about the tower. There's no need to remember where you set your quill or to look for a sponge to mop something up. You just pull out what you need at the moment, and poof! I've also found it to be a delightful means of snacking— with the truly delicious benefit of not having to loosen the robe's belt.

Shallow Grave Armor

Shallow grave armor is noteworthy for the dust and grime that is forever embedded in its padding, greaves, and joints. Although this armor looks dingy, its attunement to the grave lends it a potent magical ability. Part of the process of creating this armor requires it to be buried in a grave for a year and a day. That attunement to the grave provides it with a powerful ward against harm. If a person clad in *shallow grave armor* suffers a deadly wound, the armor's magic surges to provide a corresponding burst of healing.

Shallow Grave Armor			Level 9+ Uncommon		
This suit of armor is covered with dirt and grime. No amount of scrubbing can remove it.					
Lvl 9	+2	4,200 gp	Lvl 24	+5	525,000 gp
Lvl 14	+3	21,000 gp	Lvl 29	+6	2,625,000 gp
Lvl 19	+4	105,000 gp			
Armor: Any					
Enhancement Bonus: AC					
Utility Power (Healing) **✦ Daily** (No Action)					

Trigger: You start your turn and are dying.
Effect: You can spend a healing surge and can stand up as a free action. Until the end of the encounter, you gain necrotic resistance and radiant vulnerability equal to 5 + this armor's enhancement bonus.

Wintersnap Armor

This white armor is designed for use in climates where frigid temperatures and bitter winds freeze the flesh and steal the very life of those with warm blood in their veins. *Wintersnap armor* protects its wearer from cold temperatures and cruel winds. Further, the white-colored material it is constructed from conceals its wearer with supernatural potency while on snow and ice.

The material from which *wintersnap armor* is made seems immediately obvious to those who see it from a distance—surely came from a great polar bear, or a furred cold drake, or an albino seal—but upon closer examination of its texture and sheen, all of these possibilities are discarded, because the nature of its crafting is mystifying. The most common theory suggests that the material comes from the pelt of a unique creature known as the White One, who is eternally bound in a secret place within the ice. It is thought that this creature's fortitude is so great that it can survive being flayed and eventually produces a new skin that can be shaped into this armor.

Wintersnap Armor			Level 4+ Uncommon		
This strange white armor absorbs cold winds before they find your flesh, storing the bite of the frigid air so you can bring it forth when the time is right.					
Lvl 4	+1	840 gp	Lvl 19	+4	105,000 gp
Lvl 9	+2	4,200 gp	Lvl 24	+5	525,000 gp
Lvl 14	+3	21,000 gp	Lvl 29	+6	2,625,000 gp
Armor: Any					
Enhancement Bonus: AC					
Properties					

✦ You gain cold resistance equal to 3 + twice the armor's enhancement bonus.
✦ You gain a bonus to Stealth checks in snowy or icy environments equal to the armor's enhancement bonus.

⟳ Utility Power (Aura) **✦ Daily** (Minor Action)

Effect: You activate an aura 1 that lasts until the end of the encounter, until you deactivate it as a minor action, or until the armor is removed. Squares in the aura are difficult terrain for creatures other than you.

CHAPTER 2

Weapons

IT MIGHT *surprise some who know my reputation as a mighty wizard, but I have found that a weapon serves as well as a spell on many occasions. I speak not just of wielding a staff to ward off an enemy or using the knife kept for cutting meat to slash a sleeping throat, but also of keeping a scabbarded blade at my side. I have in my time smashed foes with maces, hacked them with axes, slashed them with swords, and impaled them upon polearms.*

We who hold discourse with demons and cull reagents from corpses should not be so effete that we fear calluses upon our palms. Indeed, every wizard should take note of the use of martial weapons. If nothing else, you will understand as you die why you should have ducked instead of parried. Why let your last thought be one of confusion?

More to the point, you should have a deep knowledge of magic weapons. So many enchanted blades, enspelled spears, arcane arrows, and other such baubles litter old battlefields that I've heard of farmers turning them up in their fields when they plow. Such objects of power should not be allowed to ricochet about the world. They must be catalogued, measured for their danger, and each tracked according to its threat.

Woe would come to us all if Blackrazor or a vorpal sword were allowed to circulate unchecked by our vigilance. By the same token, we must understand that not every dancing sword or dragonslaying lance represents a grave threat to global stability. Many magic weapons should be examined for their properties and then be allowed to move through the world as the whims of fate decree.

When you find new properties on weapons (or upon any other items, for that matter), please record them in your copy of this book. Doing that will transfer them to my master copy, and I will then disseminate that knowledge to the others who hold a copy of this work. Please include any information you gather about creating the various properties of magic items, and be assured I will keep such knowledge in the strictest confidence.

> —Mordenkainen, from his master copy
> of the *Magnificent Emporium*

Scholar's Note: Of special note is the last paragraph, which was redacted from the few copies that Mordenkainen disseminated before he reclaimed and destroyed them.

> —Qort

NEW WEAPONS

The armaments described here are somewhat less common than the typical sword or axe, but they are no less useful. Many weapons were born from necessity, such as war picks crafted from the mining implements of threatened dwarf clans. In other cases, weapons were adapted to fit a group's preferred fighting style, such as pikes crafted by gnomish militias to hold larger foes at bay.

New Weapon Category: Superior Weapons

Superior weapons are specialized swords, axes, and other weapons that require intensive training to master their use. These weapons are usually more accurate or damaging than their nonsuperior counterparts, but come at the cost of requiring advanced training and study. Many of them are also rarely seen. A warrior trained in a superior weapon might hail from an exotic land or claim membership in a small or diminishing fighting school.

You can gain proficiency with a superior weapon by taking the Weapon Proficiency feat and choosing that weapon.

Reading the Weapon Tables

An entry on the weapons table contains the following information.

Weapon: The weapon's name.

Prof.: Having proficiency with a weapon means that you are trained in the use of that weapon, which gives you a proficiency bonus to weapon attack rolls. The bonus appears in this column if applicable. Some weapons are more accurate than others, as reflected by their bonus. If you don't have proficiency with the weapon, you don't gain this bonus.

Damage: The weapon's damage die. When a power deals a number of weapon damage dice (such as 4[W]), you roll the number of the dice indicated by this entry. If the weapon's damage die is an expression of multiple dice, roll that number of dice the indicated number of times. For example, a broadsword (which has a damage die of 1d10) deals 4d10 damage when used with a power that deals 4[W] on a hit.

Range: Weapons that can strike at a distance have a range entry. The number before the slash indicates the normal range (in squares) for an attack. The number after the slash indicates the long range for an attack; an attack at long range takes a –2 penalty to the attack roll. Squares beyond the second number are considered to be out of range and can't be targeted with this weapon.

If a melee weapon has a range entry, it can be thrown and belongs to either the light thrown or the heavy thrown category.

An entry of "–" indicates that the weapon can't be used at range, except as an improvised weapon.

Price: The weapon's cost in gold pieces.

Weight: The weapon's weight in pounds.

Properties: A weapon's properties. See page 269 of the *Rules Compendium* for explanations of most of the properties. The new mounted property is explained below.

Group: A weapon's group. See the explanation on page 271 of the *Rules Compendium*.

Weapon Properties

High Crit: A high crit weapon deals more damage when you score a critical hit with it. On a critical hit, the weapon deals 1[W] extra damage at 1st–10th levels, 2[W] extra damage at 11th–20th levels, and 3[W] extra damage at 21st–30th levels. This extra damage is in addition to any critical damage the weapon supplies if it is a magic weapon.

Light Thrown: A ranged basic attack with a light thrown weapon uses your Dexterity modifier for the attack and damage rolls, unless otherwise noted in the description of the power used.

Mounted: A mounted weapon is most effective when you use it while riding a mount. When you use such a weapon while not mounted, you take a –2 penalty to attack rolls with it. While you are mounted, your charge attacks with the weapon deal 1[W] extra damage.

Off-Hand: An off-hand weapon is light enough that you can hold it and attack effectively with it while also holding a weapon in your main hand. You can't attack with both weapons in the same turn, unless you have a power that allows such an attack, but you can attack with either weapon.

Reach: With a reach weapon, you can make melee attacks against enemies that are 2 squares away from you as well as against adjacent enemies. Even so, you can make opportunity attacks only against enemies adjacent to you and can flank only enemies adjacent to you.

Small: This property describes a two-handed or a versatile weapon that a Small character can use in the same way a Medium character can. A halfling can use a shortbow, for instance, even though halflings can't normally wield two-handed weapons.

Versatile: Versatile weapons are one-handed, but you can use one two-handed. If you do so, you gain a +1 bonus to the weapon's damage rolls.

A Small creature, such as a halfling, must use a versatile weapon two-handed and doesn't gain the bonus to damage rolls.

SIMPLE MELEE WEAPONS

One-Handed

Weapon	Prof.	Damage	Range	Price	Weight	Properties	Group
Light mace	+2	1d6	–	3 gp	2 lb.	Off-hand, small	Mace
Short spear	+2	1d6	5/10	2 gp	1 lb.	Light thrown, off-hand, small	Spear

Two-Handed

Weapon	Prof.	Damage	Range	Price	Weight	Properties	Group
Morningstar	+2	1d10	–	10 gp	8 lb.	–	Mace

MILITARY MELEE WEAPONS

One-Handed

Weapon	Prof.	Damage	Range	Price	Weight	Properties	Group
Broadsword	+2	1d10	–	20 gp	5 lb.	Versatile	Heavy blade
Flail	+2	1d10	–	10 gp	5 lb.	Versatile	Flail
Lance	+2	1d10	–	12 gp	10 lb.	Mounted, small, versatile	Spear
Light war pick	+2	1d6	–	10 gp	4 lb.	High crit, off-hand, small	Pick
Rapier	+3	1d8	–	25 gp	2 lb.	–	Light blade
War pick	+2	1d8	–	15 gp	6 lb.	High crit, small, versatile	Pick

Two-Handed

Weapon	Prof.	Damage	Range	Price	Weight	Properties	Group
Falchion	+3	2d4	–	25 gp	7 lb.	High crit	Heavy blade
Glaive	+2	2d4	–	25 gp	10 lb.	Reach	Heavy blade, polearm
Halberd	+2	1d10	–	25 gp	12 lb.	Reach	Axe, polearm
Heavy flail	+2	2d6	–	25 gp	10 lb.	–	Flail
Heavy war pick	+2	1d12	–	20 gp	8 lb.	High crit, small	Pick
Pike	+2	1d10	–	15 gp	6 lb.	Reach, small	Polearm, spear

SUPERIOR MELEE WEAPONS

One-Handed

Weapon	Prof.	Damage	Range	Price	Weight	Properties	Group
Bastard sword	+3	1d10	–	30 gp	6 lb.	Versatile	Heavy blade
Serrated pick	+2	1d10	–	15 gp	4 lb.	High crit, small	Pick
Katar	+3	1d6	–	3 gp	1 lb.	High crit, off-hand	Light blade
Waraxe	+2	1d12	–	30 gp	10 lb.	Versatile	Axe
Whip	+3	1d4	–	10 gp	2 lb.	Reach	Whip

Two-Handed

Weapon	Prof.	Damage	Range	Price	Weight	Properties	Group
Spiked chain	+3	2d4	–	30 gp	10 lb.	Reach	Flail

Weapon Descriptions

Bastard Sword: This heavier variation on the longsword requires special training to cope with its weight and peculiar balance. Warriors who master the bastard sword gain the typical sword's accuracy and balance combined with the striking power of a warhammer or battle axe.

Broadsword: Compared to a longsword, a broadsword has a heavier blade more suited to brutal tactics than to quick maneuvers.

Falchion: A falchion features a long, wide blade that bends in a curve, similar to that of a scimitar.

Flail: Based on a simple agricultural tool, a flail is a wooden handle attached by a short chain to a spiked metal ball. The chain allows a skilled warrior to generate impressive force with each stroke or entangle a foe's legs or arms.

Glaive: With its long, wooden haft that ends in a swordlike cutting blade, the glaive excels at keeping enemies at a distance.

Halberd: A halberd's heavy head makes it a devastating weapon, while its long, wooden haft grants it the reach needed to deter would-be attackers.

Heavy Flail: This two-handed variation of a standard flail can bash through armor with ease.

Heavy War Pick: A longer haft and a heavier pick end make this weapon an ideal choice for a gnome or a halfling in search of a two-handed weapon.

Katar: Also known as a punching dagger, this blade has an H-shaped handle that its wielder grasps in his or her fist. By driving this weapon at a foe with

1. Halberd; 2. Falchion; 3. War pick; 4. Katar; 5. Spiked chain; 6. Rapier; 7. Morningstar; 8. Bastard sword; 9. Flail; 10. Glaive

a punching motion, the katar's wielder strikes with deep and deadly attacks.

Lance: This long, heavy spear relies on the weight and speed of a charging mount to skewer a hapless enemy. Most mounted warriors set aside their lances once they engage in close quarters fighting.

Light Mace: The smaller races often prefer this version of the mace because of its lighter weight. It can deliver a solid, if not crushing, blow to an enemy.

Light War Pick: This variation on the pick trades hitting power for speed and agility. Gnomes often favor the light war pick as an off-hand weapon.

Morningstar: This fancier take on a two-handed club consists of a wooden haft topped with a spiked metal ball. The morningstar is common among mercenaries, ogres, trolls, and others that want a heavy weapon that requires little training or maintenance.

Pike: The pike is similar to a longspear, except that its superior construction and balance make it usable by gnomes, halflings, and other Small folk.

Rapier: A weapon of choice for the sophisticated duelist, the rapier is a long, light blade ideal for parrying blows and delivering quick counterattacks.

Serrated Pick: This weapon is similar to a standard pick, except for its longer, sharper, and sawlike pick head. With proper training, a warrior can inflict terrible wounds not only with the serrated

pick's initial impact but also as the weapon is pulled free from a target.

Short Spear: Although this weapon often serves the same role as a spear, it is more handy for the smaller races. It can also be used as a thrown weapon, unlike a full-sized spear.

Spiked Chain: Eladrin duelists are thought to be the first to employ this weapon, and its combination of speed and elegance supports that theory. The spiked chain delivers raking blows from a distance. Like a whip or a flail, it can also wrap around a foe's legs to send that enemy tumbling to the ground.

War Pick: Adapted from the common mining tool, a war pick features a compact design combined with a single, sharp point to punch through armor. Gnomes and halflings favor war picks because of the weapon's small size.

Waraxe: This is a favorite weapon of dwarves, who can wield it with a shield or with two hands for greater damage. Either way, it cuts through orcs' necks very well.

Whip: Stories of novices injuring themselves with this weapon underscore the difficulty of mastering the whip, but in the hands of an expert, a whip can drag a foe down, drive away a vicious animal, or even wrap around a loose object at a distance.

NEW WEAPON FEATS

With new weapons come new techniques, tricks, and tactics to use them. The feats presented here are designed to interact with the weapons introduced in this book.

Feat Categories

Each of the feats in this section belongs to one of two groupings, or categories, based on its general theme. Feat categories were introduced in *Heroes of the Fallen Lands* and *Heroes of the Forgotten Kingdoms* as a way for players to organize and tailor their feat choices.

Weapon Training
The intense study of a single weapon allows a warrior to achieve unmatched levels of skill, though at the cost of flexibility. Three of the feats in this book are part of the weapon training category.

Weapon Training Feats
Flail Expertise
Pick Expertise
Polearm Expertise

Strike Specialization
The *power strike* power represents a sudden surge of adrenaline, a focused attack, or a savage twist of a blade. Some skilled warriors learn to incorporate it into their fighting style, using their cunning, strength, and foresight to deliver an attack that takes advantage of a weapon's unique traits.

The feats in this new category all modify the power strike power. They are ideal for rangers, fighters, and other characters who have access to that power.

Strike Specialization Feats
Axe Strike
Flail Strike
Hammer Strike
Heavy Blade Strike
Light Blade Strike
Mace Strike
Pick Strike
Spear Strike
Staff Strike

Adventurer Feats

This section presents the feats in alphabetical order.

Axe Strike
In your hands, an axe is a tool of devastation. When you focus your efforts, your attacks open deep wounds and cleave through armor, even if they're only glancing blows.

Prerequisite: *Power strike* power

Benefit: When you miss a target with a weapon attack using an axe, you can expend a use of *power strike* to deal 5 damage to the target, even if it is a minion. This damage increases to 10 at 11th level and 15 at 21st level.

Flail Expertise
The flail requires a mix of speed and power, a style that you have perfected over long hours of training. With a sweeping attack, you entangle a foe and send it tumbling to the ground.

Benefit: You gain a +1 feat bonus to weapon attack rolls that you make with a flail. This bonus increases to +2 at 11th level and +3 at 21st level.

In addition, when you hit with a melee weapon attack using a flail and the attack lets you slide the target, you can knock the target prone instead of sliding it.

Flail Strike
As a master of the flail, you have learned to make powerful strikes that take advantage

Axe strike

JEFF HIMMELMAN

Mace strike

of your cunning and guile. Your aggressive attacks are often feints, allowing you to knock your enemies to the ground using the weapon's chain and making them more vulnerable to your follow-up strike.

Prerequisite: *Power strike* power

Benefit: When you use *power strike* with a flail, you can knock the target prone, but the extra damage is reduced by 1[W]. If you do so, the target provokes an opportunity attack from you if it stands up adjacent to you during its next turn.

Hammer Strike
Your tactics are as subtle and indirect as a warhammer to the head. You line up your enemy and knock it senseless with a powerful blow.

Prerequisite: *Power strike* power

Benefit: When you use *power strike* with a hammer, you can daze the target until the end of your next turn, but the extra damage is reduced by 1[W].

Heavy Blade Strike
A heavy blade excels at holding back hordes of enemies. With great sweeps of your weapon, you hew through your foes' ranks and leave behind a trail of corpses.

Prerequisite: *Power strike* power

Benefit: When you reduce an enemy to 0 hit points with a weapon attack using a heavy blade, you can use *power strike*. Instead of gaining the power's

normal benefit, you make a melee basic attack against a different creature as a free action.

Light Blade Strike
The rapier, the short sword, and other light blades are finesse weapons that require speed rather than strength. Where other warriors rely on brute power for their attacks, you carefully strike at your foe's most vulnerable point.

Prerequisite: *Power strike* power

Benefit: When you make a melee basic attack with a light blade against a target's AC, you can use *power strike* before making the attack roll. Instead of gaining the power's normal benefit, you make the attack against the target's Reflex, rather than AC. In addition, if the attack hits, you gain a +2 bonus to the damage roll against the target. This bonus increases to +4 at 11th level and +6 at 21st level.

Mace Strike
A mace excels at delivering crushing blows against a foe's armor or protected areas. Your attacks do more than crush armor. By focusing on a vulnerable area, you can break ribs, snap bone, or hit your foes where it really hurts with a single blow.

Prerequisite: *Power strike* power

Benefit: When you make a melee basic attack with a mace against a target's AC, you can use *power strike* before making the attack roll. Instead of gaining the power's normal benefit, you make the attack against the target's Fortitude, rather than AC. In addition, if the attack hits, you gain a +2 bonus to the damage roll against the target. This bonus increases to +4 at 11th level and +6 at 21st level.

Pick Expertise
The pick is a favored weapon of dwarves, gnomes, and others that must battle giants. Its curved point makes it an excellent weapon for striking at a foe's feet, particularly against larger foes such as giants or ogres. Of course, to a halfling or gnome a human is a larger foe.

Benefit: You gain a +1 feat bonus to weapon attack rolls that you make with a pick. This bonus increases to +2 at 11th level and +3 at 21st level.

In addition, you gain a +1 bonus to pick damage rolls against any enemy that has a size category larger than yours. This bonus increases to +2 at 11th level and +3 at 21st level.

Pick Strike
A pick is built to drive deep into an enemy's armor. Its heavy, piercing head can crack through an umber hulk's hide or a hobgoblin warlord's plate armor. When you throw your weight behind a pick attack, your weapon pierces deep into your foe, hurting it very badly.

Prerequisite: *Power strike* power

Benefit: When you use *power strike* with a pick, you deal the maximum damage you could roll for *power strike* if your attack roll against the target was 18–20.

Polearm Expertise
With proper training, a polearm's length provides both an offensive and a defensive edge. When you attack, you keep your foes at a distance. When they close to attack, the polearm's size makes it ideal for parrying.

Benefit: You gain a +1 feat bonus to weapon attack rolls that you make with a polearm. This bonus increases to +2 at 11th level and +3 at 21st level.

In addition, while you hold a two-handed polearm in both hands, you gain a +2 bonus to all defenses against charge attacks.

Many wizards consider swordplay and similar pursuits to be the purview of hirelings and allies. For them, the spell is blade and bulwark. Well, take it from one wizard who has outlasted many such fools: You can run out of spells, but there are weapons enough in the world to arm everyone in it four times over. You will someday need a weapon, and when you do, you'll want to know which end to swing at your enemy.

Spear Strike
The spear was one of the first weapons developed for hunting and warfare, and for good reason. It is relatively easy to construct, and it is ideal for keeping foes at a distance and for pinning them down.

Prerequisite: *Power strike* power
Benefit: When you use *power strike* with a spear, you can immobilize the target until the end of your next turn, but the extra damage is reduced by 1[W].

Staff Strike
The staff is primarily a defensive weapon that is usually consigned to the hands of wizards or monks. In the hands of a canny warrior, a staff can be a formidable weapon thanks to its reach and the fact that either end can strike. Your unexpected strikes with this weapon allow you to knock your foes off balance and ruin their defenses.

Prerequisite: *Power strike* power
Benefit: When you use *power strike* with a staff, the target grants combat advantage until the end of your next turn.

MAGIC WEAPONS

Legend holds that the first magic weapons were crafted as gifts from wizards and clerics to their people as a token of alliance and friendship in the earliest days of history. After all, while a weapon is a warrior's tool, its crafting requires the expertise of a skilled spellcaster or an expert smith. Rarely does the hand that forges a blade wield it in battle.

Magic weapons are powerful symbols. A simple *+2 longsword* might stand as a symbol of sovereignty, granting the crown to whoever carries it. An otherwise plain magic axe might be the one weapon foretold to defeat the demon king. When an adventurer pulls a magic weapon from a treasure cache, it carries with it the legends and history forged by its previous wielders.

Captain's Weapon

These weapons gained their name from a warlord of antiquity who led a band of mercenaries known as the Wolf Raiders. Although the unit fought in many battles for various lords and countries, it always emerged from a fight with minimal casualties. The warlord claimed that between his expert skill and the power of his greatsword, which was bestowed upon him by Bane, no force could defeat his warriors. The sword gained its name from the pledge the warriors spoke before each battle: "With the captain's weapon leading us, we cannot lose."

Many weapons of simple but nonmagical virtue have been misidentified as *captain's weapons* by those who vanquished their wielders, since skilled captains often render their allies more capable through encouragement, commands, and confident presence. Such nonmagical leadership is, of course, that much more effective when combined with the capabilities of an actual *captain's weapon*.

Captain's Weapon			Level 13+ Rare
You brandish your weapon and give battle commands to your nearby comrades, who take heart knowing your side will win the day.			
Lvl 13	+3	17,000 gp	Lvl 23 +5 425,000 gp
Lvl 18	+4	85,000 gp	Lvl 28 +6 2,125,000 gp

Weapon: Any melee
Enhancement Bonus: Attack rolls and damage rolls
Critical: +1d8 damage per plus
Attack Power ✦ Daily (Standard Action)
  Effect: Choose one creature adjacent to you. Each of your allies within 3 squares of that creature can make a basic attack against it as a free action.
Utility Power ✦ Encounter (Minor Action)
  Effect: Choose one ally within 3 squares of you. That ally gains a power bonus to his or her next damage roll during this encounter. The bonus is equal to the weapon's enhancement bonus.

Flame Tongue Weapon

Many magical blades glow in darkness. Some shimmer so brightly that their light can be seen by daylight. *Flame tongue weapons* are to these what a bonfire is to a candle. When a *flame tongue weapon's* wielder speaks a command word, the weapon bursts with roaring flames capable of searing flesh and setting ablaze anything flammable.

Some *flame tongue weapons* are paired with enchanted scabbards or harnesses, allowing them to ignite immediately as they are drawn and readied. Ill suited for those who prefer the shadows, *flame tongue weapons* are made for those who lead from the front, acting as a beacon to foes and promising those enemies that searing flame awaits them should they attack.

Flame tongue

Flame Tongue Weapon		Level 10+ Rare	
This blade spews forth flames that engulf your enemies in fire.			
Lvl 10	+2	5,000 gp	
Lvl 15	+3	25,000 gp	
Lvl 20	+4	125,000 gp	
Lvl 25	+5	625,000 gp	
Lvl 30	+6	3,125,000 gp	

Weapon: Heavy blade or light blade
Enhancement Bonus: Attack rolls and damage rolls
Critical: +1d8 fire damage per plus
Properties

✦ While holding this weapon, you have fire resistance equal to 3 + twice the weapon's enhancement bonus.
✦ All untyped damage dealt by weapon attacks using this weapon changes to fire damage.
✦ Once per round when you reduce an enemy to 0 hit points with a weapon attack using this weapon, each of your enemies adjacent to that enemy takes fire damage equal to 5 + the weapon's enhancement bonus.

⚔ **Attack Power** (Fire) ✦ **Encounter** (Standard Action)
Attack: Close blast 3 (creatures in the blast); the weapon's level + 3 vs. Reflex
Hit: 1d10 fire damage, and ongoing 5 fire damage (save ends).
Level 15 or 20: 2d10 fire damage, and ongoing 10 fire damage (save ends).
Level 25 or 30: 3d10 fire damage, and ongoing 15 fire damage (save ends).

Frost Brand Weapon

An old tale so widely retold that it cannot possibly be true holds that an ancient wizard embraced the power of elemental fire so wholly that its flames animated the blood in his veins. His knowledge of that element was without peer among mortals. In the later centuries of his life, his experiments grew more speculative and more dangerous, until he succumbed to the old adage known to every child–"Play with fire and you'll get burned"–and was consumed by the very fires he had controlled for so long.

He was so powerful, however, that even this fate did not end his life, but he felt so betrayed by his favored element that he turned against fire just as it had turned against him. The *frost brand weapons* that currently exist are the results of his rage-fueled research into quenching fire and tempering the body against its burn.

Frost Brand Weapon		Level 8+ Rare	
Frost forms on your hands as you alter your grip on this icy weapon, but the cold doesn't harm you as the weapon devours all the heat around you.			
Lvl 8	+2	3,400 gp	
Lvl 13	+3	17,000 gp	
Lvl 18	+4	85,000 gp	
Lvl 23	+5	425,000 gp	
Lvl 28	+6	2,125,000 gp	

Weapon: Any melee
Enhancement Bonus: Attack rolls and damage rolls
Critical: +1d8 cold damage per plus
Properties

✦ While holding this weapon, you have fire resistance equal to 3 + twice the weapon's enhancement bonus.
✦ All untyped damage dealt by weapon attacks using this weapon changes to cold damage.

⚔ **Attack Power** (Cold) ✦ **Encounter** (Standard Action)
Attack: Close blast 3 (creatures in the blast); the weapon's level + 3 vs. Reflex
Hit: 1d10 cold damage, and the target is immobilized (save ends).
Level 13 or 18: 2d10 cold damage.
Level 23 or 28: 3d10 cold damage.

Utility Power ✦ **Encounter** (Minor Action)
Effect: Close burst 5. You can extinguish any nonmagical fire in the burst, and each ally in the burst makes a saving throw against ongoing fire damage that a save can end.

Giantslayer Weapon

Giantslayer weapons are designed to strike true and deal grievous wounds against giants and titans. The most powerful of these weapons were forged by the gods as gifts for their exarchs to help them fight in the Dawn War. In later years, the exarchs and their allies crafted lesser versions of the original weapons (as described here) to help them continue the fight against giantkind, which didn't stop harrying the mortal races after the war.

Giantslayer Weapon			Level 7+ Uncommon		
This weapon seeks out giantkind, helping you deliver vicious strikes against those foes.					
Lvl 7	+2	2,600 gp	Lvl 22	+5	325,000 gp
Lvl 12	+3	13,000 gp	Lvl 27	+6	1,625,000 gp
Lvl 17	+4	65,000 gp			

Weapon: Any melee
Enhancement Bonus: Attack rolls and damage rolls
Critical: +1d8 damage per plus, or +1d12 damage per plus against Large or larger humanoids
Property
You gain an item bonus to damage rolls against Large or larger humanoids. The bonus equals the weapon's enhancement bonus.
Utility Power ✦ Encounter (Immediate Interrupt)
  Trigger: A giant tries to push you, stun you, or knock you prone.
  Effect: You are immune to the push or the stun and do not fall prone.

Giants can cause large problems for the rest of us in the world, but those who wield giantslayer weapons would do well to remember that those who are vulnerable to such weapons can help to resolve troubles of great scope as well. I count among my allies both a tribe of stone giants and a tribe of their cloud kindred. The stone giants even aided me in the construction of my citadel, while the cloud giants will rush to my aid in return for helping them defeat a flight of dragons. I could not have hoped to gain such staunch friends while swinging about a sword dedicated to their deaths.

Greater Dancing Weapon

Some stories say that the idea of the *dancing weapon*—one able to animate itself to fight without the sword arm of a mortal behind it—was the fantasy of a vexed sergeant whose soldiers were frequently too intoxicated or hung over to fight properly when the time for battle came. One comic tale suggests that a wizard traveling with just such a frustrated commander crafted the enchantments used in all current versions of *dancing weapons* as an elaborate (but welcome) joke.

Whatever its provenance, a *greater dancing weapon* is not only magical in nature, but wondrous to behold as it whirls and dances around the field of battle as if held by an invisible but expert hand. It creates confusion and terror among the wielder's enemies by darting across the battlefield, slashing and thrusting at opponents that have no one to retaliate against.

Dark rumors persist that servants of Vecna are seeking these weapons. It's not conjectured whether they want the weapons for their own use or for some other servants of the god of secrets, or if they plan to use the weapons' magic for some other rite. The rumors suggest that Vecna's followers are willing to pay well for the weapons, but that anyone who refuses their offer comes to an ill end.

Greater Dancing Weapon			Level 15+ Rare		
This weapon leaps from your grasp, then darts and weaves through the air toward your enemies.					
Lvl 15	+3	25,000 gp	Lvl 25	+5	625,000 gp
Lvl 20	+4	125,000 gp	Lvl 30	+6	3,125,000 gp

Weapon: Any melee
Enhancement Bonus: Attack rolls and damage rolls
Critical: +1d8 damage per plus
Utility Power ✦ At-Will (Minor Action)
  Effect: The weapon animates and dances in the air in an unoccupied square adjacent to you. You can use a move action to cause the weapon to fly up to 6 squares to a square that you can see. The object occupies 1 square, and it cannot flank. Its defenses equal 10 + its level, although it cannot be harmed by any attack. If an attack hits the weapon, it returns to your hand (or it falls in your space if you don't have a hand free or in the nearest square if it can't reach you), and this power ends. You can use a minor action to end this power if the weapon is adjacent to you, causing the weapon to return to your hand.
    While you can see the weapon, you can make weapon attacks with it while it dances, using its square as the origin square of the attacks (including all attack and damage modifiers that you would normally apply).
↓ Attack Power ✦ At-Will (Opportunity Action)
  Trigger: An enemy that you can see takes an action that provokes opportunity attacks and is adjacent to the weapon while the weapon's utility power is in effect.
  Effect: You make a melee basic attack against that enemy, using the weapon.
↓ Attack Power ✦ Daily (Minor Action)
  Requirement: The weapon's utility power must be in effect, and you must be able to see the weapon.
  Effect: You make a melee basic attack using the weapon.

Greater luckblade

Greater Luckblade

Tales say that it's impossible to slay the wielder of a *greater luckblade* while he or she is holding it. Although some sages refute this claim, no record exists of the death of a warrior who clutched such a weapon.

The method by which these blades protect and assist those who wield them is strange and subtle. Although their wielders' blows land more often than not, no supernatural force guides those wielders' hands. Those who wield these weapons parry more blows than most, but a *greater luckblade*'s ability to keep its wielder safe is clearly not all-powerful. Even so, the tales claiming that it's impossible to slay the wielder of a *greater luckblade* continue to spread.

Greater Luckblade			Level 15+ Rare	
Feeling a vibration in this weapon, you spin aside. A second later, a foe's strike splits the air where your head just was.				
Lvl 15	+3	25,000 gp	Lvl 25	+5	625,000 gp
Lvl 20	+4	125,000 gp	Lvl 30	+6	3,125,000 gp

Weapon: Heavy blade or light blade
Enhancement Bonus: Attack rolls and damage rolls
Critical: +1d8 damage per plus
Utility Power ✦ Encounter (Immediate Interrupt)
Trigger: An enemy hits you with an attack while you're bloodied.
Effect: The enemy must reroll the attack and use the new result.
Utility Power ✦ Daily (No Action)
Trigger: You miss with an attack roll.
Effect: You reroll the attack roll and use the new result.

Hammer of Storms

Each of these mighty hammers is infused with the power of thunder and lightning. It is said that the effectiveness of the hammer increases when the weapon is near other weapons of its kind. Stories tell of battles in which many *hammers of storms* were brought together to sunder the walls of a fortification.

Hammer of Storms			Level 12+ Uncommon	
When you wield this weapon, the power of the storm rages around you, blasting your enemies with thunder and lightning.				
Lvl 12	+3	13,000 gp	Lvl 22	+5	325,000 gp
Lvl 17	+4	65,000 gp	Lvl 27	+6	1,625,000 gp

Weapon: Hammer
Enhancement Bonus: Attack rolls and damage rolls
Critical: +1d8 damage per plus
⚡ Attack Power (Lightning, Thunder) **✦ Encounter** (Standard Action)
Attack: Close burst 2 (enemies in the burst); the weapon's level + 3 vs. Fortitude
Hit: 5 lightning and thunder damage, and the target falls prone.
Level 22 or 27: 10 lightning and thunder damage.
Special: This power deals 2 extra damage for each *hammer of storms* that is within 10 squares of this weapon (10 extra damage maximum).

I've no doubt that dwarves crafted the hammers of storms. Many of the great axes and hammers that course with lightning or thunder with each swing were pulled from the forge by dwarf hands. It might seem odd that dwarves, largely beholden to Moradin, would have so much affinity for storms, the domain of Kord. But dwarves value Kord's emphasis on strength, and storms lash their mountain homes far more often than any other elemental force. That the dwarves should make weapons that grow stronger when used in concert should be no surprise to anyone, but why should those weapons have become separated from one another and "lost"? Perhaps the dwarves did not predict how deadly the weapons would be in their own clan wars. If you and your allies have such weapons, excellent. But as soon as your enemies have them as well . . .

Lesser Cloaked Weapon

Although more effective in combat than its nonmagical counterparts, a *lesser cloaked weapon* truly stands apart from them in the way that it disappears beyond the possibility of detection when it's sheathed, stowed, or slung. Sight, touch, and even many magical means of detection are powerless to find such a weapon that has been stored away; it is as if the weapon has ceased to exist until its wielder speaks a command word and reaches to grasp the hidden item from its place of concealment. At such command, the weapon reappears, ready for use once more. It is impossible to know how many of these weapons lie in the vaults and graves of the world, unknowingly buried along with their owners.

Lesser Cloaked Weapon			Level 2+ Common		
Seemingly unarmed as your foe approaches, you reach behind your back. Suddenly, this weapon appears in your hands, tilting the odds in your favor.					
Lvl 2	+1	520 gp	Lvl 17	+4	65,000 gp
Lvl 7	+2	2,600 gp	Lvl 22	+5	325,000 gp
Lvl 12	+3	13,000 gp	Lvl 27	+6	1,625,000 gp
Weapon: Any					
Enhancement Bonus: Attack rolls and damage rolls					
Critical: +1d6 damage per plus					
Property					
When stowed, a *cloaked weapon* cannot be detected or taken from its owner. The weapon's owner must speak a chosen word when stowing the weapon somewhere on his or her person. This word becomes the weapon's command word. As a minor action, the weapon's owner can give the command word and reach for the location where the weapon was last stowed, and it will appear in the owner's hand. The weapon's owner can use the same command word or choose a different one each time the weapon is stowed.					

Lifestealer Weapon

Made from rare materials that enhance the flow of necrotic energy, each *lifestealer weapon* was created to siphon life force from those it strikes. When a *lifestealer weapon* strikes a creature, the weapon creates a conduit of necrotic energy between the creature and its wielder, allowing the wielder to steal the creature's vitality to heal his or her wounds. Additionally, each time the weapon's wielder slays a foe, the weapon absorbs that enemy's vitality, transferring a portion of it to the wielder.

It is thought by some sages that those who enchanted *lifestealer weapons* in primeval days sought to use the extra life force absorbed from slain enemies by these weapons for some evil purpose. Enchanters and sages of the current age are unable to divine where the energy goes or to replicate the primordial magic that created these weapons.

Lifestealer Weapon			Level 4+ Uncommon		
When you strike your enemy, a small measure of your foe's life force is absorbed by this weapon and directed into you.					
Lvl 4	+1	840 gp	Lvl 19	+4	105,000 gp
Lvl 9	+2	4,200 gp	Lvl 24	+5	525,000 gp
Lvl 14	+3	21,000 gp	Lvl 29	+6	2,625,000 gp
Weapon: Any melee					
Enhancement Bonus: Attack rolls and damage rolls					
Critical: +1d12 necrotic damage per plus					
Property					
Whenever you kill an enemy with this weapon, you gain temporary hit points equal to 5 + the weapon's enhancement bonus.					
Attack Power (Healing, Necrotic) ✦ **Daily** (No Action)					
Trigger: You hit an enemy with an attack using this weapon.					
Effect: The target takes extra necrotic damage equal to 2 + the weapon's enhancement bonus, and you regain a number of hit points equal to that extra damage.					

Mace of Disruption

These weapons were forged through a combination of Moradin's metalcraft, Kord's strength, and Ioun's knowledge. Those three gods working together crafted the first *maces of disruption* to honor Pelor, whose healing magic saved their lives during the Dawn War. Since that time, similar weapons have passed among Pelor's followers.

A *mace of disruption* is utterly inimical to undead creatures. Within the center of its striking head rests a tiny ember of radiance. That shard is sealed in metal and wood—were it ever exposed, its light would blind onlookers, including the weapon's wielder—yet its power courses through the mace. The slightest touch annihilates lesser undead creatures, and vampires, wraiths, and even liches recoil from its blows.

Mace of Disruption			Level 10+ Rare		
This iron mace is scribed with a variety of holy runes. It glimmers with white light as divine magic flows through it.					
Lvl 10	+2	5,000 gp	Lvl 25	+5	625,000 gp
Lvl 15	+3	25,000 gp	Lvl 30	+6	3,125,000 gp
Lvl 20	+4	125,000 gp			
Weapon: Mace					
Enhancement Bonus: Attack rolls and damage rolls					
Critical: +1d8 damage per plus					
Properties					
✦ An evil creature that uses this weapon to make an attack takes radiant damage equal to 5 + this weapon's level.					
✦ If you attack an undead minion with this weapon, that minion is destroyed, whether the attack hits or misses. If the minion has powers or traits triggered by its destruction, they are not triggered.					
✦ If you hit an undead creature with this weapon, you gain a power bonus to the damage roll against that creature. The bonus equals the weapon's enhancement bonus.					
Attack Power ✦ **Encounter** (No Action)					
Trigger: You hit an undead creature with this weapon.					
Effect: You push the creature up to 3 squares, and it is immobilized (save ends).					

Maul of the Titans

Although the strength of titans is phenomenal, the engineering skill of dwarves and humans is capable of conceiving and constructing fortifications that can withstand even the titans' considerable might. However, nothing built by the hands of mortals, no matter how strongly reinforced by engineering or by magic, is capable of withstanding a blow from a *maul of the titans*, including solid rock.

It is said that texts detailing the expensive and time-consuming creation of these weapons still exist, the powerful incantations and formulas waiting upon their pages. If that claim is true, these texts would be more valuable than the weapons themselves. Those who spread such tales claim the texts can be found in the ancient tombs of the dwarf wizards who crafted the original mauls, but the dwarves strongly discourage such stories–as well any grave-robbers they discover disturbing their dead.

Maul of the Titans — **Level 18+ Rare**

No opposition can stand against you while you wield this mighty hammer, whether living foe or inanimate edifice.

Lvl 18	+4	85,000 gp	Lvl 28	+6	2,125,000 gp
Lvl 23	+5	425,000 gp			

Weapon: Hammer

Enhancement Bonus: Attack rolls and damage rolls

Critical: +1d8 damage per plus

Attack Power ✦ Encounter (No Action)

Trigger: You hit a creature with an attack using this weapon.

Effect: The creature also falls prone, and you gain a +10 power bonus to the damage roll against it.

Level 23 or 28: +15 power bonus.

Utility Power ✦ Encounter (No Action)

Trigger: You hit an inanimate object with an attack using this weapon.

Effect: You gain a +20 power bonus to the damage roll against the object.

Level 23 or 28: +30 power bonus.

Mighty Dwarven Thrower

Ancient songs and chants of dwarf priests tell of the mighty hammer carried by the ancient scion of the dwarf race who led the first rebellion against the dwarves' giant and titan slavemasters. The legends do not agree on that weapon's true name, but all concur that it measured more than six feet from end to end, it flew forth from its master's hand with the power of a thunderbolt, and it instantly slew any titan it struck. And not only that, before the slain foe even tumbled to the ground, the weapon appeared back in the mighty hero's hand.

That ancient weapon–if it ever truly existed–is certainly a powerful artifact. Stories of that hammer have inspired dwarf smiths and crafters to try to imitate the weapon, and many enchanted hammers have been created that possess some of that weapon's fabled traits.

In keeping with the dwarven aesthetic, all *mighty dwarven throwers* are cast in bold, geometric shapes that look as if they were never intended for flight. Some *mighty dwarven throwers* emit a whine or a hum when thrown (the dwarves say the hammer is singing). Others exude a trail of shining light, like a meteor streaking through the night sky, as they fly toward their target. Some return instantly to their owner's hand or boomerang through the air in return flight. One feature common to all is that they are especially effective against giants and titans.

Mighty Dwarven Thrower — **Level 15+ Rare**

Thunder peals as you hurl this hammer through the air on a collision course with your enemy's skull.

Lvl 15	+3	25,000 gp	Lvl 25	+5	625,000 gp
Lvl 20	+4	125,000 gp	Lvl 30	+6	3,125,000 gp

Weapon: Hammer

Enhancement Bonus: Attack rolls and damage rolls

Critical: +1d6 damage per plus, or +1d12 damage per plus against Large or larger humanoids

Property

You gain an item bonus to damage rolls against Large or larger humanoids. The bonus equals 2 + the weapon's enhancement bonus.

Attack Power ✦ Encounter (Standard Action)

Attack: Ranged 10 (one creature). You throw the weapon but make a melee basic attack against the target. On a hit, the target also falls prone. After the attack, the weapon returns to your hand.

Utility Power ✦ Daily (Free Action)

Trigger: You hit a creature adjacent to you with this weapon.

Effect: The creature is dazed (save ends).

In my experience—for all their long-winded ramblings about lineage and tradition—dwarves are a greedy and devious people. I write this not to insult them in any way. I have found greed to be a useful motivator both for myself and my underlings, and I prize the ingenious trickery that some members of the race demonstrate. Such cleverness can be seen in the creation of mighty dwarven throwers. You might see before you a dwarf holding a two-handed maul of so much heft it seems he could barely swing it, yet he hurls it fifty feet as easily as a child casts a stone. Then, in the blink of an eye, he holds it high once again.

Punishing Weapon

Every wound delivered by a *punishing weapon* brings the enemy closer to death, as each subsequent strike hits harder than the last. When someone wielding one of these weapons focuses his or her attacks upon one opponent, each successful strike takes its toll on that foe, enabling the wielder to more quickly finish off the victim.

These weapons famously received their name during Nerath's rise to power, when a group of vigilantes dedicated to Erathis used them to "punish the wicked" within their society. At first, the groups' members were seen as saviors and heroes among the common people, but eventually corruption within the group's ranks led to its downfall.

Punishing Weapon		Level 8+ Common	
After you strike your foe with this weapon, your enemy appears mote vulnerable as its will to stand up to you drains away.			
Lvl 8	+2	3,400 gp	
Lvl 13	+3	17,000 gp	
Lvl 18	+4	85,000 gp	
Lvl 23	+5	425,000 gp	
Lvl 28	+6	2,125,000 gp	

Weapon: Any
Enhancement Bonus: Attack rolls and damage rolls
Critical: +1d6 damage per plus
Property
The first time each round you hit an enemy with this weapon, you can choose to inflict a wound on the enemy. You gain a cumulative power bonus to damage rolls against the enemy for each of these wounds that you have inflicted on it. Each wound contributes half the weapon's enhancement bonus to the power bonus. The wounds end on the enemy when you hit another enemy with the weapon or at the end of the encounter.

Seeker Weapon

Seeker weapons—slings, bows, crossbows, and other ranged weapons—are deadly tools that defy physical laws in strange and unnatural ways. Although all such weapons have normal range limitations, they or the missiles they loose travel with unusual accuracy to strike their target, even if the weapon's wielder cannot see that enemy. The projectile fired by a *seeker weapon* can take a convoluted route, even streaking around a corner, over a wall, or through a window; as long as a clear route from origin to destination exists, it cannot easily be prevented from hitting its target. One legend of a master archer who was denied his true love tells of how he took his life with an arrow that he fired from his own bow.

Seeker Weapon			Level 3+ Uncommon		
The ammunition fired from this weapon weaves and changes its trajectory, snaking around obstacles to strike true.					
Lvl 3	+1	680 gp	Lvl 18	+4	85,000 gp
Lvl 8	+2	3,400 gp	Lvl 23	+5	425,000 gp
Lvl 13	+3	17,000 gp	Lvl 28	+6	2,125,000 gp

Weapon: Any ranged or any thrown
Enhancement Bonus: Attack rolls and damage rolls
Critical: +1d8 damage per plus
Utility Power ✦ Encounter (Minor Action)
Effect: The next target you attack with this weapon can be behind blocking terrain or otherwise out of line of effect, but only if a clear path can be traced to that target and the path is within range. In addition, you take no penalties for cover or concealment when you make the attack roll against that target

Shock Spear

Everyone who has seen lightning split the sky, or seen the blackened debris of a tree struck by that force, has imagined wielding its power.

A *shock spear* (or javelin) allows that dream to come true by enabling its wielder to deal lightning damage when the weapon is hurled. Its special power is much more spectacular: By calling upon the energy contained within the weapon, the wielder can expel from it a cluster of lightning bolts that fan out to hit multiple enemies.

Shock Spear			Level 3+ Uncommon		
You hold the spear aloft and stand fast before your enemies as it throws out bolts of lightning that leave those foes reeling.					
Lvl 3	+1	680 gp	Lvl 18	+4	85,000 gp
Lvl 8	+2	3,400 gp	Lvl 23	+5	425,000 gp
Lvl 13	+3	17,000 gp	Lvl 28	+6	2,125,000 gp

Weapon: Spear
Enhancement Bonus: Attack rolls and damage rolls
Critical: +1d6 lightning damage per plus
Property
All untyped damage dealt by ranged attacks using this weapon changes to lightning damage.
Attack Power (Lightning) ✦ Daily (Minor Action)
Attack: Close blast 5 (one, two, or three enemies in the blast); the weapon's level + 3 vs. Reflex
Hit: 1d8 lightning damage.
Level 13 or 18: 2d8 lightning damage.
Level 23 or 28: 3d8 lightning damage.

Stinging Spear

A *stinging spear* is cleverly enchanted to find the chinks in the armor and other protections used by your enemies. These weapons, which can be either spears or javelins, can easily find purchase in the hairline gaps between plates of steel or punch cleanly through chitinous hide armor as if it were gauze. One ancient general whose real name has been lost to history was slain by a *stinging spear* that penetrated the only trifling gap in his armor—the eyeslit in his helm. Since then, the example of the Impaled General is invoked by grizzled veterans to teach their students that no warrior should rely solely on his or her armor to ward off an enemy's attack.

Stinging Spear			Level 9+ Uncommon		
Even before you strike your foe, you can feel this weapon's tip edging up and down and back and forth, seeking the weak point in your enemy's defenses.					
Lvl 9	+2	4,200 gp	Lvl 24	+5	525,000 gp
Lvl 14	+3	21,000 gp	Lvl 29	+6	2,625,000 gp
Lvl 19	+4	105,000 gp			

Weapon: Spear
Enhancement Bonus: Attack rolls and damage rolls
Critical: +1d8 damage per plus

Utility Power ✦ Encounter (Minor Action)
Effect: Until the end of this turn, attacks made with this weapon against AC can instead be made against Reflex.

*Slings and arrows, javelins and darts—
they sound like children's games.
Then again, children play at war,
so why not with its tools? Surely, those
who will make war against them when
they are older play at war as well.
The young orc cradles a spear before
it carries an orc babe. And what
elf child has not touched a bow before
seeing ten summers? What would
the world be like if it were not so?
What if all the world's children played
bargaining games instead? Merchants
or men-at-arms, which is more
dangerous in the balance? Idle thoughts.
And idle thoughts, like idle children,
can cause mischief. Better to put
them to more profitable use.*

True Dragonslayer Weapon

Because dragons are among the most feared creatures of the world, it is natural that the magesmiths of antiquity turned their art and craft to forging weapons that would give mortal heroes the tools and strength of spirit required to slay those mighty creatures.

The varieties of *true dragonslayer weapons* are many. The most ancient (and most powerful) ones often impart the narrowest benefits. Some were forged for the sole purpose of slaying a single dragon whose horrible depredations threatened some long-forgotten kingdom. Others bear powers aligned against all dragons of a particular type; weapons antagonistic to chromatic dragons are the most common of these. The most recently forged *true dragonslayer weapons*, some of which were crafted within the memory of still-living eladrin, are said to strike true against all dragons—but nonetheless, these weapons have but a shadow of the fearsome power of the weapons of antiquity.

One tale told in Winterhaven so often it must hold some truth tells of a pair of would-be dragonslayers, the twins Lanok and Leska, who each claimed to have one of these weapons. The stories say that they traveled into the Cairngorm Peaks, following rumors of a red dragon lairing among the foul humanoids in the northern part of the Stonemarch. So far, there are no stories of the siblings' return.

True Dragonslayer Weapon			Level 9+ Rare		
You strike at a dragon, feeling this weapon thrum in anticipation as the blow sends the dragon reeling.					
Lvl 9	+2	4,200 gp	Lvl 24	+5	525,000 gp
Lvl 14	+3	21,000 gp	Lvl 29	+6	2,625,000 gp
Lvl 19	+4	105,000 gp			

Weapon: Any
Enhancement Bonus: Attack rolls and damage rolls
Critical: +1d8 damage per plus, or +1d12 damage per plus against dragons

Properties
✦ The DM chooses a damage type: acid, cold, fire, lightning, or poison. While you are holding the weapon, you have resist 5 against that damage type.
Level 14 or 19: Resist 10.
Level 24 or 29: Resist 15.
✦ Your attacks with this weapon against a dragon ignore its resistances.

Utility Power ✦ Encounter (Minor Action)
Effect: Before the end of the turn, your next attack with this weapon against a dragon gains a +3 power bonus to the damage roll against the target. On a hit, you can also knock the dragon prone.
Level 14: +6 power bonus.
Level 19: +9 power bonus.
Level 24: +12 power bonus.
Level 29: +15 power bonus.

Warning Weapon

Some legends say that the first *warning weapon* was enchanted for a mighty warrior blinded by the cruel strike of a dragon's claw. Another equally ancient saga from the lore of a seafaring empire says that the first *warning weapon* was a trident carried by the captain of the emperor's fastest messenger ship. Whatever its origin, any *warning weapon* allows whoever grasps it to be aware of the location of every enemy within a short distance—no matter what barriers might intervene, from fog to black water to solid stone.

Warning Weapon			Level 4+ Uncommon		

While you hold this weapon, every nearby enemy is known to you, standing out like a shining beacon no matter its stealth or enchantment.

Lvl 4	+1	840 gp	Lvl 19	+4	105,000 gp
Lvl 9	+2	4,200 gp	Lvl 24	+5	525,000 gp
Lvl 14	+3	21,000 gp	Lvl 29	+6	2,625,000 gp

Weapon: Any
Enhancement Bonus: Attack rolls and damage rolls
Critical: +1d6 damage per plus

Property
You gain an item bonus to Perception checks equal to the weapon's enhancement bonus.

Utility Power ✦ Daily (Minor Action)
Effect: Until the end of your next turn, you are automatically aware of each enemy within 5 squares of you, including those that are hidden or invisible. You know the squares these enemies occupy, but this knowledge does not negate the effects of cover or concealment.
Level 14 or 19: Each enemy within 10 squares of you.
Level 24 or 29: Each enemy within 20 squares of you.
Sustain Minor: The effect persists until the end of your next turn.

Magic is a fine wine, but like any good drink, you must partake of it in moderation—and keep a wary eye on its effects. I once granted a guard a warning sword. It seemed a wise precaution at the time. What better way to arm a sentry than to give him the power to sense all interlopers? However, not long after this gift, his demeanor changed. He often seemed distracted, as if his mind were elsewhere. I soon realized that his thoughts were focused not on daydreams but constantly on his surroundings. Given the ability to know the moment an enemy came close, even invisibly or in the guise of some innocent creature, he simply could not give up that advantage. He would wait as long as he could, but at the slightest noise or vague reason for suspicion, he would use the sword's magic to reassure himself that there was no threat. Once the power had been used, he became paranoid that some enemy might be bypassing him while he was "blind." Ultimately, I had to relieve him of his duty. The sword awaits a wielder who is demonstrably more stable.

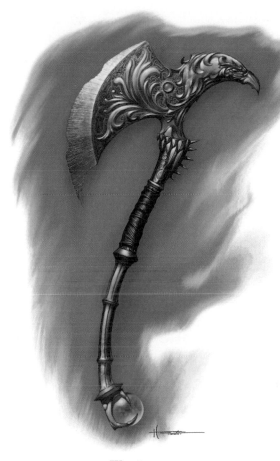

Warning weapon

Way-Leader Weapon

A *way-leader weapon* is enchanted to allow its wielder to instantly call forth nearby allies when he or she strikes true, so they can all attack the same foe at once. Thus, the one wielding this weapon leads the way to the enemy.

The primal shamans of a steppe civilization first crafted these weapons to help their hunters against the giant elephants that often assailed their people. One hunter would hurl his or her spear into an elephant, then send allies next to the beast to surround and kill it before it could trample them.

Way-Leader Weapon			Level 4+ Uncommon		

You strike your foe, designating it as prey for your allies even as you teleport them next to the surprised enemy.

Lvl 4	+1	840 gp	Lvl 19	+4	105,000 gp
Lvl 9	+2	4,200 gp	Lvl 24	+5	525,000 gp
Lvl 14	+3	21,000 gp	Lvl 29	+6	2,625,000 gp

Weapon: Spear
Enhancement Bonus: Attack rolls and damage rolls
Critical: +1d6 damage per plus
Utility Power (Teleportation) ✦ **Encounter** (Move Action)
Requirement: You must have hit an enemy with this weapon during this turn.
Effect: Close burst 5 (one or two allies in the burst). You teleport each target to a square adjacent to the enemy you hit this turn.

Weapon of defense

Weapon of Defense

A magic weapon able to strike true is greatly prized by any warrior lucky enough to have one, but there is also a lineage of weapons whose enchantments not only guide the wielder's strikes, slashing flesh and crushing bone, but also are adapt at parrying the attacks of their wielder's enemies without fail. This versatility makes *weapons of defense* appeal to a wide range of users.

Weapon of Defense			Level 4+ Uncommon		
Each of your enemy's blows finds ready opposition in this parrying weapon.					
Lvl 4	+1	840 gp	Lvl 19	+4	105,000 gp
Lvl 9	+2	4,200 gp	Lvl 24	+5	525,000 gp
Lvl 14	+3	21,000 gp	Lvl 29	+6	2,625,000 gp

Weapon: Any melee
Enhancement Bonus: Attack rolls and damage rolls
Critical: +1d6 damage per plus
Property
You gain resist 1 to all damage while you are holding the weapon.
   Level 14 or 19: Resist 2 to all damage.
   Level 24 or 29: Resist 3 to all damage.
Utility Power ✦ Daily (Immediate Interrupt)
   Trigger: You take damage from a melee attack that hits you.
   Effect: You take only half of the damage.

Weapon of Submission

Every wise general and veteran warrior has learned that the morale of both allies and enemies is a critical dimension to any battle. A *weapon of submission* brings a sense of despair to a creature struck by it, as that foe finds itself propelled across the battlefield at the whim of the attacker. In the spot where the creature ends up, it cowers in fearful anticipation of another strike.

Weapon of Submission			Level 4+ Uncommon		
Your enemy flinches and cowers, allowing itself to be thrown around when you strike it with this weapon.					
Lvl 4	+1	840 gp	Lvl 19	+4	105,000 gp
Lvl 9	+2	4,200 gp	Lvl 24	+5	525,000 gp
Lvl 14	+3	21,000 gp	Lvl 29	+6	2,625,000 gp

Weapon: Any melee
Enhancement Bonus: Attack rolls and damage rolls
Critical: +1d6 damage per plus
Attack Power (Fear) ✦ **Daily** (No Action)
   Trigger: You hit an enemy adjacent to you with an attack using this weapon.
   Effect: You push that enemy up to 5 squares, and it is immobilized (save ends).

Weapon of Surrounding

The wielder of a *weapon of surrounding* blinks out of sight for a split second, reappearing to strike his or her disoriented target from some other direction, whether from the rear or even from above. Those who have faced a foe that wielded a *weapon of surrounding* and lived to tell the tale report that they felt like they were being attacked by a host of enemies all at once though they faced only one.

Weapon of Surrounding			Level 3+ Uncommon		
When you strike with this weapon, you blink out of sight, then instantly reappear on the other side of your foe.					
Lvl 3	+1	680 gp	Lvl 18	+4	85,000 gp
Lvl 8	+2	3,400 gp	Lvl 23	+5	425,000 gp
Lvl 13	+3	17,000 gp	Lvl 28	+6	2,125,000 gp
Weapon: Any melee					
Enhancement Bonus: Attack rolls and damage rolls					
Critical: +1d6 damage per plus					
Utility Power (Teleportation) ✦ **Encounter** (Free Action)					
Trigger: You hit an adjacent enemy with an attack using this weapon.					
Effect: You teleport to a different square adjacent to the enemy.					

Weapons of Accuracy, Long Range, and Speed

It is said that the road wardens of a long-fallen empire never failed to hit their mark given a ready crossbow and pair of eyes to see. Although the training regimen of the wardens was nearly without match in all the empire, their famed precision with ranged attacks—whether with a bow, crossbow, sling, or dagger—also relied on the enchantments placed on their weapons by the empire's master wizards.

These weapons carried three types of enchantments. *Weapons of accuracy* rarely missed their mark, striking foes at fifty paces as easily as at ten. *Weapons of long range* launched their missiles twice or even three times as far as their mundane equivalents. *Weapons of speed* allowed their users to fire and reload so quickly that their hands blurred with the shots.

Weapon of Accuracy			Level 3+ Uncommon		
This weapon or its projectiles strike with unerring precision.					
Lvl 3	+1	680 gp	Lvl 18	+4	85,000 gp
Lvl 8	+2	3,400 gp	Lvl 23	+5	425,000 gp
Lvl 13	+3	17,000 gp	Lvl 28	+6	2,125,000 gp
Weapon: Any ranged or any thrown					
Enhancement Bonus: Attack rolls and damage rolls					
Critical: +1d6 damage per plus					
Utility Power ✦ **Encounter** (Minor Action)					
Effect: You gain a +2 power bonus to your next attack roll with this weapon during this encounter.					

Weapon of Long Range			Level 2+ Common		
Though your allies can barely see your enemies approaching, your attacks with this weapon are already finding their targets.					
Lvl 2	+1	520 gp	Lvl 17	+4	65,000 gp
Lvl 7	+2	2,600 gp	Lvl 22	+5	325,000 gp
Lvl 12	+3	13,000 gp	Lvl 27	+6	1,625,000 gp
Weapon: Any ranged or any thrown					
Enhancement Bonus: Attack rolls and damage rolls					
Critical: +1d6 damage per plus					
Properties					
✦ This weapon's long range increases by 10 squares.					
✦ You do not take the penalty to attack rolls for attacking at long range with this weapon.					

Weapon of Speed			Level 5+ Rare		
Even before your first attack with this weapon hits its mark, you follow it up with another one.					
Lvl 5	+1	1,000 gp	Lvl 20	+4	125,000 gp
Lvl 10	+2	5,000 gp	Lvl 25	+5	625,000 gp
Lvl 15	+3	25,000 gp	Lvl 30	+6	3,125,000 gp
Weapon: Any ranged or any thrown					
Enhancement Bonus: Attack rolls and damage rolls					
Critical: +1d8 damage per plus					
Property					
While holding this weapon, you gain an item bonus to initiative checks equal to the weapon's enhancement bonus.					
⤳ **Attack Power** ✦ **Encounter** (Minor Action)					
Effect: You make a ranged basic attack with this weapon.					

Wind Weapon

Wind weapons are attuned to the power of elemental air and awaken the air around them when swung, giving rise to gusts of wind that drive back their wielder's foes and compelling defenders to give ground. The wielder of a *wind weapon* can use those same gusts to carry an ally into the battle, allowing that comrade to gain superior positioning.

True *wind weapon* masters are capable of intricate and delicate effects. One of the greatest eladrin *wind weapon* fencers in all the Feywild was said to have been able to blow a love letter from a courier's pouch across his master's throne room with the barest flick of his blade, though such tales are most likely the fancies of romantic bards.

Wind Weapon			Level 14+ Rare		
You twist this weapon just so as your strike, calling forth gusts of wind to toss your enemies about.					
Lvl 14	+3	21,000 gp	Lvl 24	+5	525,000 gp
Lvl 19	+4	105,000 gp	Lvl 29	+6	2,625,000 gp
Weapon: Any melee					
Enhancement Bonus: Attack rolls and damage rolls					
Critical: +1d8 damage per plus					
⇐ **Attack Power** ✦ **Encounter** (Move Action)					
Attack: Close blast 3 (enemies in the blast), the weapon's level + 3 vs. Fortitude					
Hit: You slide the target up to 2 squares.					
Utility Power ✦ **At-Will** (Move Action)					
Effect: Close burst 5 (one ally in the burst). You slide the target up to 2 squares.					

MAGIC AMMUNITION

Arrows, bolts, and sling bullets can all have enchantments. Though the power of these items rarely matches that provided by a magic ranged weapon, they can prove useful in a number of situations.

Enchanted arrows, bolts, and sling bullets are activated and fired from ranged weapons. You must load magic ammunition before you can activate and fire it (spending whatever action is necessary to do so), and it's used up when fired. When used with powers that target multiple enemies, magic ammunition affects only the first attack roll or target after it's loaded. In certain circumstances (such as when loading is a free action), however, a ranged attacker can load more magic ammunition during an attack against multiple targets if desired.

Ammunition applies an enhancement bonus to an attack roll and damage roll when used. If the projectile weapon is magical, use the ammunition's enhancement bonus in place of the weapon's enhancement bonus. The weapon's critical bonus and the properties from both the weapon and the ammuniton still apply. Using magic ammunition doesn't prevent you from activating a magic weapon's powers.

You can fire magic ammunition without activating it, using your weapon's enhancement bonus and receiving no benefit from the ammunition's magic. The ammunition is still expended.

Armor-Sapping Ammunition

The first *armor-sapping ammunition* was imbued with primal power, but the secret of crafting these deadly projectiles quickly spread throughout all magical traditions. Primal warriors often fight best in light or no armor, which can put them at a disadvantage against heavily armored foes. This ammunition evens the odds by stripping a creature of its armor's strength.

Armor-Sapping Ammunition		Level 17+ Uncommon	
When this arrow strikes, your foe's armor appears to fade away.			
Lvl 17	+4	2,600 gp	
Lvl 22	+5	13,000 gp	
Lvl 27	+6	65,000 gp	
Ammunition			
Enhancement Bonus: Attack rolls and damage rolls			
Property			
When you hit an enemy with an attack using this ammunition, that enemy's defense is decreased (save ends). Until this effect ends, attacks against that enemy by you or your allies that normally target AC can instead target Reflex, as the attacker chooses.			

Firesight Ammunition

An unseen foe can turn an evenly matched fight into a deadly rout in a heartbeat. For the heroes who hunted the most powerful magical monsters of ancient days, they dreaded most the creatures that had the ability to become invisible. To even the odds, those heroes crafted the first *firesight ammunition*. Carved of sturdy oak and pulsing with a soft white glow, this ammunition bursts into brilliant white specks that cling to any creature it touches, making that creature visible despite its efforts to vanish once more.

Firesight Ammunition		Level 10+ Uncommon		
When this bolt strikes its target, the shaft explodes in a burst of white, illuminating specks that cover your foe.				
Lvl 10	+2	200 gp	Lvl 25 +5	25,000 gp
Lvl 15	+3	1,000 gp	Lvl 30 +6	125,000 gp
Lvl 20	+4	5,000 gp		
Ammunition				
Enhancement Bonus: Attack rolls and damage rolls				
Property				
When you make an attack using this ammunition, your attack takes no penalty due to cover or concealment. When you hit an enemy with an attack using this ammunition, that enemy cannot gain the benefit of cover, concealment, or invisibility (save ends).				

Foe-Seeker Ammunition

Foe-seeker ammunition is usually crafted from a piece of ebony inlaid with glowing runes that make the projectile strike true. It is said that no one is safe once *foe-seeker ammunition* is fired. Even if the target should avoid its doom, another enemy will succumb to the projectile's magic as it seeks out a target.

Foe-Seeker Ammunition		Level 12+ Uncommon		
This arrow creates a magical link between you and your enemies, making each of your shots more accurate than the last until you strike home.				
Lvl 12	+3	500 gp	Lvl 22 +5	13,000 gp
Lvl 17	+4	2,600 gp	Lvl 27 +6	65,000 gp
Ammunition				
Enhancement Bonus: Attack rolls and damage rolls				
Property				
When you make an attack using this ammunition, you gain a +1 item bonus to the attack roll. If you miss, during your next turn, choose another target within range of the original square you attacked from and make the attack again as a minor action, increasing the item bonus by 1. You can repeat the attack this way each round (and increase the item bonus) until the attack hits or until the end of the encounter.				

Reaving Ammunition

Too many times in the heat of battle, an enemy will shrug off a wound from a ranged attack. An attacker using *reaving ammunition* has no such worries. Its rough-carved shape makes this projectile seem unlikely to fly true, let alone hit with deadly force.

Reaving ammunition

Shadowshaft Ammunition			Level 5+ Uncommon		
A dark haze trails behind this arrow as you fire it, exploding in a burst of clinging shadow upon impact.					
Lvl 5	+1	50 gp	Lvl 20	+4	5,000 gp
Lvl 10	+2	200 gp	Lvl 25	+5	25,000 gp
Lvl 15	+3	1,000 gp	Lvl 30	+6	125,000 gp
Ammunition					
Enhancement Bonus: Attack rolls and damage rolls					
Property					
When you make an attack using this ammunition, whether the attack hits or misses, it creates a zone in a burst 1 centered on the target. The zone is heavily obscured, and it lasts until the end of the encounter.					

Shiver-Strike Ammunition

This ammunition was first crafted by the elite high guard of the eladrin realms, whose members prided themselves on their ability to fight against superior numbers. When foes push in, archers can unleash these plain steel projectiles, which suddenly shiver and split upon impact, unleashing a hail of destruction upon everything nearby.

Shiver-Strike Ammunition			Level 5+ Uncommon		
When it strikes, this bolt splits, spraying nearby creatures with shards of steel.					
Lvl 5	+1	50 gp	Lvl 20	+4	5,000 gp
Lvl 10	+2	200 gp	Lvl 25	+5	25,000 gp
Lvl 15	+3	1,000 gp	Lvl 30	+6	125,000 gp
Ammunition					
Enhancement Bonus: Attack rolls and damage rolls					
Property					
When you hit an enemy with an attack using this ammunition, each other creature in a burst 2 centered on that enemy takes 4 damage.					
Level 15 or 20: 8 damage.					
Level 25 or 30: 12 damage.					

Stonehold Ammunition

A single moment to regroup and reposition is sometimes all that's needed to turn the tide of combat. The dwarves who created *stonehold ammunition* used thin black stone in its crafting. Upon impact, the projectile shatters, showering the target in a haze of piercing stone and rooting it in place for a short time.

Stonehold Ammunition			Level 14+ Uncommon		
A shroud of stone fragments erupts from this bolt when it hits, holding your foe in place.					
Lvl 14	+3	800 gp	Lvl 24	+5	21,000 gp
Lvl 19	+4	4,200 gp	Lvl 29	+6	105,000 gp
Ammunition					
Property					
When you hit an enemy with an attack using this ammunition, that enemy is also immobilized until the end of your next turn.					

However, after *reaving ammunition* strikes, it twists and turns within the wound. A foe so injured must either cope with the pain as the arrow bores into it, or spend precious time tearing it free.

Reaving Ammunition			Level 8+ Uncommon		
When this arrow finds its target, it burrows deep, causing great pain.					
Lvl 8	+2	125 gp	Lvl 23	+5	17,000 gp
Lvl 13	+3	650 gp	Lvl 28	+6	85,000 gp
Lvl 18	+4	3,400 gp			
Ammunition					
Enhancement Bonus: Attack rolls and damage rolls					
Property					
When you hit an enemy with an attack using this ammunition, that enemy also takes ongoing 5 damage until it spends a move action (without moving) to end the ongoing damage.					
Level 13 or 18: Ongoing 10 damage.					
Level 23 or 28: Ongoing 15 damage.					

Shadowshaft Ammunition

A piece of *shadowshaft ammunition* has a blunt head that appears to shimmer and flow as though made of dark mist. Shadar-kai explorers first crafted this ammunition in the mortal realm after realizing the disadvantage they faced when fighting in the clear light of the sun.

CHAPTER 3

Implements

WHERE WOULD *we wizards be without the aid of wands, staffs, and orbs? Who among us does not draw comfort from donning the creaking leather of a brace of wands or from feeling the wear-smoothed heft of a familiar staff in hand? Just as the paladin stabs at evil more powerfully with a holy avenger, so do our spells increase in potency when we direct them with a magic implement.*

Of course, the tools of our trade can be used by others, and there are implements beyond our favored three. The holy symbols of warriors of the gods are the most obvious example, but magic implements come in a variety of other forms. Some people utilize primitive totems imbued with the ability to connect with spirits of the natural world. Others wield blades as we wield wands, or even find a way to channel magical energy through meditation.

I have collected an array of the most powerful of these items, and those that serve no purpose for me I subject to disjunction. You might find this act cruel. How, you might ask, can I deprive the world of such treasures, callously destroying pieces of often-priceless magical craftwork passed down through the generations?

Yet I know you better than that. You would have them for your own sake, perhaps one day to use them against me.

Although it's true that powerful implements are works of incomparable beauty, so too can a displacer beast be thought of as lovely or the appearance of a wyvern inspire awe. And like those beasts, such items should not be loosed upon children. You are not yet ready to wield all the powers at my disposal. I protect you from yourself. Count yourself lucky that I provide you with knowledge of those implements described herein.

—Mordenkainen, from his master copy
of the *Magnificent Emporium*

Scholar's Note: The final three paragraphs of Mordenkainen's introduction to this chapter showed a marked stress in his typically fluid pen strokes. Though it cannot be confirmed, it is the belief of this scholar that the paranoia evinced in his words might be due to a curse or even possession by some foreign spirit. Doubtless Mordenkainen could have held thoughts such as those he expresses here, but it is unlike him to betray such concerns so candidly.

—Qort

WILLIAM O'CONNOR

Superior Implements

Formed of exotic materials and created using magical crafting techniques, superior implements enhance a wielder's magic. Despite their magical origin, superior implements aren't magic items per se, and like non-superior implements, they can be enchanted with the Enchant Magic Item ritual.

Each type of superior implement has one or more properties that enhance its wielder's attack powers, such as granting improved accuracy or increasing forced movement. These properties are comparable to the properties that many weapons have.

Wielding a Superior Implement

You need the Superior Implement Training feat (below) to gain the benefits of a specific superior implement. If you wield a superior implement and don't have the feat for it, you don't gain the benefits of its properties, but you can use it as a normal implement of its type, assuming you have proficiency with implements of that type.

Superior Implement Training With careful study and practice, you have unlocked the magical potential in an implement.

Benefit: You can use a single superior implement of your choice. The implement must be of a type with which you have proficiency.

Special: You can take this feat more than once. Each time you take this feat, choose a different superior implement.

SUPERIOR IMPLEMENTS

Daggers	Price	Weight	Properties
Accurate dagger	25	1	Accurate
Incendiary dagger	22	1	Energized (fire), unerring
Lancing dagger	15	1	Empowered crit, energized (lightning)
Resonating dagger	25	1	Energized (thunder), forceful

Holy Symbols	Price	Weight	Properties
Accurate symbol	25	1	Accurate
Astral symbol	18	1	Distant, energized (radiant)
Warding symbol	21	1	Shielding, unstoppable
Wrathful symbol	23	1	Empowered crit, undeniable

Ki Focuses	Price	Weight	Properties
Accurate ki focus	25	–	Accurate
Inexorable ki focus	35	–	Energized (force), unstoppable
Iron ki focus	30	–	Deadly, forceful
Mighty ki focus	25	–	Empowered crit, unerring
Mountain ki focus	30	–	Forceful, shielding
Serene ki focus	35	–	Energized (psychic), undeniable

Orbs	Price	Weight	Properties
Accurate orb	30	2	Accurate
Crystal orb	27	2	Energized (psychic), undeniable
Greenstone orb	27	2	Energized (acid), unstoppable
Petrified orb	25	2	Energized (force), forceful

Rods	Price	Weight	Properties
Accurate rod	25	2	Accurate
Ashen rod	22	2	Energized (fire), unerring
Deathbone rod	22	2	Energized (necrotic), undeniable
Defiant rod	18	2	Energized (radiant), shielding

Staffs	Price	Weight	Properties
Accurate staff	20	4	Accurate
Guardian staff	13	4	Energized (force), shielding
Mindwarp staff	16	4	Distant, energized (psychic)
Quickbeam staff	15	4	Energized (thunder), forceful

Tomes	Price	Weight	Properties
Echo tome	15	3	Distant, unerring
Forbidden tome	15	3	Deadly, unstoppable
Unspeakable tome	15	3	Empowered crit, undeniable

Totems	Price	Weight	Properties
Accurate totem	20	2	Accurate
Farseeing totem	14	2	Deadly, distant
Icicle totem	15	2	Empowered crit, energized (cold)
Storm totem	18	2	Energized (thunder), unstoppable

Wands	Price	Weight	Properties
Accurate wand	20	–	Accurate
Cinder wand	18	–	Empowered crit, energized (fire)
Dragontooth wand	18	–	Deadly, unerring
Rowan wand	15	–	Distant, energized (lightning)

Properties

Accurate: You gain a +1 bonus to implement attack rolls made with an accurate implement.

Deadly: You gain a +1 bonus to the damage rolls of implement attacks made with a deadly implement. The bonus increases to +2 at 11th level and +3 at 21st level.

Distant: The range of your area and ranged implement attack powers increases by 2 when they're used through a distant implement.

Empowered Crit: When you score a critical hit with an implement attack using an empowered crit implement, the attack deals 1d10 extra damage (this damage is not maximized). The extra damage increases to 2d10 at 11th level and 3d10 at 21st level.

Energized: When you use an implement attack power with an energized implement, you gain a +2 bonus to damage rolls if the power has a keyword that matches the implement's damage type. The bonus increases to +3 at 11th level and +4 at 21st level.

Forceful: Whenever you pull, push, or slide a target with an implement attack using a forceful implement, you can increase the distance of the forced movement by 1 square.

Shielding: Whenever you hit at least one target with an implement attack power using a shielding implement, you gain a +1 shield bonus to AC and Reflex until the start of your next turn.

Undeniable: You gain a +1 bonus to the attack roll when you make an implement attack against Will using an undeniable implement.

Unerring: You gain a +1 bonus to the attack roll when you make an implement attack against Reflex using an unerring implement.

Unstoppable: You gain a +1 bonus to the attack roll when you make an implement attack against Fortitude using an unstoppable implement.

Descriptions

Daggers: An accurate dagger is a weapon with a very narrow blade, resembling a stiletto. An incendiary dagger features a wavy blade that was forged by tiefling weapon makers using ancient techniques of Bael Turath. A lancing dagger is made of metal drawn from tall mountains and features two jagged edges, giving it the shape of a lightning bolt. A resonating dagger has a thick, wide blade that narrows only slightly as it approaches the tip.

Holy Symbols: An accurate symbol is carved with symbols of power that channel divine energy more precisely. An astral symbol is crafted of solidified mist from the Astral Sea and glows with a faint silvery light. A warding symbol has protective glyphs carved into its adamantine surface. A wrathful symbol is made from black iron mined in Chernoggar and engraved with runes of divine fury.

Ki Focuses: An accurate ki focus takes the form of a small, smooth stone disc, etched with the ancient divided-circle symbol. An inexorable ki focus consists of a small scroll containing a single calligraphic character, preserved in a leather tube. An iron ki focus is a teardrop-shaped piece of iron about the size of a thumb, covered with small etchings. A mighty ki focus is a hand-sized square of wood, about an inch thick, that has been cut from a plank split or struck by a famous master. A mountain ki focus is a small stone statuette of a guardian monster, such as a dragon or a sphinx. A serene ki focus is a clear quartz crystal, mounted in a reliquary of bronze or silver.

Orbs: An accurate orb is made of clear blown glass, with tiny runes engraved around its equator. A crystal orb looks similar, but has a faceted surface and might appear in any color. A greenstone orb is carved from a heavy metallic stone that has an affinity for acid magic. A petrified orb is made from petrified wood.

Rods: An accurate rod is made from a shaft of silver, bound with golden bands. An ashen rod is made from fire-blackened hardwood and laced with veins of crystallized red sap. A deathbone rod is formed from the bone of an undead creature that is no longer animate. A defiant rod is made of white gold and studded with crystals or gemstones.

Staffs: An accurate staff is smooth and straight, balanced for easy handling and made of polished hardwood. A guardian staff is formed from an uncut branch of a watcher tree, a variety of oak that grows only in the Feywild. A mindwarp staff is made of light, strong wood, topped with a many-faceted crystal. A quickbeam staff is made of rowan wood cut from a tree that has been struck by lightning.

Tomes: The cover of an echo tome is a plate of iron inlaid with silver, and its pages are thin sheets of mithral engraved with arcane secrets. A forbidden tome has a heavy cover and binding, with a lock to keep it closed to prying eyes. An unspeakable tome is bound in straps of iron so that it cannot be opened, but it imparts the knowledge it contains through sinister whispers in the night.

Totems: An accurate totem is a short rod of light wood wrapped in snakeskin. A farseeing totem consists of eagle feathers tied at one end of a roc's bone. An icicle totem is a shaft of unmelting ice, freezing cold to the touch but wrapped with white fur to protect the wielder's hand. A storm totem is made from wood scorched by lightning and adorned with a thunderhawk's feather.

Wands: An accurate wand is a smooth and straight length of light wood, honed to a point at the tip. A cinder wand, in contrast, is blackened and crooked, and warm to the touch. A dragontooth wand is smooth ivory that is bound with bands of gold. A rowan wand is polished wood engraved with lightning motifs.

Magic Implements

Soon after mortals mastered the art of magic, they learned to focus their arts to produce implements imbued with magic. Any magic implement adds might and accuracy to magical attacks, but more unusual versions are painstakingly crafted to add unique flourishes to such attacks.

HOLY SYMBOLS

A holy symbol of a deity serves as both an icon of that god's power and a conduit of divine energy. The design or physical nature of some magic holy symbols makes obvious the faith, or at least the moral stance, of whoever wields them. Most holy symbols come in a form that can be appropriate for a number of different deities.

Many religious people consider it blasphemous for someone to wield a holy symbol dedicated to an enemy god, but some who use holy symbols treasure such items. After all, a cleric of Pelor bearing a symbol of Lolth stands as a clear sign sign that the god of the sun can overcome the Spider Queen and her followers.

Candle of Invocation

This holy symbol takes the form of a simple candle, its power and sanctity evident to all who are attuned to the divine. When the candle is lit, it enhances the wielder's ability to make his or her faith manifest. That faith fills one of the wielder's allies with courage, allowing him or her to turn a failed attempt into a success.

Candle of Invocation				Level 8+ Uncommon	
The radiance of this holy symbol both lights your way and helps you overcome the challenges that block the path.					
Lvl 8	+2	3,400 gp	Lvl 23	+5	425,000 gp
Lvl 13	+3	17,000 gp	Lvl 28	+6	2,125,000 gp
Lvl 18	+4	85,000 gp			
Implement: Holy symbol					
Enhancement Bonus: Attack rolls and damage rolls					
Critical: +1d6 radiant damage per plus					
Utility Power ✦ Encounter (Minor Action)					
Effect: The candle casts bright light in a radius of 4 squares. The light lasts until you extinguish it as a minor action or until you are no longer holding the candle.					
Utility Power ✦ Encounter (Immediate Interrupt)					
Trigger: An ally within 5 squares of you fails a skill check while the candle is lit.					
Effect: The candle's light is extinguished, and the ally gains a power bonus to the skill check equal to 2 + the candle's enhancement bonus.					

Necklace of Prayer Beads

This strand of semiprecious stones appears to be humble jewelry until it is worn by one who can channel its power. Typically made of three kinds of enchanted stones, a *necklace of prayer beads* enables its wearer to choose from the same number of benefits each time the magic of the necklace is called upon. Some crafters have tried to make necklaces with different features, but without any success to date.

Necklace of Prayer Beads				Level 10+ Rare	
The beads that hang from this necklace glow with divine power that you can call upon to overcome any challenge.					
Lvl 10	+2	5,000 gp	Lvl 25	+5	625,000 gp
Lvl 15	+3	25,000 gp	Lvl 30	+6	3,125,000 gp
Lvl 20	+4	125,000 gp			
Implement: Holy symbol					
Enhancement Bonus: Attack rolls and damage rolls					
Critical: +1d8 damage per plus					
Utility Power ✦ Encounter (Minor Action)					
Effect: Choose one of the following benefits.					
✦ You and each ally within 5 squares of you can make a saving throw.					
✦ Until the end of this turn, your healing powers restore the maximum number of hit points possible.					
✦ Once before the end of your next turn, when you miss with a divine attack power, you can reroll the attack roll. You must use the second result.					

Candle of invocation

Phylactery of Faithfulness

The wielder of this holy symbol gains the power to perceive strands of the future and to realize when a possible action would adversely affect the wielder's standing with his or her deity. Such actions might include failing to complete a divine quest or allowing a companion to fall before that person had played his or her part in the gods' grand design.

Phylactery of Faithfulness				Level 14+ Rare
You attune yourself to this symbol of your god and gain insight into your deity's will.				
Lvl 14	+3	21,000 gp	Lvl 24 +5	525,000 gp
Lvl 19	+4	105,000 gp	Lvl 29 +6	2,625,000 gp

Implement: Holy symbol
Enhancement Bonus: Attack rolls and damage rolls
Critical: +1d8 damage per plus

Utility Power ✦ Daily (Standard Action)
 Effect: You ask a single question about two possible courses of action, and a feeling of certainty informs you which course of action is most consistent with your deity's will, or if neither is consistent with it. At the DM's discretion, your deity's answer might provide some insight into the dangers and risks that course involves. These insights are never more than vague hints.

Utility Power ✦ Encounter (Immediate Interrupt)
 Trigger: An attack hits an ally within 5 squares of you.
 Effect: The ally gains a power bonus to all defenses against that attack. The bonus equals the phylactery's enhancement bonus.

If you know the word "phylactery," you probably associate it with that vile curse of magic set loose upon the world, lichdom. Yet it comes from an archaic language wherein the root of the word means "to guard" or "guard post." Thus, the lich who creates a phylactery is quite literally guarding its immortality. Today the term is rightly more broadly used for various amulets and small containers worn about the neck or head. A locket worn about your neck with a lover's hair clasped inside is, in all senses of the word, a phylactery.

To take the analogy back to the topic at hand: The phylactery of faithfulness therefore serves as a guardian of the wearer's faith. Ironic that faith should need guarding. Is not unshakable belief the very definition of faith?

Symbol of the sun

Symbol of the Sun

The undead are considered sacrilegious by most non-evil faiths, and the *symbol of the sun* was created to help cleanse the world of such abominations. During creation, these items are plated with gold beneath the noontime sun on a cloudless day, imbuing them with the ability to enhance the wielder's attacks against undead creatures.

Symbol of the Sun				Level 4+ Common
Crafted from polished gold, this holy symbol intensifies and reflects light like a mirror.				
Lvl 4	+1	840 gp	Lvl 19 +4	105,000 gp
Lvl 9	+2	4,200 gp	Lvl 24 +5	525,000 gp
Lvl 14	+3	21,000 gp	Lvl 29 +6	2,625,000 gp

Implement: Holy symbol
Enhancement Bonus: Attack rolls and damage rolls
Critical: +1d6 radiant damage per plus

Properties
 ✦ When you pull, push, or slide an undead creature with an attack using this implement, you can increase the distance of the forced movement by 1 square.
 ✦ You gain a +2 item bonus to the damage rolls you make with this implement against undead creatures.
 Level 14 or 19: +4 item bonus.
 Level 24 or 29: +6 item bonus.

BRIAN HAGAN

Ki Focuses

As a tool designed to sharpen the mind and train the body to adapt to a unique fighting style, the ki focus is unusual among implements. The wielder of a ki focus rarely uses it in battle directly. Instead, its wielder draws upon the knowledge and magical patterns intrinsic in his or her motions and actions to gain the benefits of the ki focus's enchantment.

Body of Fire Ki Focus

The physical form of this ki focus is a colorless oil. To unlock its power, the user spreads the oil over his or her hands and visualizes fighting a hated enemy until the oil bursts into flame for a brief, painless second. The user must contain and internalize the flame through an act of will each time the inner fire is unleashed. In times of anger or stress, smoke rises from the user's skin.

KI FOCUS RULES

A ki focus is an implement that certain characters use as a focus for their inner magical energy, known as ki. A ki focus might take the form of a training manual, a scroll of ancient secrets, a battered training weapon, or a cherished memento.

Attunement: Before you can use a ki focus, you must attune yourself to it. To attune yourself to a ki focus, you must have the item on your person during a short or an extended rest and must have proficiency with ki focuses. Some characters study their ki focus to attune themselves to it. Others meditate with it or wield it as they practice using fighting techniques. The ki focus that you are attuned to occupies your ki focus item slot.

Whenever you take a rest, you can attune yourself to a ki focus in your possession, but you can be attuned to only one ki focus at a time. Also, only one creature at a time can be attuned to a particular ki focus. Once you attune yourself to a ki focus, no one else can become attuned to it until you are no longer attuned to it or you are dead.

Using a Ki Focus: Once you have attuned yourself to a ki focus, you must either wear it or hold it in order to use it as an implement.

Ki Focuses and Weapon Attacks: If you use a magic ki focus, you can add its enhancement bonus to the attack rolls and the damage rolls of weapon attacks you make using a weapon with which you have proficiency. If you have both a magic ki focus and a magic weapon, you choose before you use an attack power whether to draw on the magic of the ki focus or that of the weapon. Your choice determines which enhancement bonus, critical hit effects, and magic item properties and powers you can apply to that power. You can't, for example, use the enhancement bonus of your ki focus and the critical hit effect of your magic weapon on the same attack.

Body of Fire Ki Focus			Level 4+ Uncommon	
This oil fuels a fire within you that might smolder or might blaze forth, but will never be extinguished.				
Lvl 4	+1	840 gp	Lvl 19 +4	105,000 gp
Lvl 9	+2	4,200 gp	Lvl 24 +5	525,000 gp
Lvl 14	+3	21,000 gp	Lvl 29 +6	2,625,000 gp

Implement: Ki focus
Enhancement Bonus: Attack rolls and damage rolls
Critical: +1d6 fire damage per plus

Property

All damage dealt by attacks using this implement is fire, unless the damage already has a type.

Utility Power (Fire) ✦ **Daily** (Minor Action)

Effect: Until the end of the encounter, you gain resist 5 fire and vulnerable 5 cold. If a creature is grabbing you or being grabbed by you at the start of its turn, it takes 5 fire damage.
Level 14 or 19: Resist 10 fire, vulnerable 10 cold, and 10 fire damage.
Level 24 or 29: Resist 15 fire, vulnerable 15 cold, and 15 fire damage.

Steadfast Stone Ki Focus

The *steadfast stone ki focus* is a simple stone that represents the value of patience and tenacity applied with relentless discipline. Focusing ki into this item involves taking it into your hand and slowly applying more and more pressure. The stone's unyielding strength molds the wielder's ki to emulate the unyielding nature of rock.

Steadfast Stone Ki Focus			Level 9+ Common	
This plain, round stone reveals the secrets of strength and tenacity, allowing you to mimic its impervious nature.				
Lvl 9	+2	4,200 gp	Lvl 24 +5	525,000 gp
Lvl 14	+3	21,000 gp	Lvl 29 +6	2,625,000 gp
Lvl 19	+4	105,000 gp		

Implement: Ki focus
Enhancement Bonus: Attack rolls and damage rolls
Critical: +1d6 damage per plus

Property

Attacks made with this ki focus ignore 5 of any resistance.
Level 14 or 19: Ignore 10 of any resistance.
Level 24 or 29: Ignore 15 of any resistance.

Steadfast stones

EVA WIDERMANN

Tidal Wave Ki Focus

The monastery that originated the use of this ki focus—a scroll bearing the image of a wave—teaches the importance of remaining centered through a parable: "Towers stand fast before the tidal wave and are destroyed; the leaf rides the crest because it flows with the wave's power." Devotees of the school are famed for using a foe's momentum to send the enemy crashing into other enemies, knocking them all sprawling.

Tidal Wave Ki Focus			Level 8+ Uncommon		
You hit an enemy and concentrate on this ki focus, sending that foe staggering backward to the ground.					
Lvl 8	+2	3,400 gp	Lvl 23	+5	425,000 gp
Lvl 13	+3	17,000 gp	Lvl 28	+6	2,125,000 gp
Lvl 18	+4	85,000 gp			
Implement: Ki focus					
Enhancement Bonus: Attack rolls and damage rolls					
Critical: +1d6 damage per plus					
Attack Power ✦ Daily (No Action)					
Trigger: You hit an enemy with a melee attack using this ki focus.					
Effect: You push that enemy up to a number of squares equal to the ki focus's enhancement bonus. At the end of the push, that enemy and each of your enemies adjacent to it fall prone.					

ORBS

An orb channels magic in a manner reminiscent of its shape. Arcane power flows around its surface, seeming to gain strength with each revolution, until that power is unharnessed.

Orb of Enduring Magic

The archmage Bigby is renowned for his skill in weaving conjurations. He created *Bigby's grasping hand*, *Bigby's icy grasp*, and similar powers that call forth fist-shaped constructs of arcane magic to hold enemies at bay. To help him employ such spells, Bigby created the *orb of enduring magic*. It enables its wielder to keep his or her spells active even if he or she is hampered or otherwise unable to focus full attention on them. As a side benefit, drawing on such magic lends the orb's wielder a measure of vitality that helps him or her shrug off attacks.

Orb of Enduring Magic			Level 7+ Uncommon		
Carved from iron to resemble a clenched gauntlet, this orb allows you to extend your magical abilities while absorbing your foes' attacks.					
Lvl 7	+2	2,600 gp	Lvl 22	+5	325,000 gp
Lvl 12	+3	13,000 gp	Lvl 27	+6	1,625,000 gp
Lvl 17	+4	65,000 gp			
Implement: Orb					
Enhancement Bonus: Attack rolls and damage rolls					
Critical: +1d6 damage per plus					
Utility Power ✦ Encounter (Minor Action)					
Effect: You sustain all of your active powers that can be sustained with a minor action. In addition, you gain temporary hit points equal to 2 + the orb's enhancement bonus.					

Although I know of many wizards who use them, I've never been fond of orbs. Most are too large to fit in a pocket, too round to comfortably hold, and too cumbersome by half. I've had better results bowling an orb in a game of skittles than employing one on a battlefield. However, I cannot deny that many orbs of tremendous power exist. My friend Otiluke has always had a peculiar fondness for them. A few tankards short of a keg, that one. Anything circular excited his interest. It's good he never met a beholder while alone. He'd probably have prattled on to it, fascinated by its nature and caught firmly under the gaze of its central eye until it gobbled him up. Otiluke himself created many magical orbs. Often they possessed the power to cast his many sphere and orb spells. I'd use an orb made by Otiluke. I miss his whimsy.

Orb of Forceful Magic

At first glance, an *orb of forceful magic* looks like a sphere of transparent glass, but touching this item reveals its true nature. The orb is a focused sphere of coalesced force, held in place by the magic that created the item. Spells channeled through it batter their targets with greater impact, sending enemies staggering.

Orb of Forceful Magic			Level 3+ Common		
This transparent orb shimmers and glows with golden energy that you can channel to hurl your enemies about.					
Lvl 3	+1	680 gp	Lvl 18	+4	85,000 gp
Lvl 8	+2	3,400 gp	Lvl 23	+5	425,000 gp
Lvl 13	+3	17,000 gp	Lvl 28	+6	2,125,000 gp
Implement: Orb					
Enhancement Bonus: Attack rolls and damage rolls					
Critical: +1d6 force damage per plus					
Property					
When you pull, push, or slide an enemy with an attack using this orb, you can increase the distance of the forced movement by 1 square.					

Orb of Relentless Sympathy

This orb often takes the form of a head sculpted in bronze or clay. Its wielder can link the sensations of nearby minds through it. An enemy that harms one of the wielder's friends feels the pain it has inflicted—and that pain is magnified. The wielder is not entirely detached from the process, however; the orb's shielding cannot entirely protect him or her if any mind within range suffers a grievous wound.

Orb of Relentless Sympathy			Level 4+ Uncommon		

This orb empathically links you and your allies' physical senses to your enemy's mind, causing it to feel your pain when it harms you.

Lvl 4	+1	840 gp	Lvl 19	+4	105,000 gp
Lvl 9	+2	4,200 gp	Lvl 24	+5	525,000 gp
Lvl 14	+3	21,000 gp	Lvl 29	+6	2,625,000 gp

Implement: Orb
Enhancement Bonus: Attack rolls and damage rolls
Critical: +1d6 psychic damage per plus

Property

You gain an item bonus to Insight checks equal to the orb's enhancement bonus.

Attack Power (Psychic) ✦ **Daily** (No Action)

Trigger: You hit a target with an attack using this orb.

Effect: The target takes psychic damage equal to 2 + the orb's enhancement bonus at the end of any of its turns during which it hit you or one of your allies. This effect lasts until the end of the encounter or until you end it as a minor action. If the target drops to 0 hit points while this power is in effect, you lose a healing surge (or you take damage equal to your healing surge value if you have no surges remaining).

Prismatic Orb

The seven pure colors of the rainbow decorate the surface of this orb. Each hue is represented by a shell of luminous force formed by the crystal at the orb's heart. The wielder can channel each of the shells in turn and hurl them at a target, enclosing it in a hindering globe of brightly hued energy. Although the sequence of alternating colors appears to be random, some texts claim that certain shades presage danger or opportunity.

Many who live in the Feywild claim that the first *prismatic orb* was crafted in their realm. A human mage from the world who loved the magic and the primal energy of the Feywild often traveled to that realm, taking special delight in the amazing rainbows that always emerged after a storm passed (and sometimes without a storm). The mage discovered a way to harness the power of the lingering rainbows, infusing their light in an orb carved from a type of crystal from the Feydark. Whether this story is true or not, those who face the power held within a *prismatic orb* quickly learn to fear anyone wielding this powerful item.

Prismatic orb

Prismatic Orb			Level 15+ Rare		

Each of the spectral colors flickering on the surface of this orb is a shell of energy that can engulf a foe.

Lvl 15	+3	25,000 gp	Lvl 25	+5	625,000 gp
Lvl 20	+4	125,000 gp	Lvl 30	+6	3,125,000 gp

Implement: Orb
Enhancement Bonus: Attack rolls and damage rolls
Critical: +1d8 damage per plus

Attack Power (Teleportation) ✦ **Daily** (No Action)

Trigger: You hit a target with an attack using this orb.

Effect: You teleport the target up to a number of squares equal to the orb's enhancement bonus.

Attack Power ✦ **Daily** (No Action)

Trigger: You hit a target with an at-will or encounter attack power using this orb.

Effect: The target is dazed or immobilized (save ends). You choose the effect.

Utility Power ✦ **Encounter** (No Action)

Trigger: You hit a target with an attack using this orb.

Effect: Choose acid, fire, lightning, or poison. Until the target saves against this effect, attacks that deal damage of the chosen type to the target gain an item bonus to their damage rolls against the target. The bonus equals the orb's enhancement bonus.

Stone of Good Luck

The first gnome clan to experiment with luck stones learned to their sorrow that fate often acts decisively to restore the balance between good luck and bad. To avoid tempting fate, a well-crafted *stone of good luck* rearranges the wielder's luck so that good fortune arrives when it is most needed.

Stone of Good Luck		Level 14+ Uncommon	
This orb, typically made from rough polished agate, grants its wielder control over the ups and downs of fortune.			
Lvl 14	+3	21,000 gp	
Lvl 19	+4	105,000 gp	
Lvl 24	+5	525,000 gp	
Lvl 29	+6	2,625,000 gp	

Implement: Orb
Enhancement Bonus: Attack rolls and damage rolls
Critical: +1d6 damage per plus
Utility Power ✦ Daily (No Action)
Trigger: You fail a saving throw.
Effect: You gain a +10 power bonus to your next saving throw during this encounter.
Utility Power ✦ Daily (No Action)
Trigger: You make an attack or a damage roll using this orb and dislike the result.
Effect: You gain a power bonus to the roll. The bonus equals the orb's enhancement bonus.

RODS

The rod is the signature implement for warlocks, although some other practitioners of the mystic arts employ implements of this sort. Compact and easy to handle, a rod also makes a good choice for a warrior who dabbles in spellcasting.

Rod of Absorption

This rod, which typically takes the form of an elaborately carved metal cylinder, appears otherwise unremarkable until one notices how lights dim and sounds become muted in its vicinity. The ability of these rods to negate hostile energy was highly valued during the Dawn War. Some immortals who fought in those battles, and whose perceptions of reality and memory often mix, might mistake anyone wielding a *rod of absorption* for an enemy officer from that ancient war.

Rod of Absorption		Level 4+ Rare	
This rod is prized for its power to negate all forms of energy.			
Lvl 4	+1	840 gp	
Lvl 9	+2	4,200 gp	
Lvl 14	+3	21,000 gp	
Lvl 19	+4	105,000 gp	
Lvl 24	+5	525,000 gp	
Lvl 29	+6	2,625,000 gp	

Implement: Rod
Enhancement Bonus: Attack rolls and damage rolls
Critical: +1d8 damage per plus
Attack Power ✦ Encounter (No Action)
Trigger: You hit a creature with an attack using this rod and the creature has an active aura.
Effect: The aura is deactivated, and the creature can't reactivate the aura (save ends).
Utility Power ✦ Daily (Immediate Interrupt)
Trigger: You are targeted by a close attack power or an area attack power that has a damage keyword.
Effect: The attacker takes a −5 penalty to all of the power's attack rolls.

Warlocks make strange bargains. Although many claim to have stolen their might from some source, I have a hard time believing anyone can get something for nothing. Plus, it's hard to trust the word of an admitted thief—and one that would take the easy route to magical power rather than go through the long process of study or religious devotion.

No, warlocks are not to be trusted, nor are their tools. While some other spellcasters take up the skill of manipulating magic with rods, I cannot recommend that anyone do so. The taint of warlocks' pacts cling to these objects.

What promises were made to imbue them with power? Whose souls were lost in order to make a creature's bone or a bar of iron into a weapon of magic? Of course, many dark deeds have been done to create great magic—by myself included—but a rod might still be linking its wielder to whatever entity imbued its creator with power.

Rod of absorption

WAYNE ENGLAND

Rod of Beguiling

This rod gives its wielder control over an enemy by playing on the foe's greed and reflexive submission to authority. The rod seems to be a crude lead scepter until its power is activated, at which point others see its shaft turn golden and its gem-covered head sparkle. Enemies that view the rod in this transformed state are briefly fooled into thinking that the wielder is on their side. Even when the power is not called forth, mere possession of the rod gives its owner an advantage when dealing with others.

Rod of Beguiling			Level 10+ Rare		
This rod displays the trappings of wealth and status, persuading your foes to see you as one of their own.					
Lvl 10	+2	5,000 gp	Lvl 25	+5	625,000 gp
Lvl 15	+3	25,000 gp	Lvl 30	+6	3,125,000 gp
Lvl 20	+4	125,000 gp			
Implement: Rod					
Enhancement Bonus: Attack rolls and damage rolls					
Critical: +1d8 psychic damage per plus					
Property					
You gain an item bonus to Bluff checks, Diplomacy checks, and Intimidate checks equal to the rod's enhancement bonus.					
Utility Power (Charm) ✦ **Daily** (Minor Action)					
Effect: Until the end of your next turn, enemies cannot attack you, or target you with any effect that targets an enemy. An enemy ignores this effect if you attack it, if it is marked by you, or if it is in your *defender aura*.					

Rod of Death

These grim rods are often made of wood from a gallows where someone sentenced to be hanged escaped the noose. The wielder of this rod can empower it by choosing to step closer to the grave. There is no obvious cost to doing so twice, as long as the wielder is not brought to death's door by bodily harm. Those who do so on a third occasion discover that the rod becomes less useful for a time.

Rod of Death			Level 8+ Uncommon		
Wielding this rod lets you cheat death to harm your foes more quickly.					
Lvl 8	+2	3,400 gp	Lvl 23	+5	425,000 gp
Lvl 13	+3	17,000 gp	Lvl 28	+6	2,125,000 gp
Lvl 18	+4	85,000 gp			
Implement: Rod					
Enhancement Bonus: Attack rolls and damage rolls					
Critical: +1d8 damage per plus					
Property					
Whenever you make a damage roll for an attack with this rod and don't like the result, you can reroll the damage roll and must use the new result. If you make the reroll, you are considered to have failed a death saving throw. If this is your third failure since your last rest, the failure does not cause you to die until you are dying, and you cannot use this property again until you have fewer than three failures.					

Rod of death

Rod of Revenge

Crafted from wood harvested from the darkest corners of the Feywild, a *rod of revenge* enables its wielder to lash out effectively against an enemy that has just landed a blow on that individual. Any foe that's the target of the rod's power might be less likely to seek out the wielder as the battle continues, having seen firsthand what can happen if that creature presses its attack.

Rod of Revenge			Level 2+ Uncommon		
This rod resembles a short spear carved from black wood. With it, you can gain the upper hand against any foe that dares to attack you.					
Lvl 2	+1	520 gp	Lvl 17	+4	65,000 gp
Lvl 7	+2	2,600 gp	Lvl 22	+5	325,000 gp
Lvl 12	+3	13,000 gp	Lvl 27	+6	1,625,000 gp
Implement: Rod					
Enhancement Bonus: Attack rolls and damage rolls					
Critical: +1d6 damage per plus					
Utility Power ✦ **Encounter** (Immediate Reaction)					
Trigger: An enemy hits you.					
Effect: Until the end of your next turn, you gain combat advantage against that enemy when you attack it using this rod.					

WAYNE ENGLAND

Rod of Smiting

This rod is nearly unbreakable. Stories abound of those who wield such items catching an opponent off guard with a seemingly weak swing that cracks bones and smashes skulls. A *rod of smiting* bestows the strength of an enchanted mace upon attacks made through it, imparting tremendous force to those blows.

Rod of Smiting			Level 2+ Common	
The head of this rods flares outward like a mace. It weighs heavily in your hand, allowing you to make heavy strikes with it like a weapon.				
Lvl 2	+1	520 gp	Lvl 17	+4	65,000 gp
Lvl 7	+2	2,600 gp	Lvl 22	+5	325,000 gp
Lvl 12	+3	13,000 gp	Lvl 27	+6	1,625,000 gp

Implement: Rod
Enhancement Bonus: Attack rolls and damage rolls
Critical: +1d10 force damage per plus
Property
This rod can be used as a melee weapon, functioning as a mace. You add its enhancement bonus to the attack rolls and damage rolls of melee weapon attacks that you make with it.

STAFFS

A staff is perhaps the most commonly recognized magic implement, because of both its size and its place in folklore and legend. Some of the mightiest wizards in history have used staffs to channel and focus magical power. A staff's size and heft make it the ideal choice for a defensive implement that can ward off attacks while delivering powerful spells.

Greater Staff of Power

Though firm knowledge of its origin has been lost, many believe the first *greater staff of power* to be a copy of a copy of a staff wielded by Corellon in the Dawn War. The thousands of runes that cover this gnarled staff glow with an eerie green light and hint at the versatility of the magic harnessed within. Those wielders who are cognizant of the fundamental nature of energy find many ways to mold and manipulate the staff's features to great benefit.

Greater staff of power

I have seen many sticks called a staff of power in my time. It seems like any mage that gets a hold of a magic staff wants to call it his "staff of power." I suppose that lacking real power gives one the desire for its trappings. Know that a true staff of power is no trifling thing. They contain a raw might uncommon in other enchanted items. Their power can turn aside blows, change fate, and preserve the wilder's life in the most dire circumstances. Great things can be accomplished by a mage with a staff of power. Great and terrible things.

Greater Staff of Power		Level 25+ Rare	
Covered in eldritch runes, this staff exudes raw magical might that you can harness for your defense or to attack your foes.			
Lvl 25	+5	625,000 gp	Lvl 30	+6	3,125,000 gp

Implement: Staff
Enhancement Bonus: Attack rolls and damage rolls
Critical: +1d10 damage per plus
Attack Power (Force) ✦ **Daily** (Immediate Reaction)
   Trigger: An enemy within 20 squares of you hits you with an attack.
   Effect: The enemy takes force damage equal to 25 + the level of your highest-level unused daily arcane attack power.
Utility Power ✦ **Encounter** (Minor Action)
   Effect: You gain a +5 power bonus to all defenses against the next attack against you during this encounter.
Utility Power ✦ **Daily** (No Action)
   Trigger: You miss with an attack roll for an at-will or an encounter arcane attack power using this staff.
   Effect: You reroll that attack roll and must use the second result.

Staff of Command

To create this staff, arcane crystals are dissolved in a solution. The supersaturated solution is kept in absolute silence until the crafter speaks a word in Primordial. The vibrations of his or her voice ordering the staff to form cause the solution to draw forth from its container and crystallize into a long, tapering shard. Anyone who carries a *staff of command* is viewed by others with a measure of respect, and when the item is used in battle it greatly enhances the efficacy of the wielder's charm powers.

Staff of Command

Staff of Command			Level 4+ Uncommon		
This staff is a useful tool for imposing your will on others.					
Lvl 4	+1	840 gp	Lvl 19	+4	105,000 gp
Lvl 9	+2	4,200 gp	Lvl 24	+5	525,000 gp
Lvl 14	+3	21,000 gp	Lvl 29	+6	2,625,000 gp

Implement: Staff

Enhancement Bonus: Attack rolls and damage rolls

Critical: +1d6 psychic damage per plus

Property

You gain an item bonus to Diplomacy checks equal to the staff's enhancement bonus.

Attack Power ✦ Encounter (No Action)

Trigger: You hit a target with a charm power using this staff.

Effect: You slide the target up to a number of squares equal to the staff's enhancement bonus, and the target grants combat advantage to you until the end of your next turn.

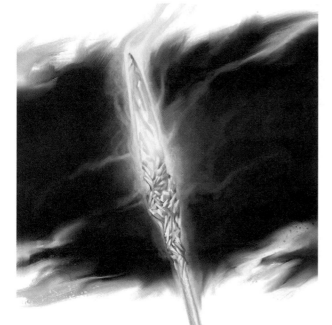

Staff of command

Staff of Striking

When its special power is ready for use, a *staff of striking* emits a deep, ominous hum until its wielder delivers a blow to his or her foe. Even unintelligent enemies instinctively recognize the danger inherent in a *staff of striking*, making it as effective for performing feints and threats as for making actual strikes in melee. Wizards in particular favor these implements, since the gentlest tap from a *staff of striking* sends an enemy stumbling away.

Staff of Striking			Level 4+ Uncommon		
Fashioned of unadorned metal in a symmetrical and severe design, this staff delivers forceful blows to your enemies.					
Lvl 4	+1	840 gp	Lvl 19	+4	105,000 gp
Lvl 9	+2	4,200 gp	Lvl 24	+5	525,000 gp
Lvl 14	+3	21,000 gp	Lvl 29	+6	2,625,000 gp

Implement: Staff

Enhancement Bonus: Attack rolls and damage rolls

Critical: +1d8 damage per plus

Attack Power ✦ Encounter (No Action)

Trigger: You hit a creature adjacent to you with an implement or a weapon attack using this staff.

Effect: You push the creature 1 square and knock it prone.

Staff of the Viper

Some lore-gatherers among the yuan-ti have claimed that the first *staff of the viper* was made in memory of the snake that taught mortals the secret of constructing magic items. Despite the item's most commonly known name and its appearance when it is used, other scholars and historians do not agree that the staff expressly captures the essence of a snake—after all, they say, poisonous attacks are not the domain of ophidians alone.

The wielder of this sinuous, rough-carved wooden staff can cause the staff's head to shape itself into the head of a snake that delivers a venomous strike.

Staff of the Viper			Level 7+ Uncommon		
The head of this wooden staff animates when you lash out at a foe, delivering a poisonous wound.					
Lvl 7	+2	2,600 gp	Lvl 22	+5	325,000 gp
Lvl 12	+3	13,000 gp	Lvl 27	+6	1,625,000 gp
Lvl 17	+4	65,000 gp			

Implement: Staff

Enhancement Bonus: Attack rolls and damage rolls

Critical: +1d8 poison damage per plus

Attack Power (Poison) **✦ Daily** (No Action)

Trigger: You hit a creature with an attack using this staff.

Effect: The creature takes ongoing 5 poison damage (save ends).

Level 12 or 17: Ongoing 10 poison damage.

Level 22 or 27: Ongoing 15 poison damage.

Staff of Withering

This staff resembles an old, gnarled tree branch blackened with rot and mold. A cruel wizard-prince who had no need for a dungeon or a prison in his realm created the original *staff of withering*. He used the staff, which was the symbol of his power, upon criminals and rebels in his realm, aging them to infirmity with a single touch.

In time, the tyrant fell to the might of druids and elves whose forest he sought to conquer and despoil. The triumphant druids destroyed the original staff, but lesser copies employed by his inquisitors spread across the world. Any spellcaster bearing a *staff of withering* can expect a hostile reaction to the symbol of tyranny he or she carries.

Staff of Withering			Level 3+ Uncommon		
This staff appears to be little more than a rotting tree branch, but one touch of it saps the strength from any foe.					
Lvl 3	+1	680 gp	Lvl 18	+4	85,000 gp
Lvl 8	+2	3,400 gp	Lvl 23	+5	425,000 gp
Lvl 13	+3	17,000 gp	Lvl 28	+6	2,125,000 gp
Implement: Staff					
Enhancement Bonus: Attack rolls and damage rolls					
Critical: +1d6 necrotic damage per plus					
Attack Power ✦ Daily (No Action)					
Trigger: You hit a target with an attack using this staff.					
Effect: The target is weakened (save ends).					

TOMES

A rare sort of implement for an adventuring wizard, the tome offers great flexibility and power. Wizards ensconced in their towers typically employ tomes. Most adventuring wizards find a tome too bulky and unwieldy compared to an orb, a staff, or a wand, but all wizards see the great value in the lore that tomes contain.

Wizards are automatically proficient with using tomes as implements.

Emerald Tome of the Devourer

The first *emerald tome of the devourer* is said to have fallen from the sky as a shooting star. Many of those who have borne one of these implements have met untimely ends, and although this tome is often seen as an ill omen for that reason, it offers great benefits to those willing to use it.

When a nearby enemy is close to death, the bearer of this implement can invoke its special power to more easily dispatch that foe—but if the owner's death blow fails to land, the tome will devour the essence it seeks from within the one who holds it.

In everyday use, the tome appears to contain only blank pages for anyone but its owner, who can perceive magical writing that reveals insights into the world. That the tome comes from the realm of the fell stars is indisputable. Whoever grasps one of these tomes sees darkness fall away, his or her vision illuminated by the cold, pale light of a distant star.

Emerald Tome of the Devourer			Level 10+ Rare		
This green tome's cover and pages have a strange metallic feel. An eldritch yellow sigil marks its cover and emanates a sense of foreboding.					
Lvl 10	+2	5,000 gp	Lvl 25	+5	625,000 gp
Lvl 15	+3	25,000 gp	Lvl 30	+6	3,125,000 gp
Lvl 20	+4	125,000 gp			
Implement: Tome					
Enhancement Bonus: Attack rolls and damage rolls					
Critical: +1d8 damage per plus					
Properties					
✦ You gain darkvision.					
✦ You gain an item bonus to Arcana checks, History checks, and Religion checks. The bonus equals the tome's enhancement bonus.					
Utility Power ✦ Encounter (Minor Action)					
Effect: You gain a +2 item bonus to your next attack roll before the end of your next turn. If that attack hits, you gain an item bonus to its damage roll. The bonus equals 4 + the tome's enhancement bonus. If you do not kill a creature before the end of your next turn, you take damage equal to your healing surge value at the end of that turn. If this damage drops you below 1 hit point, you die.					

I have little doubt that the so-called emerald tome of the devourer has its origins in what we have come to know as the Far Realm. There exist certain stellar beings—mistakes of the gods, victims of strange fates, vestiges of defeated beings of immense power, leftovers from the time of creation—that are somehow tied to that hidden plane. And it might be that the tome comes as a kind of message—or, more worryingly, as a spy—for one or more of these entities. That the Far Realm has spawned such horrors as mind flayers and aboleths is enough to convince me that such tomes present a threat regardless of the intent of their creators. I have expunged every such item I can find, but I'm certain that more lurk throughout the land, hidden in the cracks of the world or the robes of misguided spellcasters.

Magic tome

Magic Tome

The typical magic tome relies on the enchantments contained within the paper and ink that were used to craft it. Ingredients such as ink from dragon's blood, paper crafted from trees found within astral domains, and similarly rare materials combine to lend strength to spells cast through such a tome.

Magic Tome		Level 1+ Common	
Scribed with rare inks and printed on paper crafted from trees nourished with magical power, this tome amplifies your spellcasting ability.			
Lvl 1	+1	360 gp	
Lvl 6	+2	1,800 gp	
Lvl 11	+3	9,000 gp	
Lvl 16	+4	45,000 gp	
Lvl 21	+5	225,000 gp	
Lvl 26	+6	1,125,000 gp	
Implement: Tome			
Enhancement Bonus: Attack rolls and damage rolls			
Critical: +1d6 damage per plus			

Manual of Expansive Learning

This little-seen tome is a compilation of mystic exercises and mnemonic techniques. The original one was crafted by a long-nameless adventuring mage who managed to infuse an ordinary object with the remarkable ability to "remember" a useful spell he had already cast.

When he tried to take his experiment one step further while on an adventure, the wizard found that he could even use the tome to summon forth an attack spell he had not thought to prepare. The strain of performing this act left the wizard sapped of some of his inner strength, which he considered a small price to pay.

Manual of Expansive Learning			Level 14+ Rare	
This tome expands your ability to prepare and use spells.				
Lvl 14	+3	21,000 gp	Lvl 24 +5	525,000 gp
Lvl 19	+4	105,000 gp	Lvl 29 +6	2,625,000 gp
Implement: Tome				
Enhancement Bonus: Attack rolls and damage rolls				
Critical: +1d8 damage per plus				

Utility Power ✦ Daily (Minor Action)
Effect: You regain the use of one wizard encounter or daily utility power that you have already used. The power must be in your spellbook, and its level must be lower than the tome's level.

Utility Power ✦ Daily (Minor Action)
Requirement: You must be taking a short rest, have a spellbook, have at least one healing surge, and have expended all your wizard daily attack powers.
Effect: You lose a healing surge, but you gain the use of one wizard daily attack power from your spellbook that you did not prepare after your last extended rest. The power's level must be lower than the tome's level.

Manual of Puissant Skill

This tome's features, such as a waterproof cover, sturdy bindings, and stain-resistant pages, suggest it was designed for wizards who lead an unusually active lifestyle. Its codification of the best ways to overcome problems with skilled deeds reflects a quest for formulas by which all mortal knowledge might be studied and prepared in the same way as spells.

Manual of Puissant Skill			Level 9+ Rare	
This tome contains lore to improve your performance by training your mind and body.				
Lvl 9	+2	4,200 gp	Lvl 24 +5	525,000 gp
Lvl 14	+3	21,000 gp	Lvl 29 +6	2,625,000 gp
Lvl 19	+4	105,000 gp		
Implement: Tome				
Enhancement Bonus: Attack rolls and damage rolls				
Critical: +1d8 damage per plus				

Property
You gain a +2 item bonus to skill checks.

Utility Power ✦ Daily (No Action)
Trigger: You make a skill check and dislike the result.
Effect: You reroll the skill check and must use the second result.

Utility Power ✦ Encounter (Minor Action)
Effect: You gain a +2 item bonus to the next attack roll you make before the end of the current turn.

Tome of Undeniable Might

An unremembered yet brilliant mage wrote this tome as a treatise on a theory she developed: that arcane magic taps into a state of being beyond the physical. According to her research, the physical world is merely an illusion, while arcane magic provides the true structure of the world. Although the archmage's name is now forgotten, the secrets contained within this tome allow casters to overcome some of the physical limits to their combat spells, keeping her legacy intact.

Tome of Undeniable Might		Level 8+ Common	
This plain, leather-bound tome appears to be a simple treatise on arcane magic, but at your touch, it gives your powers the ability to affect creatures not of the world.			
Lvl 8	+2	3,400 gp	
Lvl 13	+3	17,000 gp	
Lvl 18	+4	85,000 gp	

| Lvl 23 | +5 | 425,000 gp |
| Lvl 28 | +6 | 2,125,000 gp |

Implement: Tome
Enhancement Bonus: Attack rolls and damage rolls
Critical: +1d6 damage per plus
Property
When you gain this tome, choose acid, cold, fire, lightning, necrotic, psychic, or thunder. Your arcane attacks made with this tome ignore the insubstantial quality if they have the chosen damage keyword. You can change your choice at the end of an extended rest.

TOTEMS

Totems allow druids and other users of primal magic to gather and direct energy. Most totems are linked to a symbolic event, creature, or concept in the natural world.

Totem of Thorns

All living things feel pain. This totem is based on that truth, storing up the wielder's pain to unleash it upon his or her enemies as a concentrated wave of agony. Owners of a *totem of thorns* are typically eager to enter combat, since battle is a constructive way to keep the totem supplied with the hurt it channels.

Totem of Thorns		Level 5+ Uncommon	
This totem is carved from a briar vines with their thorns left intact, so that it cannot be gripped without drawing blood.			
Lvl 5	+1	1,000 gp	
Lvl 10	+2	5,000 gp	
Lvl 15	+3	25,000 gp	

Lvl 20	+4	125,000 gp
Lvl 25	+5	625,000 gp
Lvl 30	+6	3,125,000 gp

Implement: Totem
Enhancement Bonus: Attack rolls and damage rolls
Critical: +1d6 psychic damage per plus, or +1d10 psychic damage per plus if you are bloodied
Attack Power (Psychic) ✦ **Encounter** (No Action)
  Trigger: You hit a target with an attack using this totem while you are bloodied.
  Effect: The target takes extra psychic damage equal to the number of healing surges you have spent since your last extended rest.
Utility Power ✦ **Daily** (Minor Action)
  Requirement: You must be bloodied.
  Effect: You lose a healing surge, and you gain temporary hit points equal to 5 + your healing surge value + the totem's enhancement bonus.

Totem of thorns

I must admit to some ignorance surrounding magical totems. I've always seen them as the cursed domain of grubby, shamanistic savages like orcs and gnolls. Apparently, there exist some druids who utilize them, although I doubt very much that such druids differ much from orcs. Perhaps that was too unkind, but I find myself at odds with druids as often as not. While many druids talk of the need for balance in the world, we of the Circle of Eight desire a balance of power, not a balance between wilderness and civilization. The world is deadly. It needs taming, not protecting.

Totem of Trailblazing

Legends tell of a time when human tribes fled into the high mountains to escape a great calamity. The first *totems of trailblazing* were crafted to help explorers who ventured back to the lowlands, trying to find their way home. Supposedly, secret phrases or other passwords create a map on the totem, showing the location of the refuges where the tribes took shelter.

Totem of Trailblazing				Level 2+ Common	
This simple stone has the faded image of a campsite painted upon it.					
Lvl 2	+1	520 gp	Lvl 17	+4	65,000 gp
Lvl 7	+2	2,600 gp	Lvl 22	+5	325,000 gp
Lvl 12	+3	13,000 gp	Lvl 27	+6	1,625,000 gp

Implement: Totem
Enhancement Bonus: Attack rolls and damage rolls
Critical: +1d6 damage per plus
Property
You gain an item bonus to Nature checks equal to the totem's enhancement bonus.

Totem of the Woodlands

This beautifully carved length of oak, ash, or yew is a symbol of the forest's abundance. Even when not channeled by its wielder, the totem's power is always active. Tales say that if one of these totems is left unattended next to a fence or a chair, it can cause vines and leaves to sprout from the once-living material.

Totem of the Woodlands				Level 5+ Rare	
This carved wooden totem lets you call forth the power of the forest to block and restrain your enemies.					
Lvl 5	+1	1,000 gp	Lvl 20	+4	125,000 gp
Lvl 10	+2	5,000 gp	Lvl 25	+5	625,000 gp
Lvl 15	+3	25,000 gp	Lvl 30	+6	3,125,000 gp

Implement: Totem
Enhancement Bonus: Attack rolls and damage rolls
Critical: +1d6 damage per plus, and the target is slowed (save ends).
Attack Power ✦ Daily (No Action)
Trigger: You hit a target with an attack using this totem.
Effect: The target is restrained (save ends).
Utility Power ✦ Encounter (Minor Action)
Effect: You create a vine in your square that stretches to one unattended object you can see within 10 squares of you and twines around it. The vine is as strong as a rope and lasts until the end of the encounter or until you spend a minor action to cause the vine to retract. If the vine is twined around an object weighing less than 5 pounds, it can pull that object into your space when the vine retracts.
Utility Power (Zone) ✦ Encounter (No Action)
Trigger: You use a close or an area primal attack power with this totem.
Effect: The power's area of effect also creates a zone of difficult terrain that lasts until the end of your next turn.

WANDS

The wand is one of the most common kinds of implement, particularly among wizards. Wands are usually crafted with an attunement to a specific energy type or category of effect. A wand's size and design typically allow it to contain a limited range of magical abilities, but within that range it offers flexibility and expertise.

Apprentice's Wand

This simple wooden wand is a typical gift from a master to an apprentice. To ensure that an apprentice is never without an implement, this wand can be attuned to its user. With a simple gesture, the wand appears in its owner's hand, ready for use.

Apprentice's Wand				Level 2+ Common	
This simple length of wood appears in your hand when you need it most.					
Lvl 2	+1	520 gp	Lvl 17	+4	65,000 gp
Lvl 7	+2	2,600 gp	Lvl 22	+5	325,000 gp
Lvl 12	+3	13,000 gp	Lvl 27	+6	1,625,000 gp

Implement: Wand
Enhancement Bonus: Attack rolls and damage rolls
Critical: +1d6 damage per plus
Properties
✦ You gain an item bonus to Arcana checks to sense the presence of magic. The bonus equals the wand's enhancement bonus.
✦ You can attune this wand to yourself during a short rest. It can be attuned to only one person at a time, and attuning it to one person breaks the attunement to anyone else.
Utility Power ✦ Encounter (Minor Action)
Effect: If the wand is attuned to you and on the same plane, it is transported to your hand, regardless of distance.

Wand of Conjuring

The few who are able to craft these items claim that they can be made only from a single source of metal found in the Feydark. The metal, taken from a vein of ore in a large underground cavern filled with waterfalls and other wonders, is unique because it is infused with magic from the blood of Corellon. That deity's blood fell upon the vein of ore when Lolth struck him during the surprise attack that sundered the alliance between Corellon, Sehanine, and Lolth that existed in antiquity. Those who tell these tales also speak of many terrible monsters that inhabit the cavern, warning off those who would try to replicate this wand.

Wand of Conjuring — Level 8+ Rare

This metal wand is covered in silvery runes that glow with arcane might. Here and there, strands and crystals seem to exude from it.

Lvl 8	+2	3,400 gp	Lvl 23	+5	425,000 gp
Lvl 13	+3	17,000 gp	Lvl 28	+6	2,125,000 gp
Lvl 18	+4	85,000 gp			

Implement: Wand

Enhancement Bonus: Attack rolls and damage rolls

Critical: +1d6 damage per plus, or +1d10 damage per plus when used with a conjuration attack

Utility Power (Varies, Zone) ✦ Encounter (Standard Action)

Effect: You create a zone in a wall 5 within 10 squares of you. The zone lasts until the end of your next turn. When you use this power, choose one of the following effects (a creature can take damage from the zone only once per turn):

Flame (Fire): Any creature that enters the zone or ends its turn there takes 5 fire damage.

Frost (Cold): Any creature that enters the zone or ends its turn there takes 2 cold damage, and it is slowed (save ends).

Darkness: The zone is heavily obscured.

Venom (Poison): The zone is lightly obscured, and any creature that enters the zone or ends its turn there takes 2 poison damage.

Level 13 or 18: Add 5 to the effect's damage, if any.

Level 23 or 28: Add 10 to the effect's damage, if any.

Wand of Fear

Pale light flickers along the length of this fractured crystal wand. Faces viewed in this light resemble skulls, while the visions seen by foes struck by the wand's energy are too horrible to be put into words. Those who wield a *wand of fear* often suffer nightmares. Sometimes these dreams contain omens of future events, although they are rarely interpreted in time to prevent them from coming true.

Wand of Fear — Level 3+ Uncommon

The only thing more unnerving than holding this pale wand is experiencing its horrific effects.

Lvl 3	+1	680 gp	Lvl 18	+4	85,000 gp
Lvl 8	+2	3,400 gp	Lvl 23	+5	425,000 gp
Lvl 13	+3	17,000 gp	Lvl 28	+6	2,125,000 gp

Implement: Wand

Enhancement Bonus: Attack rolls and damage rolls

Critical: +1d6 damage per plus

Property

You gain an item bonus to Intimidate checks equal to the wand's enhancement bonus.

Attack Power (Fear) ✦ Encounter (No Action)

Trigger: You hit a target with an attack using this wand.

Effect: You push the target up to a number of squares equal to the wand's enhancement bonus.

Wand of Fire

Typical materials used in the construction of these wands include flame-blackened wood, phoenix feathers, and salamander scales. Sages claim that the wizard Kelgore crafted a handful of these wands after becoming so angry that he sequestered himself from all mortal contact for a year. Although Kelgore himself was a bit of a comical figure, his enemies fled in terror when they saw him approaching in a fit of rage with one of these wands in hand.

Wand of Fire — Level 15+ Rare

Thin wisps of smoke curl from the surface of this pyrotechnic wand.

Lvl 15	+3	25,000 gp	Lvl 25	+5	625,000 gp
Lvl 20	+4	125,000 gp	Lvl 30	+6	3,125,000 gp

Implement: Wand

Enhancement Bonus: Attack rolls and damage rolls

Critical: +1d8 fire damage per plus

Attack Power ✦ Daily (No Action)

Trigger: You hit a target with an at-will or encounter attack power that has the fire keyword using this wand.

Effect: The attack's fire damage is maximized against the target.

Utility Power ✦ Encounter (Minor Action)

Effect: The next area or close fire attack that you use during this turn with this wand does not target any of your allies who would otherwise be targeted by the attack.

Utility Power (Fire) ✦ Encounter (Minor Action)

Effect: You cause one unattended, inanimate, flammable object (up to 1 square foot) that is adjacent to you to catch on fire.

Where would wizards be without wands? The wand is to the wizard what the sword is to the warrior. Yet how did it come to be such? Which came first, the wizard or the wand? As long as one has existed, it seems so has the other, but surely in some world at some time there must have been the first wizard and the first wand. The first sword was probably a piece of junk barely better than a club, but the first wand would have been magic incarnate. If it still exists, what powers might that first wand have? What features might it have collected over the eons and from the thousands who have wielded it? Such is the stuff of all wizards' dreams.

Wand of Frost

Some of these wands are carved of white dragon bone, while others are icicles made permanent and unbreakable. In use, a silver ray springs forth from the wand's tip to freeze a single enemy, or a single touch instantly turns water to ice. According to legend, each *wand of frost* is constructed to destroy a specific creature that is vulnerable to cold. Even if this is untrue, the tale is widespread enough to make it an effective threat.

Wand of Frost					Level 4+ Rare
Snow drifts to the ground in the wake of this wand's silvery ray, as it freezes the air it passes through before striking your enemy.					
Lvl 4	+1	840 gp	Lvl 19	+4	105,000 gp
Lvl 9	+2	4,200 gp	Lvl 24	+5	525,000 gp
Lvl 14	+3	21,000 gp	Lvl 29	+6	2,625,000 gp
Implement: Wand					
Enhancement Bonus: Attack rolls and damage rolls					
Critical: +1d8 cold damage per plus					
Property					
You gain cold resistance equal to 3 + twice the wand's enhancement bonus.					
Attack Power ✦ Daily (No Action)					
Trigger: You hit a target with a cold attack using this wand.					
Effect: The target is immobilized (save ends).					
Utility Power ✦ Encounter (Minor Action)					
Effect: You touch an adjacent container, pool, or other body of water with the wand, and a number of contiguous squares within the body of water equal to 1 + the wand's enhancement bonus freeze into solid ice. Only one of the frozen squares has to be adjacent to you. The squares of ice are difficult terrain and remain solid until the end of the encounter. This effect cannot freeze a square if it contains any creatures.					

Wand of Inevitability

This wand gathers spent magical energy to make its next attack more accurate. The springy, flexible wood used to construct the wand reflects its ability to absorb and redirect energy. In some lands, a *wand of inevitability* is standard equipment for wizards who are members of a city watch or a group of noble's bodyguards.

Wand of Inevitability					Level 3+ Common
This wand, crafted from light, supple wood, allows you to accurately strike your enemies with a flick of the wrist.					
Lvl 3	+1	680 gp	Lvl 18	+4	85,000 gp
Lvl 8	+2	3,400 gp	Lvl 23	+5	425,000 gp
Lvl 13	+3	17,000 gp	Lvl 28	+6	2,125,000 gp
Implement: Wand					
Enhancement Bonus: Attack rolls and damage rolls					
Critical: +1d6 damage per plus					
Property					
If you miss every target of an at-will attack power using this wand, you gain a +2 item bonus to the attack rolls of that power the next time you use it before the end of your next turn.					

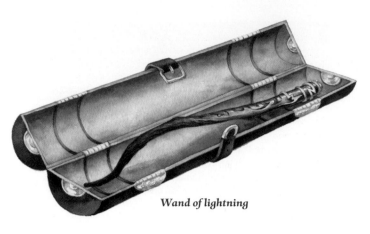

Wand of lightning

Wand of Lightning

Each of these wands is made from a slender glass or iron cylinder with metal bands spaced along its length. The *wand of lightning* is a self-renewing source of electrical energy that can be made to expel that energy to harmful effect.

In its most spectacular function, the wand embellishes its wielder's lightning attacks so that they also shock those nearby. It can also be used to electrify a metal object, making that object dangerous to the next creature that touches it. Even when otherwise dormant, the wand gives off a static shield that delivers a rebuking shock to attackers.

Wand of Lightning					Level 8+ Rare
Whenever you use this wand to send arcs of lightning among your foes, the smell of ozone fills the air and your hair stands up on end.					
Lvl 8	+2	3,400 gp	Lvl 23	+5	425,000 gp
Lvl 13	+3	17,000 gp	Lvl 28	+6	2,125,000 gp
Lvl 18	+4	85,000 gp			
Implement: Wand					
Enhancement Bonus: Attack rolls and damage rolls					
Critical: +1d8 lightning damage per plus					
Property					
When you use this wand to make a lightning attack, if any adjacent creature hits you with an attack before the start of your next turn, that creature takes lightning damage equal to 2 + the wand's enhancement bonus.					
Attack Power (Lightning) **✦ Daily** (No Action)					
Trigger: You hit a target with a lightning attack using this wand.					
Effect: Each creature adjacent to the target takes 10 lightning damage.					
Level 13 or 18: 20 lightning damage.					
Level 23 or 28: 30 lightning damage.					
Utility Power (Lightning) **✦ Encounter** (Minor Action)					
Effect: You touch the wand to one adjacent, unattended metal object no larger than a Medium suit of armor. The next time a creature touches the object within the next 5 minutes, that creature takes lightning damage equal to 5 + the item's enhancement bonus.					

BETH TROTT

Wand of Thunder

Crafted from brass and designed to maximize the damage unleashed by a thunder attack, a *wand of thunder* is a favorite of mages who favor brute force over a subtle approach. When used to focus a spell, the wand creates echoing blasts that, to the discriminating ear, resemble chords of music and sequences taken from ancient songs. Tales suggest that some of these wands are attuned to secret doors, hidden passages, and other locations deep within ancient arcane colleges and wizard's towers. Accessing these areas requires casting a specific spell with this wand to produce the tone or tune needed to unlock it.

The most common story of this sort suggests that one of these wands can be used to grant its owner access to Azarel's Tower, the abode of a long-dead archmage, which supposedly lies somewhere within the Dawnforge Mountains. It also suggests that anyone attempting to access the tower without such a wand to open the tower's hidden passages will find a quick end from the magic traps and immortal guardians still defending the place.

Wand of Thunder					Level 13+ Rare

This brass wand, which resembles a miniaturized horn, will drive your enemies back with a wave of thunder, or drop them with a shock wave.

Lvl 13	+3	17,000 gp	Lvl 23	+5	425,000 gp
Lvl 18	+4	85,000 gp	Lvl 28	+6	2,125,000 gp

Implement: Wand
Enhancement Bonus: Attack rolls and damage rolls
Critical: +1d8 thunder damage per plus

Property
Once during each of your turns, when you hit with a thunder attack using this wand, you can push one creature adjacent to you 1 square.

✦ Attack Power ✦ Encounter (Standard Action)
Attack: Close blast 5 (creatures and objects in the blast); the wand's level + 3 vs. Fortitude.
Hit: You push the target up to a number of squares equal to the wand's enhancement bonus and knock it prone.

Attack Power (Thunder) **✦ Daily** (No Action)
Trigger: You hit a target with a thunder attack using this wand.
Effect: Each creature adjacent to the target takes 10 thunder damage and falls prone.
Level 23 or 28: 20 thunder damage.

Wand of Wonder

This strange and unpredictable device usually looks like some other type of wand. Most magewrights who craft one of these wands delight in surprising first-time wielders with its strange side effects. Over time, the wielder of a *wand of wonder* is likely to become familiar with its oddities, but it is impossible to predict when they will appear.

The mad warlock Loon, who delved too deeply into the secrets of the Far Realm, always carried one of these wands. To him, the wand's randomness was a measuring stick of the true order of the universe (or lack thereof), as he had been taught through dark dreams sent by those from the place beyond. Before his demise during the war between Bael Turath and Arkhosia, many claimed that he had been able to shape his own powers to match the randomness of his *wand of wonder*.

Legends tell of more powerful *wands of wonder*. These items are potentially powerful artifacts, but none can guess what might happen when the magic they contain is unleashed.

Wand of Wonder					Level 7+ Rare

Few can call on the powers of this wand without a mingled sense of amazement and dread.

Lvl 7	+2	2,600 gp	Lvl 22	+5	325,000 gp
Lvl 12	+3	13,000 gp	Lvl 27	+6	1,625,000 gp
Lvl 17	+4	65,000 gp			

Implement: Wand
Enhancement Bonus: Attack rolls and damage rolls
Critical: +1d6 damage per plus. For each of these dice that rolls a 6, teleport the target 1 square. For each of these dice that rolls a 1, teleport yourself 1 square.

Property
When you use a daily attack power with this wand, roll a d6 to determine an additional effect, which lasts until the end of your next turn.
1. You gain a fly speed of 5.
2. Butterflies create a zone of partial concealment in your space.
3. You become invisible.
4. 2d20 fake, brightly colored gems appear in the space of the next target hit by the wand, temporarily creating difficult terrain.
5. Leaves grow from each target hit by the attack, causing it to be slowed.
6. You and each target hit by the attack are dazed.

Really, there's nothing wonderful about the mad warlock's wand. One studies magic to master it, to bend the forces of the universe to one's will. Toying with those forces is not wonderful, and it's not fun. It's dangerous.

CHAPTER 4

Magical Gear

TO CATALOGUE *all the wondrous items that exist would take a book of infinite pages, but it does us all well to have a firm grasp upon both the most common items and the rare items of incredible efficacy. Though some wondrous items are simple and of little impact, such as a lock opened only by a magic key, others have strange properties that defy the mind's attempt to grasp them, such as the portable hole.*

What a wonder magic is! Unhindered by the rules that bind the physical universe or by the laws of mortals, it can routinely make the impossible possible.

A pair of wings on a pair of boots, each wing no bigger than a dove's, can lift the wearer of the boots into the air. A band of metal placed on a finger can provide the power to see through stone. A belt can grant its wearer the strength of a giant. You no doubt wonder how can magic do so much with such strange materials. Despite my many years, magic often surprises me as well. The occasions when it does are the delights of my life.

An inexperienced wizard, such as I myself once was, sees magic as a system—a secret set of instructions for rebuilding reality as you see fit. And it's true that even the most rudimentary uses of magic involve learning its language: how to say the right words, make the right gestures, and pull upon the threads of the skeins of arcane, divine, and primal energy that flow invisibly all around us.

Yet the true master knows the system to be false. The patterns we see in various forms of energy, the languages we learn to speak to manipulate them, the differences between one phenomenon and another, even the division between what is magic and what is mundane—all are false. Perhaps only the gods can fully grasp this concept, but the truth is that all things are part of the same continuum. Why else would magic of so many types accomplish much the same end, and why else are so many things—from old gloves to living beings to entire planes—able to be created and imbued with magic?

The true pity is that even upon recognizing that we are imprisoned by our faulty understanding of magic, none of us can escape it. We are like babes that for the first time realize a world exists outside our crib. Even if we had the wherewithal to explore beyond our boundaries, we could not conceive of the dangers that await us.

Perhaps that is what the gods are for. Certainly they've proved themselves good for little else.

—Mordenkainen, from his master copy
of the *Magnificent Emporium*

HOWARD LYON

Arms Slot Items

The items in this category are usually coveted for their protective qualities—though some of them, such as the aptly named *bracers of infinite blades*, are good for more than just defense.

Bracers of Infinite Blades

Some dragonborn know these gold-inlaid armbands as *Menyra's bracers,* for the Arkhosian court assassin who first commissioned them. Menyra was said to have drawn from the power of the *bracers of infinite blades* only to protect those in her charge. Most of the heroes who make use of this armgear have a more wide-reaching definition of self defense.

Bracers of Infinite Blades		Level 11+ Common	
With a flick of your wrist, a gleaming blade appears in your previously empty hand.			
Lvl 11	9,000 gp	Lvl 21	225,000 gp
Lvl 16	45,000 gp	Lvl 26	1,125,000 gp
Arms Slot			
Property			

You can draw a +2 *magic dagger* from these bracers as though drawing it from a sheath (typically a minor action). The dagger lasts until the end of the current turn.
Level 16: +3 *magic dagger.*
Level 21: +4 *magic dagger.*
Level 26: +5 *magic dagger.*
Special: These bracers can be crafted to produce a different light thrown weapon, such as a shuriken.

Gleaming Diamond Bracers

Like many magic items made from gem and stone, *gleaming diamond bracers* were first crafted by the dwarves, and were worn as badges of honor by their most powerful clan lords. In battle, the bracers flare with a bright light when their magic absorbs an attack that might otherwise fell their wearer. In the Underdark, dwarf scouts who have become separated from their fellows look for this beacon in the darkness, which signals both a warning and a call to arms.

Gleaming Diamond Bracers		Level 9+ Uncommon	
These clear crystal bracers blaze with light as you shrug off your foe's attack.			
Lvl 9	4,200 gp	Lvl 29	2,625,000 gp
Lvl 19	105,000 gp		
Arms Slot			
Property			

These bracers cast bright light in a 5-square radius. You can extinguish the light or restore it as a minor action.
Utility Power ✦ Daily (Immediate Reaction)
Trigger: An attack deals a particular type of damage to you.
Effect: You gain resist 5 to that damage type until the end of the encounter.
Level 19: Resist 10.
Level 29: Resist 15.

Greater Stonewall Shield

Dwarf arcane crafters built the first *greater stonewall shield,* and among many of their clans, this essential defensive item is carried with the respect of a sacred relic. Its lacquered steel shell is inlaid with a tight mosaic of granite and marble chips, adding to its already considerable heft. Among the dwarves, it is said that each warrior who falls while wielding a *greater stonewall shield* imbues a fragment of his or her spirit into the shield's stonework. For this reason, the dwarves consider it a great honor to wield one of these shields, and they will go out of their way to retrieve one from a warrior who falls on the field of battle.

Greater Stonewall Shield		Level 13+ Rare	
At your command, this stone shield becomes a solid wall that hems in your foes.			
Lvl 13	17,000 gp	Lvl 23	425,000 gp
Arms Slot: Any shield			
Utility Power ✦ Encounter (Minor Action)			

Effect: You create a wall 3 in unoccupied squares within 5 squares of you. At least 1 square of the wall must be adjacent to you, and the wall must be on a solid surface. The wall is blocking terrain. It can be up to 2 squares high, and has AC/Reflex 5, Fortitude 10, and resist 10 to all damage. A square of the wall is destroyed if it takes any damage.
Level 23: Wall 5 within 10 squares of you; resist 15 to all damage.

Greater Storm Shield

The all-wooden construction of this shield, which is bound in black leather and set with studs of white marble, features not a single pin, nail, or clip of metal. Said to have first been employed by druids, the *greater storm shield* is a stalwart defense against—and conduit for—the power of the storm. When the shield's power is used, the images of shifting clouds on its surface animate, becoming dark and riddled with lightning.

Greater Storm Shield		Level 8+ Uncommon	
When a foe dares to attack you, you summon the power of the storm through this shield to smite your enemy.			
Lvl 8	3,400 gp	Lvl 28	2,125,000 gp
Lvl 18	85,000 gp		
Arms Slot: Any shield			
Property			

You gain resist 5 lightning and resist 5 thunder.
Level 18: Resist 10 lightning and resist 10 thunder.
Level 28: Resist 15 lightning and resist 15 thunder.
Attack Power (Lightning, Thunder) ✦ Daily (Immediate Reaction)
Trigger: An enemy within 10 squares of you hits you with an attack.
Effect: The triggering enemy takes 10 lightning and thunder damage. If the enemy's attack deals lightning or thunder damage, you do not expend this power.
Level 18: 15 lightning and thunder damage.
Level 28: 20 lightning and thunder damage.

Ranging Defender Shield

As the story goes, an ancient merchant prince commissioned seven identical shields for his bodyguards to help them protect him, because he was despised so widely that more than ten thousand people had vowed to kill him. Whether or not the story is true, all seven known shields of this type bear a weasel rampant, the emblem of the trading house the merchant ruled.

In addition to its strong protective magic, a *ranging defender shield* has an additional enchantment that makes it well suited for its original purpose of defending another. With a command word, its wielder can transfer the shield's protective aegis to a nearby ally; a shimmering duplicate shield appears in the air next to that person to protect him or her from harm.

Ranging Defender Shield		Level 4+ Uncommon

You protect a comrade in danger by extending this shield's magical defenses to that ally.

Lvl 4	840 gp	Lvl 24	525,000 gp
Lvl 14	21,000 gp		

Arms Slot: Any shield

Utility Power ✦ Encounter (Minor Action)

Effect: Close burst 5 (one ally in the burst). Until the end of your next turn, the target gains the shield's bonuses to AC and Reflex, and you lose them.

Utility Power ✦ Daily (Minor Action)

Effect: Close burst 5 (one bloodied ally in the burst). The target gains resist 5 to all damage until he or she is no longer bloodied or until the end of the encounter.
Level 14: Resist 10 to all damage.
Level 24: Resist 15 to all damage.

Robilar once told me that if given a choice of a weapon or a shield, a warrior should always pick the shield. The premise, I presume, is that the shield guards your life and also can be used to strike a foe. It has not escaped my notice, however, that Robilar always wore his sword, even in peaceful company, but carried a shield only in times of known danger. The shield protects, but the sword swiftly kills that which threatens.

Searing shield

Searing Shield

To outward appearances, this shield seems nothing more than a finely made defensive item, perhaps holding some minor enchantment. But when the command word is spoken, the shield emanates a wall of light in front of its wielder to drive away the darkness like a beacon in the night. The light is so bright and pure that undead caught within its glare quail before it.

With a second word, the *searing shield* blazes with a halo of light that extends upward to the heavens. That radiance is so pure that it will sear the flesh of any undead creature that gets too close.

Searing Shield	Level 13 Uncommon

You send a wave of brilliant light outward from this shield to illuminate the darkness.

Arms Slot: Any shield — 17,000 gp

Utility Power (Zone) **✦ Encounter** (Minor Action)

Effect: Close blast 5. The blast creates a zone of bright light that lasts until the end of the encounter or until you are no longer holding the shield. When you move, the zone moves with you, keeping the same orientation. Undead creatures grant combat advantage while in the zone. Once per round during your turn, you can reorient the zone as a free action.

Utility Power (Aura, Radiant) **✦ Daily** (Minor Action)

Effect: You activate an aura 1 that lasts until the end of the encounter or until you are no longer holding the shield. Any undead enemy that ends its turn in the aura takes 2 radiant damage. At night, the aura also sheds bright light in a column that extends upward, stopped only by blocking terrain.

JIM NELSON

Shield of Aversion

Though halflings are as fierce as any other warriors, many of them believe that the best way to win a fight is to avoid it altogether. Playing to this philosophy, the *shield of aversion* is one of the few magic items whose creation originated within the halfling clans, and it suits that race well. The halflings' predilection for lore sees many warriors of that race engrave these shields with carefully scribed tales of their own valor, allowing a warrior's prowess to be easily seen by his or her enemies. Halfling clans highly value *shields of aversion*, and they do not take it well when they see a member of another race carrying one as the spoils taken from a fallen halfling warrior.

Shield of Aversion	Level 15 Uncommon
Even as your foe closes in to attack, you see its eyes cloud with uncertainty.	
Arms Slot: Any shield	25,000 gp
Property	
You gain a +4 item bonus to all defenses against charge attacks.	
Utility Power (Charm) ✦ **Daily** (Immediate Interrupt)	
Trigger: An enemy hits you with a melee attack while you are adjacent to another creature.	
Effect: Choose a creature adjacent to you, other than the triggering enemy. The attack hits that creature instead of you.	

Shield of the Doomed

For most warriors, the promise to fight to the death in the service of liege, country, and comrades is the ultimate expression of loyalty. For the elite imperial guard of Nerath, such a vow was not enough—they pledged to fight beyond death, using the magic of the *shield of the doomed* to fulfill that oath. It is said that no single blow can lay low the wielder of this battered steel and adamantine shield, and many foes have been shocked by the counterattack of a hero wielding one who should have breathed his or her last.

Shield of the Doomed	Level 23 Rare
Thanks to the protective magic of this shield, you shrug off a fatal blow, giving you time to put your foe down.	
Arms Slot: Heavy shield	425,000 gp
Utility Power ✦ **Daily** (Immediate Interrupt)	
Trigger: An attack drops you to below 1 hit point.	
Effect: You instead have 1 hit point, and you gain temporary hit points equal to the damage dealt by the triggering attack.	
Utility Power ✦ **Daily** (Minor Action)	
Effect: Choose one enemy within 5 squares of you. The next time you drop below 1 hit point before the end of the encounter, you instead have 1 hit point, but only if the chosen enemy has at least 1 hit point. However, if you are at 1 hit point or lower when that enemy drops below 1 hit point, you must roll a d20. If you roll a 9 or lower, you die.	

Tusk Shield

At first glance, a *tusk shield* looks like something that was quickly constructed from scrap materials. A pair of thick tusks of bloodstained ivory are set in a V shape and banded with strips of black oak, but with gaps between them wide enough to drive a great-sword through. Enemies that face a charging warrior protected by a *tusk shield* quickly come to understand the potency of the item—despite the fact that it doesn't seem capable of turning aside any blows.

Tusk Shield	Level 2 Common
With this shield on your arm, your deadly charge shatters your enemies' attacks.	
Arms Slot: Light shield	520 gp
Property	
Whenever you charge, you gain a +2 item bonus to all defenses until the start of your next turn.	

Twilight Shield

A *twilight shield* is crafted from black glass that is exposed only to the light of the setting sun during the month required to craft the item. By absorbing the growing shadows of the oncoming night, a *twilight shield* is imbued with the magic of shadow. On command, a halo of shadows emerges from it, cloaking those within against attacks made at a distance.

Twilight Shield	Level 8 Uncommon
This shield looks like a polished black pane of glass set in a sturdy metal frame.	
Arms Slot: Any shield	3,400 gp
Utility Power (Aura) ✦ **Encounter** (Minor Action)	
Effect: You activate an aura 1 that lasts until the end of the encounter or until you move. You and each creature in the aura have partial concealment against ranged attacks.	

Vanguard's Shield

High in their rocky redoubts, the dwarves present an implacable defense to those who would plunder their vast treasures. Typically outnumbered by invading goblins and orcs, the dwarves learned to craft weapons and armor that would help even the odds. Named for the elite dwarf fighting units that stand at the front of any battle, a *vanguard's shield* emits a pulse of magical power that blunts a charging enemy's attack. By keeping their foes from breaking through the front lines, the dwarves can pulverize them with fire from the back ranks.

Vanguard's Shield	Level 3 Common
When an enemy charges, this steel shield hinders the attack.	
Arms Slot: Any shield	680 gp
Property	
You gain a +4 item bonus to all defenses against charge attacks.	

Feet Slot Items

Boots and shoes are popular forms of enchanted items not just for what they can do but also because much magical footgear is innocuous in appearance: Not until you use your *boots of levitation* to surprise your foes do they realize what they're up against.

Boots of Elvenkind

This supple leather footwear lets its wearer pass without leaving a trace or making a sound over any ground, no matter how unsuited to stealth or how cluttered the path might be. Dry leaves, spongy soil, and even fresh, squelching mud are no challenge to secrecy for someone wearing *boots of elvenkind*.

One legend tells of an elf who was so proud of his skill in crafting a pair of these boots that he walked silently across a pile of bells, gongs, and cymbals before the court of an eladrin noble. Whether that tale is true or not, the items made in his family's workshops are still in high demand to this day.

Boots of Elvenkind			Level 7+ Uncommon
You pass without notice, leaving neither footprint nor echo.			
Lvl 7	2,600 gp	Lvl 27	1,625,000 gp
Lvl 17	65,000 gp		
Feet Slot			
Property			
You gain a +2 item bonus to Stealth checks.			
Level 17: +4 item bonus.			
Level 27: +6 item bonus.			
Utility Power (Illusion) ✦ **Daily** (Move Action)			
Effect: You move up to your speed, and you are hidden (invisible and silent) during the move.			

Boots of Leaping

Most *boots of leaping* are ugly, thick-soled footwear that use simple materials, but their appearance belies their nature. The wearer can jump over enemies without a running start, vault up city walls, clear a broad river in one bound—and make it look effortless.

Boots of leaping are unusually uniform in appearance and function, because all were made by the same enchanter. This unlucky mage spent a century doing nothing but crafting the same item over and over again at the behest of the dwarf warlord who held him captive and wanted every member of his army's vanguard to have a pair.

Boots of Leaping	Level 9 Rare
Empowered by these boots, you fling yourself into the air, clearing your foes and landing behind them.	
Feet Slot	4,200 gp
Property	
You gain a +2 item bonus to Athletics checks to jump.	
Utility Power ✦ **Encounter** (Move Action)	
Effect: You jump to a square within 10 squares of you. The jump does not provoke opportunity attacks.	

Boots of Levitation

The most powerful (and thus most famous) pair of *boots of levitation* was made for one of the most notorious political agitators in ancient Nerath. The rabble rouser in question was renowned for delivering scathing speeches in public places, but as crowds gathered, those who arrived later had a difficult time hearing this speaker. With the boots, however, he was able to rise above the ground so that large crowds could see him and hear his words. This method of gaining height had the additional benefit of raising him above the city guards who were typically dispatched to arrest him, once the authorities got wind that he was speaking. The Floating Demagogue, as he came to be known, was eventually arrested and put to death—his boots getting burned publicly right after him.

Boots of Levitation	Level 9 Uncommon
You rise into the air thanks to these soft leather boots, able to see and be seen across a broader area.	
Feet Slot	4,200 gp
Utility Power ✦ **Encounter** (Move Action)	
Effect: You fly up to 4 squares vertically and 1 square horizontally, and you can hover there until the end of your next turn. When the levitation ends, you descend to the ground without taking falling damage.	

Boots of the Shadowed Path

These magic boots are attuned to the ebb and flow of shadow magic. On command, a creature wearing them can step through shadow to appear somewhere else nearby. Although this teleportation effect is limited in its range, the boots' enduring magic allows their wearer to use them time and time again.

Boots of the Shadowed Path	Level 13 Uncommon
These leather boots are utterly black and seem to absorb light.	
Feet Slot	17,000 gp
Utility Power (Teleportation) ✦ **Encounter** (Move Action)	
Effect: You teleport up to 3 squares. You must end this teleportation adjacent to a creature or an object that is Small or larger.	

Halfling Boots

Halflings are known to prefer flight or stealth to a direct fight, and these magic boots reflect their desires. Crafted by a cabal of halfling wizards, these boots allow a creature to move with a subtle balance of speed, agility, and foresight. With the aid of the boots, a creature can slip between a giant's stomping feet or glide past a dragon's grasping talons with ease.

Halfling Boots	Level 9 Uncommon
These boots look like they are sized for a child, but when you attempt to pull them on, they grow just large enough to fit you. Still, they feel tight around your feet.	
Feet Slot	4,200 gp
Property	
You can move through the space of any enemy that has a size category larger than yours.	

Shoes of the Tireless Gait

The *shoes of the tireless gait* are well named; one who travels while wearing them is able to continue walking without fatigue for as long as he or she perseveres and maintains momentum. Even sleep can be forestalled by the magic of this footwear.

Adventurers must be wary when seeking these shoes, because cursed versions also exist that compel those who wear them to travel without pause. Those unfortunate enough to don such footgear find themselves unable to stop and rest, walking themselves to their doom.

Shoes of the Tireless Gait	Level 8 Common
While you stay in motion, these shoes keep your body fresh for the challenges ahead.	
Feet Slot	3,400 gp
Property	
You can walk without fatigue or the need to stop for sleep. However, if you walk for more than 24 hours, you take a -5 penalty to all skill checks, ability checks, and attack rolls until the end of your next extended rest.	

Shoes of Water Walking

For anyone wearing this footwear, oceans are like land and can be crossed as easily. Lakes, rivers, and swampland are little different from firm earth. Being on the water's surface can be a drawback, however, when bad weather strikes or evil magic is employed. In hurricane conditions, for instance, rather than being able to sink beneath the turmoil, the wearer is battered by wind and waves (but presumably only until he or she has managed to remove the shoes).

Shoes of water walking were originally developed to protect aristocrats who traveled on small ships in rough seas, but were soon after put to less noble uses by the pirates who stole them.

Shoes of water walking

Shoes of Water Walking	Level 6 Common
While in these shoes, you tread across water as if it were land.	
Feet Slot	1,800 gp
Property	
You can move on water as if it were solid ground (rough water counts as difficult terrain). You can break through the surface of the water as a free action, whether you're descending or ascending.	

The simple boot represents a stunning innovation. The most primitive people run barefoot through the world, but when they discover sandals, they can walk farther with fewer troubles.
A simple closed toe on the sandal can add miles to the distance an army can march in a day. And when your soldiers' cracked and bleeding feet are armored by a true shoe as they walk for miles along dung-spattered trails, the benefits are multifold. When you realize all this, it's no wonder that spellcasters have lavished enchantments upon footwear.

Hands Slot Items

For obvious reasons, anyone can benefit from even a mundane pair of gloves or gauntlets. When they're supplemented with a magical quality, so much the better.

Gauntlets of Remote Action

These fine chainmail gauntlets set with ruby studs come in a pair matched for the same hand, which often confuses those who discover them. With one gauntlet worn, the wearer can launch the other into the air, where it floats and moves under mental command. This second hand mimics the movements of the first, allowing the wearer to perform a number of simple activities at a distance. The user can also sometimes switch places with the floating gauntlet.

These gauntlets are sometimes worn by alchemists who find it useful to mix dangerous components from a safe distance.

Gauntlets of Remote Action	Level 9 Uncommon

You send one of these gauntlets into the air, where it waits for you to control its actions from a safe distance.

Hands Slot	4,200 gp

Utility Power ✦ At-Will (Minor Action)
Effect: You cause one of the gauntlets to lift off your hand and float in a square adjacent to you. The gauntlet does not occupy its square. While the gauntlet is floating, you can perform actions with it as if your hand were still in it, such as opening doors, picking up objects, and making Thievery checks. You cannot use the floating gauntlet to make attacks or to perform any action requiring two hands.

You can take a move action to move the gauntlet up to 10 squares, and it must end the move within 10 squares of you. If the gauntlet is adjacent to you, you can return it to your hand as a minor action. If you drop below 1 hit point or remove the gauntlet that you're wearing, the floating gauntlet returns to your hand.

Utility Power (Teleportation) ✦ Daily (Move Action)
Requirement: One of the gauntlets must be floating.
Effect: You teleport, swapping positions with the floating gauntlet.

Gauntlets of Swimming and Climbing

A creature wearing these gauntlets moves with supernatural grace in the forest canopy or beneath the surface of a lake or a stream. Made of well-creased leather and ornamented with studs of steel and jet, *gauntlets of swimming and climbing* appear damp to both sight and touch, though they leave no trace of water on anything they touch. The ancient ranger orders of the wood elves once gifted these gauntlets as a sign of rank and accomplishment, but they are now seldom found among the forest folk.

Gauntlets of Swimming and Climbing	Level 10 Common

Primal strength flows through your limbs when you don these gauntlets.

Hands Slot	5,000 gp

Property
You gain a climb speed and a swim speed both equal to half your speed.

Gloves of Missile Snaring

These fine white leather gloves seem to fade away when worn, becoming little more than a paper-thin sheath over the hands. The benefit of *gloves of missile snaring* emerges only in the thick of combat, when arrows, bolts, sling bullets—and even the deadly spears of giants—can be caught by the wearer with almost supernatural grace. Of greater surprise to a startled foe that witnesses this act is seeing its own projectile hurtling back toward it.

Gloves of Missile Snaring	Level 15 Uncommon

Your gloved hand moves in a blur, plucking your foe's arrow out of midair before you hurl it back as a deadly missile.

Hands Slot	25,000 gp

Utility Power ✦ Daily (Immediate Interrupt)
Trigger: An enemy hits you with a ranged weapon attack.
Effect: You gain a +4 power bonus to all defenses against the attack. If this bonus causes the attack to miss you, the enemy is hit by the attack instead.

Hero's Gauntlets

Kavad, a renowned warlord and famous champion of the second-to-last Nerathan emperor, was the first to wear *hero's gauntlets*. Those who follow his example know that the true mark of a hero lies in one's ability to push past all limits—to the point where life and death, reputation and honor, and fame and infamy cease to matter.

Hero's Gauntlets		Level 17+ Common	

When you push past your limits, the magic of these gauntlets backs up the fury of your attack.

Lvl 17	65,000 gp	Lvl 27	1,625,000 gp

Hands Slot
Properties
✦ Whenever you spend an action point to make an attack, you gain a +1 bonus to attack rolls with that attack.
✦ Whenever you spend an action point to make an attack and the attack deals damage, you gain temporary hit points equal to one-half your healing surge value.
Level 27: +2 bonus to the attack rolls, and temporary hit points equal to your healing surge value.

Life-Draining Gauntlets

A patchwork of bone-dry leather strips of unknown origin, these gauntlets are seldom worn by the overly moral or faint of heart. Those who know the function of this macabre handwear understand that its creation requires the flayed skin of sentient humanoids. Daring to wear the flesh of the dead gives dark power to the wearer—power over life and death, and the ability to feed from both.

Life-Draining Gauntlets		Level 6+ Rare	
The dead flesh of these grisly gauntlets draws strength from your enemies.			
Lvl 6	1,800 gp	Lvl 26	1,125,000 gp
Lvl 16	45,000 gp		
Hands Slot			
Property			
You gain a +2 item bonus to necrotic damage rolls.			
Level 16: +4 item bonus.			
Level 26: +6 item bonus.			
Utility Power ✦ Daily (No Action)			
Trigger: You hit a creature with an attack and deal necrotic damage to it.			
Effect: You gain temporary hit points equal to 4 + the gauntlets' level.			

While the material they are made of might cause some to become queasy, life-draining gauntlets can be a boon to anyone. The secret to their most effective use is that you need only spill a few drops of blood from a creature, friend or foe. Of course no ally likes being attacked, but if you ensure the harm you inflict is minimal, the benefit you gain from such an act can be quite substantial.

True Gauntlets of Ogre Power

Although *true gauntlets of ogre power* are best known for granting their wearer phenomenal strength, they also feature a more subtle magic that adapts to the armor worn by their wielder, making them nearly impossible to detect by casual sight or contact. A rogue in leather wears the gauntlets as matching gloves of heavy calfskin; a knight in full plate wears them as steel gauntlets that perfectly match his or her armor's hue and alloy. Doffed, they appear as plain leather gauntlets set with rusting studs, and careless adventurers might realize too late that they missed this rare treasure.

Gauntlets of ogre power

True Gauntlets of Ogre Power	Level 17 Rare
When the brutal strength of the ogre courses through you, nothing can stand in your way.	
Hands Slot	65,000 gp
Property	
You gain a +4 item bonus to Athletics checks and Strength ability checks.	
Utility Power ✦ Encounter (No Action)	
Trigger: You make a Strength check to break or lift an object.	
Effect: You gain a +4 power bonus to the Strength check.	
Utility Power ✦ Encounter (No Action)	
Trigger: You hit a creature with a melee attack.	
Effect: You gain a +4 power bonus to the damage roll against that creature for this attack.	

I've heard that the creator of gauntlets of ogre power was a godlike being known as Vaprak the Destroyer. Whether true deity or exarch, Vaprak is worshiped by trolls and ogres in many worlds. Though this entity appears to be little more than a brutish and mean being, the creation of the gauntlets could imply some strategy of subtlety and scope. Beyond that, I do not speculate.

CHRIS SEAMAN

Head Slot Items

Hats and helms are what many people think of when they consider the purchase of an item in this category. The most unusual enchanted objects in this group, however, might be those that don't touch the owner's head at all.

Crown of Leaves

The first elves to migrate from the Feywild to the world brought this headwear with them to their new homes. These Feywild-infused circlets allowed the elves to establish mastery over the unspoiled forests.

Crown of Leaves	Level 7 Common

The fey energy imbued into this delicate crown unveils nature and its secrets to your sight and touch.

Head Slot 2,600 gp
Property
You gain a +2 item bonus to Nature checks and Insight checks.

Exceptional Factotum Helm

The beautiful and capricious Queen Ailion had many suitors, but she vowed to wed only the one who could master a series of twelve tasks of intellectual and physical skill. But while countless heroes tried and failed, a stripling adventurer named Parrin met Ailion's challenge and became her king and consort—with the help of this elaborately etched silver helm, which he found by chance in some old eladrin ruins.

Exceptional Factotum Helm			Level 4+ Rare

The knowledge stored within this silver helm is imparted to you when you need it most.

Lvl 4	840 gp	Lvl 24	525,000 gp
Lvl 14	21,000 gp		

Head Slot
Property
You gain a +1 item bonus to untrained skill checks.
  Level 14: +2 item bonus.
  Level 24: +3 item bonus.
Utility Power ✦ Daily (Minor Action)
  Effect: You gain training in one skill until the end of your next turn, or for 1 minute when not in an encounter.
  Level 14: You gain training until the end of the encounter, or for 1 hour when not in an encounter.
  Level 24: You gain training in two skills until the end of the encounter, or for 1 hour when not in an encounter.

Eyes of Charming

The gnome enchanter Warallako was known for both his arcane crafting and his ability to manipulate the will of any creature of his choosing (at least according to the tales he told). This set of stylish silver spectacles was discovered to be the source of the enchanter's alleged charm after he tried to use them on the wife of Aloryan, a fiery-tempered elf chieftain. Aloryan inherited the *eyes of charming* after Warallako's unexpected and violent demise, and put them to better use turning his fractious tribes into a nation.

Eyes of Charming			Level 6+ Rare

These silver spectacles let you either assert subtle influence on others, or force them to do your bidding.

Lvl 6	1,800 gp	Lvl 26	1,125,000 gp
Lvl 16	45,000 gp		

Head Slot
Property
You gain a +2 item bonus to Bluff checks and Diplomacy checks.
  Level 16: +4 item bonus.
  Level 26: +6 item bonus.
➹ Attack Power (Charm) ✦ **Daily** (Standard Action)
  Attack: Ranged 5 (one creature); the eyes' level + 5 vs. Will
  Hit: The target is dominated (save ends). The target is not aware that you used this power against it.

Eyes of charming often prove more difficult to use than their wearers first surmise. Just because a victim of the magic does not know you used a power to control it does not mean the victim cannot recognize it was controlled. To use the eyes successfully, you must use them subtly. Lay the groundwork for the charmed action, and the victim might not even suspect it was ensorcelled.

Eyes of the Eagle

These minute crystal lenses magically attach themselves directly to the eyes of the wearer, making them all but impossible to detect when they are worn. The existence of these lenses was first recorded in legends of the ancient druid war leader Ohartu, but his tribe's lack of crafters suggests that the eyewear was probably a relic from an older age that he discovered.

Eyes of the Eagle	Level 11+ Uncommon

After an initial surge of vertigo, these magic lenses, which rest unseen on your eyes, bring the farthest objects into sharp relief.

Lvl 11	9,000 gp	Lvl 21	225,000 gp

Head Slot
Property
You gain a +3 item bonus to Perception checks. When spotting creatures or phenomena 20 or more squares away from you, the bonus increases by 2. In addition, you have normal visual acuity at a range of 5 squares. For example, an inscription or parchment 5 squares away from you can be read as if it was held up close.
  Level 21: +5 item bonus.

Helm of Brilliance

Crafted of brilliant silver and polished steel, this helm appears to be a mundane piece of armored headgear when first found. Only close study reveals the secret of its precious gems, each channeling the powerful magic of the helm's unknown makers. The resistance to fire that the helm bestows cannot be sustained indefinitely, however, and the helm's magic can be overwhelmed by exposure to intense heat and flames, causing it to focus that energy inward.

Helm of Brilliance			Level 18+ Rare
The gems of this helm flare in a corona of brilliant light as you prepare to unleash their power.			
Head Slot			
Lvl 18	85,000 gp	Lvl 28	2,125,000 gp
Lvl 23	425,000 gp		
Property			
You gain resist 15 fire. If an attack deals more fire damage than 20 + one-half your level before your resistance is applied, you instead have vulnerable 15 fire against that attack.			
➷ **Attack Power** (Radiant) ✦ **Daily** (Standard Action)			
Attack: Ranged 10 (one creature); the helm's level + 3 vs. Will			
Hit: 10 radiant damage, and the target is dazed until the end of your next turn.			
Level 23: 15 radiant damage.			
Level 28: 20 radiant damage.			
❋ **Attack Power** (Fire) ✦ **Daily** (Standard Action)			
Attack: Area burst 2 within 10 (each creature in the burst); the helm's level + 3 vs. Reflex			
Hit: 15 fire damage, and ongoing 10 fire damage (save ends).			
Level 23: 15 fire damage, and ongoing 15 fire damage.			
Level 28: 20 fire damage, and ongoing 20 fire damage.			
Utility Power ✦ **At-Will** (Minor Action)			
Effect: The helm casts bright light in a 10-square radius until you extinguish it as a minor action or until the helm is removed.			

Helm of Languages

The ambassadors of the famous warrior Beharrin first created and made use of this unassuming war helmet. The power of the *helm of languages* was critical to the diplomatic efforts that allowed Beharrin to forge the kingdom that bore his name, and these precious items have aided countless lords, nobles, and adventurers in the long years since.

Helm of Languages	Level 10 Common
When you slip on this helm, the haze of garbled voices around you quickly gives way to perfect understanding.	
Head Slot	5,000 gp
Property	
You can speak and understand any spoken language (the helm does not grant literacy or the ability to speak Abyssal or Supernal).	

Helm of Seven Deaths

Legends of the Shadowfell speak of gems and their ability to capture and hold the souls of recently slain creatures. A gem's facets can, with the proper infusion of divine or arcane magic, become a twisting, winding maze that captures a soul and forces it to travel in endless circles rather than depart to the afterlife. The helm of seven deaths incorporates several such gems. When the helm's wearer defeats a foe, the gems mounted upon it capture the departing soul and store it for use in fueling the helm's powers.

Magic was never meant to make us lazy. There's no substitute for the discipline and effort involved in actually learning a language that's not your own. If you lean on magic items to do all your work for you, you will someday find yourself badly disappointed.

Helm of brilliance

Helm of Teleportation

The *helm of teleportation* is known far and wide even though very few of these items have ever existed. In fact, its reputation might even predate its creation: Explorers have discovered ancient pictograms that show two images of the same individual some distance apart from one another. One of the images is bareheaded, and the other is wearing a helmet. Some experts take this to mean that the headgear had something to do with the individual's movement, while critics of that view are quick to point out that it's not necessary to take off a *helm of teleportation* to prevent it from working.

Whatever the case, it's not unusual for bystanders to believe they've just seen a *helm of teleportation* in action when what they truly saw was someone using a teleport power while wearing a hat.

Helm of seven deaths

Helm of Seven Deaths	Level 5 Rare

This black helm has seven green gems set above its brow. They are dull, dead things, as if they once held magical power that has long since been spent.

Head Slot   1,000 gp

Utility Power ✦ At-Will (Minor Action)
Effect: Choose one bloodied creature you have hit with an attack during this turn. You learn that creature's current hit point total.

Utility Power ✦ At-Will (Free Action, 1/Turn)
Trigger: You kill a living creature with an attack.
Effect: One of the helm's seven gems captures the creature's soul. A gem can hold no more than one soul at a time and glows with a green radiance while it contains a soul. A dead creature cannot be returned to life while its soul is captured in this manner.

Utility Power (Healing) ✦ Encounter (Minor Action)
Requirement: At least three of the seven gems must each contain a soul.
Effect: You regain hit points equal to 5 + one-half your level, and two of the gems release their souls.

Utility Power ✦ Daily (Minor Action)
Requirement: All seven gems must contain souls.
Effect: On your next damage roll, maximize the results of up to four of the dice you roll. All seven gems then release their souls.

Helm of Teleportation	Level 15+ Rare

This headwear makes you preternaturally aware of the space around you, allowing you to step to other nearby locations in the blink of an eye.

Lvl 15	25,000 gp	Lvl 25	625,000 gp

Head Slot
Property
When you teleport on your turn and end the move adjacent to any enemies, you gain combat advantage against those enemies until the end of your next turn.
Utility Power (Teleportation) ✦ Encounter (Move Action)
Effect: You teleport yourself or an adjacent ally up to 6 squares.
Level 25: You teleport yourself or an adjacent ally up to 12 squares.

Ioun Stones

The oldest legends speak of *Ioun stones* as gifts given by the god of knowledge and prophecy to the greatest heroes. *Ioun stones* as a group encompass a wide range of wondrous powers, and each stone in its own right is very powerful. All of them have one characteristic in common: The stone's power is activated by setting it in motion around its wearer's head, where it orbits continuously.

Priests of Ioun argue over their deity's motives in creating the stones and believe that anyone who comes into contact with one should take it as a sign of prophecy. If someone is seen with two of the stones in his or her possession, the priesthood marks that person as destined for great (and sometimes terrible) events. For this reason, many adventurers shun the stones despite their power, fearing that they might be swept up in events outside their control.

WARREN MAHY

Ioun stone

Ioun Stone of Perfect Language — Level 22 Rare

This white and pink rhombic prism makes you more persuasive and gives you a knack for language.

Head Slot   325,000 gp

Property

You gain a +5 item bonus to Bluff, Diplomacy, Intimidate, and Streetwise checks. In addition, you can understand any spoken language, and when you speak, all creatures hear your words in their native language.

Utility Power ✦ Daily (Free Action)

Trigger: You make an Insight check.

Effect: You treat the check as if you rolled a natural 20.

Ioun Stone of Sustenance — Level 21 Common

This iridescent spindle lessens your need for rest and removes your body's base needs for air and nourishment.

Head Slot   225,000 gp

Property

You do not need to eat, drink, or breathe. In addition, when you take an extended rest, you do so in half the normal time.

Ioun Stone of Might — Level 21 Rare

This pale blue rhomboid augments your physical strength.

Head Slot   225,000 gp

Property

You gain a +4 item bonus to Strength-based skill checks and Strength ability checks. You also gain a +5 item bonus to the damage rolls of Strength-based attacks.

Ioun Stone of Agility — Level 21 Rare

This deep red sphere increases your reaction time and quickness.

Head Slot   225,000 gp

Property

You gain a +4 item bonus to Dexterity-based skill checks and Dexterity ability checks. You also gain a +5 item bonus to the damage rolls of Dexterity-based attacks.

Ioun Stone of Vigor — Level 21 Rare

This pink rhomboid lends its magic to your bodily health.

Head Slot   225,000 gp

Property

You gain a +4 item bonus to Constitution-based skill checks and Constitution ability checks. You also gain a +5 item bonus to the damage rolls of Constitution-based attacks.

Ioun Stone of Intellect — Level 21 Rare

This scarlet and blue sphere sharpens the power of your mind.

Head Slot   225,000 gp

Property

You gain a +4 item bonus to Intelligence-based skill checks and Intelligence ability checks. You also gain a +5 item bonus to the damage rolls of Intelligence-based attacks.

Ioun Stone of Insight — Level 21 Rare

This iridescent blue sphere hones your instincts to a fine edge.

Head Slot   225,000 gp

Property

You gain a +4 item bonus to Wisdom-based skill checks and Wisdom ability checks. You also gain a +5 item bonus to the damage rolls of Wisdom-based attacks.

Ioun Stone of Allure — Level 21 Rare

This pink and green sphere increases your presence and force of personality.

Head Slot   225,000 gp

Property

You gain a +4 item bonus to Charisma-based skill checks and Charisma ability checks. You also gain a +5 item bonus to the damage rolls of Charisma-based attacks.

Reading Spectacles

The first *reading spectacles* were crafted in lost antiquity but are recorded as having been in the possession of a human playwright named Monieta. In the early days of Nerath, his work as a dramatist heralded a groundbreaking and illustrious career—until it was revealed that his entire body of work was plagiarized from a dozen lost cultures, translated into Common with the help of his spectacles.

Reading Spectacles — Level 2 Common

Your vision blurs the first time you put on these spectacles, then all written text comes into perfect focus and clarity.

Head Slot   520 gp

Property

You can read any language (the spectacles do not grant the ability to speak or write a language).

Neck Slot Items

Magic items worn on or around the neck are so varied in physical form that almost anyone you meet might be wearing one. Who's to say whether someone's dirty cloak has a hidden power, or the small charm around one's neck is more than mere decoration?

Amulet of Aranea

The first of these clustered settings of mithral, ebony, and black glass were worn by the drow during the earliest days of the war that sundered them from their elf and eladrin kin. The enemies of the drow typically destroyed *amulets of aranea* they found on their hated foes, along with any other items that might contain the magic of Lolth, but a few surviving examples of this amulet made their way to the fomorian kingdoms, and from there to the world. Because these items emulate the venom and viciousness of the Spider Queen, assassins and others who seek any dark advantage in combat often seek them out.

Amulet of Aranea		Level 10+ Uncommon			
This neck charm protects you from poison even as it cripples your enemies with a venomous rebuke.					
Lvl 10	+2	5,000 gp	Lvl 25	+5	625,000 gp
Lvl 15	+3	25,000 gp	Lvl 30	+6	3,125,000 gp
Lvl 20	+4	125,000 gp			
Neck Slot					
Enhancement Bonus: Fortitude, Reflex, and Will					
Property					
You gain resist 5 poison.					
Level 15 or 20: Resist 10 poison.					
Level 25 or 30: Resist 15 poison.					
Utility Power (Poison) ✦ **Daily** (Immediate Reaction)					
Trigger: An enemy hits you with a melee attack.					
Effect: The enemy that hit you takes 1d10 poison damage, and ongoing 5 poison damage (save ends). The enemy also takes a –2 penalty to saving throws against poison effects until the end of the encounter.					
Level 15 or 20: 1d10 poison damage, and ongoing 10 poison damage (save ends).					
Level 25 or 30: 2d10 poison damage, and ongoing 20 poison damage (save ends).					

Amulet of Life Protection

A rough-cut chunk of clear crystal set on a golden chain, an *amulet of life protection* is a powerful ward against possession and death. The talisman's wearer is bound to the item in such a way that it creates a safe haven for that person's mind and soul. In some dark circles, tales are told of necromancers who have learned how to use evil versions of these amulets to bring a person back as a slave to the necromancer.

Amulet of Life Protection		Level 2+ Common			
Each time you take damage to body or mind, this amulet pulses warmly, reminding you of the protection it holds for you, even in death.					
Lvl 2	+1	520 gp	Lvl 17	+4	65,000 gp
Lvl 7	+2	2,600 gp	Lvl 22	+5	325,000 gp
Lvl 12	+3	13,000 gp	Lvl 27	+6	1,625,000 gp
Neck Slot					
Enhancement Bonus: Fortitude, Reflex, and Will					
Property					
If you die while wearing the amulet and it is left on your body, the time that your corpse can lie dead and still be revived by a power or a ritual is multiplied by 10. In addition, you cannot be raised as an undead creature. If the amulet is removed from your corpse, these benefits end. Placing the amulet on an already dead body has no effect.					

If you are so fortunate as to possess an amulet of life protection (and friends willing to revive you), I suggest you change the chain on the amulet to something other than gold. It's not good wearing the amulet if your killer or some other scavenger strips it from you before your friends reclaim your body.

Brooch of Unerring Defense

Nerathan war mages knew that not even the strongest armor or magical protection could guard against all attacks. The *brooch of unerring defense*, an ordinary-looking clasp of silver and gold, was crafted to soften the blows that do get through.

Brooch of Unerring Defense		Level 9+ Common			
This clasp flares with white light each time you shrug off an otherwise unavoidable strike.					
Lvl 9	+2	4,200 gp	Lvl 24	+5	525,000 gp
Lvl 14	+3	21,000 gp	Lvl 29	+6	2,625,000 gp
Lvl 19	+4	105,000 gp			
Neck Slot					
Enhancement Bonus: Fortitude, Reflex, and Will					
Property					
When an attack deals damage to you on a miss, that damage is halved, unless it is ongoing damage.					

Cloak of Displacement

Originally essential equipment of the elite Bael Turath warriors known as the Fiendguard, the *cloak of displacement* is cut from the hide of the dreaded displacer beast. Its black leather shimmers in waves of unsettling shadow as its wearer sidesteps even the deadliest blows.

Cloak of Displacement			Level 10+ Uncommon	
When you wrap this shimmering cloak around yourself, your enemies' attacks strike empty air.				
Lvl 10	+2	5,000 gp	Lvl 25	+5	625,000 gp
Lvl 15	+3	25,000 gp	Lvl 30	+6	3,125,000 gp
Lvl 20	+4	125,000 gp			

Neck Slot

Enhancement Bonus: Fortitude, Reflex, and Will

Property

At the start of each encounter, you gain a +2 item bonus to AC and Reflex until an attack against either of those defenses hits you.

Utility Power (Teleportation) ✦ **Daily** (Immediate Interrupt)

Trigger: You are hit by a melee or a ranged attack.

Effect: The triggering attacker must reroll the attack roll and use the second result. If the attack misses you, you can teleport 1 square.

Cloak of the Manta Ray

Adventurers who ply the world's wide oceans, the black waters of the Underdark, or the fierce seas of the Elemental Chaos all can benefit from this unusual gray leather cloak. Always wet to the touch, the *cloak of the manta ray* is said to have been created by acolytes of the primal water spirits, who granted a measure of their power to heroes defending the creatures that dwell beneath the waves.

Cloak of the Manta Ray			Level 18+ Rare
When you enter the water, this cloak enfolds you, with its edges acting like the powerful wings of a fast-moving ray.			
Lvl 18	+4	85,000 gp	Lvl 28	+6	2,125,000 gp
Lvl 23	+5	425,000 gp			

Neck Slot

Enhancement Bonus: Fortitude, Reflex, and Will

Property

You gain a swim speed of 8 and can breathe underwater. You also have the aquatic keyword, so in aquatic combat, you gain a +2 bonus to attack rolls against nonaquatic creatures.

Attack Power ✦ **Encounter** (Immediate Reaction)

Trigger: A creature hits you with a melee attack.

Effect: The triggering creature takes 2d6 damage. If you are underwater, that creature is also dazed until the end of its next turn.

Level 23: 3d6 damage.

Level 28: 4d6 damage.

Cloak of the phoenix

Cloak of the Phoenix

This relic is said to have originated in the arcane court of an empire whose name now lies beyond memory. The *cloak of the phoenix* is a fine weave of pure gold thread loomed with white silk that cannot be marred by dirt or stain. Its clasp is a single golden feather from the tail of the fabled phoenix, whose mastery of life and death is shared by any hero fortunate enough to claim one of these cloaks.

Cloak of the Phoenix			Level 20+ Uncommon	
As your enemy's deadly attack hits home, this cloak flares with a blast of scouring fire that seems to devour you . . . until you return, ready for battle again.				
Lvl 20	+4	125,000 gp	Lvl 30	+6	3,125,000 gp
Lvl 25	+5	625,000 gp			

Neck Slot

Enhancement Bonus: Fortitude, Reflex, and Will

Utility Power (Fire, Healing) ✦ **Daily** (No Action)

Trigger: You drop below 1 hit point.

Effect: Each enemy within 3 squares of you takes 1d10 fire damage, and you are removed from play. At the start of your next turn, you reappear in your former space, or the nearest unoccupied space if that space is occupied. All effects on you end, you regain hit points equal to your healing surge value, and you lose all remaining healing surges.

Level 25: 2d10 fire damage, and you regain hit points equal to your bloodied value.

Level 30: 3d10 fire damage, and you regain all your hit points.

Cloak of the Shadowthief

When faced with a fight worth believing in, a halfling warrior will take on foes three times his or her size—and win. However, the halflings' small stature inspires their warriors to choose stealthy tactics and roguish combat arts more often than a fighter's boldness. The *cloak of the shadowthief* was designed to even the odds for a stealthy combatant, enabling its wearer to make surprisingly effective attacks from within its protective confines.

Cloak of the Shadowthief		Level 14+ Uncommon	

A veil of shadows erupts from this cloak, delaying your enemies' reactions as they try to pinpoint your location.

Lvl 14	+3	21,000 gp	Lvl 24	+5	525,000 gp
Lvl 19	+4	105,000 gp	Lvl 29	+6	2,625,000 gp

Neck Slot

Enhancement Bonus: Fortitude, Reflex, and Will

Utility Power ✦ Encounter (Minor Action)

Effect: Until the end of your next turn, each enemy that you have any concealment or cover against grants combat advantage to you.

Cloak of the Stalking Shadow

A *cloak of the stalking shadow* is crafted from strands of shadows cast between rays of moonlight, each carefully strung together over the course of a month to produce a garment of utter darkness. When worn, the cloak shifts and moves around its wearer, cloaking him or her from sight. By focusing on the cloak's magic, its wearer allows the cloak's form to merge with his own. For a moment, the wearer becomes a creature of insubstantial shadows.

Cloak of the Stalking Shadow		Level 14+ Uncommon	

This flimsy, black cloak is cool to the touch. In your hands it flows and shifts, as if it were a liquid barely being held in solid form.

Lvl 14	+3	21,000 gp	Lvl 24	+5	525,000 gp
Lvl 19	+4	105,000 gp	Lvl 29	+6	2,625,000 gp

Neck Slot

Enhancement Bonus: Fortitude, Reflex, and Will

Property

You gain an item bonus to Stealth checks equal to the cloak's enhancement bonus.

Utility Power ✦ Daily (Minor Action)

Effect: Until the end of your next turn, you are insubstantial and gain a +5 power bonus to Stealth checks.

Greater Medallion of the Mind

Many claim that these items were created by an order of psychics to help in their training of new recruits. Those familiar with cladrin magical lore offer a different story, saying that the eladrin crafted the original *medallions of the mind* to make fey enchantments even more powerful. They later refined the power of these amethyst amulets to focus and shape their thoughts into tools.

Greater Medallion of the Mind		Level 15+ Rare	

The medallion's gem glows softly as your thoughts take root in the minds of those around you.

Lvl 15	+3	25,000 gp	Lvl 25	+5	625,000 gp
Lvl 20	+4	125,000 gp	Lvl 30	+6	3,125,000 gp

Neck Slot

Enhancement Bonus: Fortitude, Reflex, and Will

Properties

✦ You gain an item bonus to Insight checks equal to the medallion's enhancement bonus.

✦ You can communicate telepathically with any creature you can see. Those willing to communicate with you can send thoughts back to you, allowing two-way communication. This telepathic communication fulfills the requirement of any feature or power that a target be able to hear you.

Utility Power ✦ Encounter (Free Action)

Trigger: An enemy attacks you.

Effect: The triggering enemy grants combat advantage until the end of your next turn.

Greater medallion of the mind

CHRIS SEAMAN

Greater Necklace of Fireballs

Masked by special enchantments, this necklace appears to be nothing but a piece of cheap jewelry. However, a character who places the item around his or her neck can see the necklace as it really is—a series of golden-red globes hanging from a fine gold chain. The *greater necklace of fireballs* is one of the more devastating devices of arcane magic known to exist, allowing its wearer to evoke the power of arcane fire by making the motion of plucking off a globe and hurling it. A burst of fiery terror comes into being at the spot indicated by the wearer, scorching everything it touches.

Greater Necklace of Fireballs		Level 15+ Rare	
The globes of this necklace are warm to the touch, hinting at the deadly fire they can unleash upon your foes.			
Lvl 15	+3	25,000 gp	Lvl 25 +5 625,000 gp
Lvl 20	+4	125,000 gp	Lvl 30 +6 3,125,000 gp
Neck Slot			
Enhancement Bonus: Fortitude, Reflex, and Will			
❈ **Attack Power** (Fire) ✦ **Encounter** (Standard Action)			
Attack: Area burst 2 within 10 squares (each creature in the burst); the necklace's level + 3 vs. Reflex			
Hit: 5d6 + the necklace's enhancement bonus fire damage.			
Level 20: 6d6 + enhancement bonus fire damage.			
Level 25: 7d6 + enhancement bonus fire damage.			
Level 30: 8d6 + enhancement bonus fire damage.			
Miss: Half damage.			

I must express some misgivings about those magic items that give the spells cast by wizards to any ordinary fool. Of course, magic items by their nature grant nearly anyone powers beyond what they might normally accomplish, but the greater necklace of fireballs seems particularly egregious in that it so obviously provides a wizard's power. Then again, lightning bolts, flight, teleportation, charm, and sleep effects all reside in items usable by anyone. I suppose I should just be grateful that there exist no gloves of magic missile. Actually, I should look into that.

Greater Talisman of Repulsion

Wizards and others who try to avoid melee favor this useful pendant and its singular power. Known to have been in common use among the first eladrin mages to explore the mortal realm, the talisman ensures that creatures foolish enough to engage the wearer in combat pay a potentially deadly price.

Greater Talisman of Repulsion			Level 13+ Uncommon		
When an enemy strikes you, you release a pulse of magical force from this amulet that drives your foe back.					
Lvl 13	+3	17,000 gp	Lvl 23	+5	425,000 gp
Lvl 18	+4	85,000 gp	Lvl 28	+6	2,125,000 gp
Neck Slot					
Enhancement Bonus: Fortitude, Reflex, and Will					
Utility Power ✦ Daily (Immediate Reaction)					
Trigger: A creature hits you with a melee attack.					
Effect: You push the triggering creature up to a number of squares equal to the talisman's enhancement bonus, and the creature is immobilized until the end of your next turn.					

Lesser Badge of the Berserker

In the aftermath of the Dawn War, the world was given over to the care of humanoid tribes that had long been pawns in the battles between gods and primordials. The greatest of the tribes' early leaders were the first to wear the *lesser badge of the berserker*—a token crafted from the flesh and bone of heroes who had gone before them, and which granted them the determination of those fallen heroes during the heat of battle.

Lesser Badge of the Berserker		Level 2+ Common			
The jagged bone of this macabre badge digs into your flesh as you race into battle, the pain inspiring you to greater fury.					
Lvl 2	+1	520 gp	Lvl 17	+4	65,000 gp
Lvl 7	+2	2,600 gp	Lvl 22	+5	325,000 gp
Lvl 12	+3	13,000 gp	Lvl 27	+6	1,625,000 gp
Neck Slot					
Enhancement Bonus: Fortitude, Reflex, and Will					
Property					
When you charge, you gain a +4 bonus to all defenses against opportunity attacks provoked by the charge's movement.					

Periapt of Health

This charm is set with a blue-white diamond that pulses faintly with each beat of its wearer's heart. A *periapt of health* protects against all disease, whether inflicted by mundane squalor, the power of magic, or the foulest monsters. Many tales tell of adventurers finding these periapts within hidden lairs secreted among the sewer systems of the more wealthy cities.

Periapt of Health — Level 3+ Common

This charm gives off a sweet scent that only you can detect, masking any odor of noxiousness or corruption.

Lvl 3	+1	680 gp	Lvl 18	+4	85,000 gp
Lvl 8	+2	3,400 gp	Lvl 23	+5	425,000 gp
Lvl 13	+3	17,000 gp	Lvl 28	+6	2,125,000 gp

Neck Slot

Enhancement Bonus: Fortitude, Reflex, and Will

Property

You gain a +2 item bonus to saving throws against disease. You also gain an item bonus to Endurance checks against disease. That bonus equals the periapt's enhancement bonus.

Periapt of Wound Closure

Invented by dragonborn spellcasters (and still commonly found among their most headstrong warriors), each of these blood-red crystals is set with a heavy steel clasp. When worn, a *periapt of wound closure* allows its wearer to shrug off injuries that would fell a lesser creature.

Periapt of Wound Closure — Level 15+ Uncommon

When you suffer a grievous wound, this gem releases a burst of stored vitality, helping your body quickly heal itself.

Lvl 15	+3	25,000 gp	Lvl 25	+5	625,000 gp
Lvl 20	+4	125,000 gp	Lvl 30	+6	3,125,000 gp

Neck Slot

Enhancement Bonus: Fortitude, Reflex, and Will

Property

You gain an item bonus to saving throws against untyped ongoing damage. The bonus equals the periapt's enhancement bonus.

Utility Power (Healing) ✦ Daily (No Action)

Trigger: An attack drops you below 1 hit point.

Effect: You spend a healing surge and regain additional hit points equal to your healing surge value.

Level 20: 5 + your healing surge value.

Level 25: 10 + your healing surge value.

Level 30: 15 + your healing surge value.

Beware scarabs of insanity. Many carry curses imbued within them on their creation in the ancient empire of Bael Turath. From what I've learned of that realm, its curses will be like many of its citizens: perverse, deceptive, and pernicious. I would not put it past a scarab's creator to link the item to a particular bloodline so that only members of one family can use it— a wise precaution in the treacherous society that gave birth to such a devilish item.

Scarab of Insanity

The elite dragonborn warriors who fought against Bael Turath feared no physical pain. However, even some of Arkhosia's greatest heroes would quail when tiefling spellcasters wearing *scarabs of insanity* joined the battle. It is said that only the strongest creatures can shake off the dread effects of a *scarab of insanity.*

Scarab of Insanity — Level 17+ Uncommon

When an enemy dares attack your mind, you lash out with the power of this red-and-black scarab, driving a spike of madness into your foe's mind.

Lvl 17	+4	65,000 gp	Lvl 27	+6	1,625,000 gp
Lvl 22	+5	325,000 gp			

Neck Slot

Enhancement Bonus: Fortitude, Reflex, and Will

Property

You gain a +2 item bonus to saving throws against effects that dominate you or otherwise allow an enemy to control what you do with your actions.

Utility Power (Charm) ✦ Daily (Immediate Reaction)

Trigger: An enemy makes an attack against your Will.

Effect: Until the end of the encounter, whenever the triggering enemy makes a melee or a ranged attack against you or any of your allies, it must make a saving throw. On a failure, it must target your enemy that is closest to it, instead of its chosen target (the enemy can attack as normal if no other enemies can be targeted). On a successful saving throw, this effect ends.

Sneak's Cloak

A creature wearing this thick wool cloak can be seen only when it wants to be, and so those who favor stealth in combat particularly appreciate this item. The court assassins of Bael Turath are credited as the first to make extensive use of the *sneak's cloak*—often in the course of bringing down their own corrupt regents and kings.

Sneak's Cloak — Level 9+ Uncommon

As you wrap this voluminous cloak around you, its magic conceals your presence from your enemies.

Lvl 9	+2	4,200 gp	Lvl 24	+5	525,000 gp
Lvl 14	+3	21,000 gp	Lvl 29	+6	2,625,000 gp
Lvl 19	+4	105,000 gp			

Neck Slot

Enhancement Bonus: Fortitude, Reflex, and Will

Property

You gain an item bonus to Stealth checks equal to the cloak's enhancement bonus.

Utility Power (Illusion) ✦ Daily (No Action)

Trigger: You hit a creature with a melee or a ranged attack while you have any cover or concealment.

Effect: The creature treats you as invisible (save ends).

Rings

Rings are everywhere: Even the lowliest peasant might have a crude adornment of this sort. The truly magnificent magical specimens, however—those capable of altering reality in stunning ways—are exceedingly hard to find.

Incendiary Ring of Fireblazing

The flame-loving mage Zagrisar created the first *incendiary ring of fireblazing* in a failed attempt to craft a more powerful *ring of fire resistance*. The attempt nearly destroyed Zagrisar's tower and workshop, but from his spectacular failure came a new discovery that allowed him to become a living inferno on the battlefield.

With his new ring, Zagrisar's power increased greatly, and he attempted even greater feats of daring, many of them dangerous and foolhardy, such as the burning of the undead at Ungol Keep, where he gained the nickname "Flame Scourge." Whether Zagrisar's original ring survives is unknown, because he disappeared during a trip to the City of Brass after vowing to destroy a powerful efreet lord. One of his apprentices was able to duplicate the feat of creating these rings when Zagrisar didn't return.

Incendiary Ring of Fireblazing	Level 14 Rare
A shroud of living flame emanates from this ring without harming you. On your command, you can send it blazing outward to sear your enemies.	
Ring Slot 21,000 gp	
Property	
When you make a basic attack, that attack can deal fire damage instead of its normal damage type.	
Attack Power (Fire) ✦ Daily (No Action)	
Trigger: You hit with an attack that deals fire damage.	
Effect: The target and each creature, other than you, adjacent to it take ongoing 10 fire damage (save ends).	
Milestone: If you've reached at least one milestone today, the ongoing damage increases to 20.	
Utility Power ✦ At-Will (Minor Action)	
Effect: You can ignite any unattended combustible object that you touch, including cloth, oil, paper, tinder, a torch, and so on. You cannot use this power to deal damage to any creature.	

Lesser Ring of Feather Fall

First forged by the dwarf clans charged with guarding the passes of the treacherous Razorpeaks, this filigreed mithral band enables its wearer to ignore the laws of gravity. The secrets of the ring's creation passed into the wider world when the forgemaster's apprentice was kidnapped by a drow raiding party, and the *lesser ring of feather fall* is now coveted by adventurers of all stripes.

Lesser Ring of Feather Fall	Level 12 Common
You barely notice the weight of this delicately filigreed metal band, but you appreciate the lightness it confers to you whenever you take a fall.	
Ring Slot 13,000 gp	
Property	
You take no damage from a fall.	

Ring of Borrowed Spells

At the height of the wars that led to Nerath's founding, the armies that fought for domination of the human lands depended on the talent of their arcane spellcasters. Since those casters were typically less experienced than the troops they fought, they died quickly. In response, the war mages of Veoran designed and perfected this rune-scribed circle of black ebony, granting their warriors the ability to combine arcane magic and martial prowess to deadly effect.

Ring of Borrowed Spells	Level 17 Uncommon
This band of rune-carved ebony holds arcane power in reserve for you to call upon in time of need.	
Ring Slot 65,000 gp	
Property	
This ring contains two arcane encounter attack powers of level 17 or lower that the wearer can employ using the ring's power. The powers contained in the ring are determined when it is created and cannot be changed.	
Attack Power ✦ Daily (Standard Action)	
Effect: You use one of the powers stored in the ring.	
Milestone: If you've reached at least one milestone today, you gain a +2 bonus to the attack rolls of the stored power you use.	

Ring of Humanoid Influence

The despotic warlock Orada was feared both for his might and his hideous countenance, which had been disfigured by long years of channeling the twisted essence of the Far Realm. After his death, his exultant servitors discovered on his withered finger a band of pure crystal set with chips of amethyst and emerald. The powers of persuasion granted by the ring were believed to be an essential part of the warlock's rise to power, and the item was successfully replicated a handful of times by those servants.

Ring of Humanoid Influence — Level 21 Rare

A dark self-confidence fills you as you slip on this ring, emboldening you to manipulate the feelings of others.

Ring Slot   225,000 gp

Property

You gain a +2 item bonus to Charisma-based skill checks and Charisma ability checks.

Utility Power (Charm) ✦ Daily (Standard Action)

Effect: You make a single Bluff check or Diplomacy check opposed by the passive Insight checks of each humanoid creature within 3 squares of you. If you win the opposed check, the creature treats you as a trusted friend until the end of the encounter. The creature is not dominated and does not automatically follow your orders. However, it reacts to your suggestions in the most favorable way. The creature is not aware that you used this power against it. If you or your allies attack a creature under the effect of this power, the effect ends on that creature.

A creature engaged in combat with you or your allies gains a +10 bonus to its Insight check.

Milestone: If you've reached at least one milestone today, the effect lasts until the end of your next extended rest.

Ring of Resourceful Wizardry

This ring appears as a band of plain steel to anyone except a wizard, who sees it as a blue sapphire band set with a star and engraved with arcane glyphs—and only a wizard handling a *ring of resourceful wizardry* can determine its function. Crafted by a guild of master mages known as the Red Circle, the *ring of resourceful wizardry* allows its wearer to improve his or her spellcasting prowess—and on occasion to access magic that would otherwise be denied.

The Red Circle used these bands in its fight against the early invasions of the world by githyanki pirates, helping the mages offset the strength of those astral raiders.

Ring of Resourceful Wizardry — Level 21 Uncommon

You feel the fullness of your arcane potential while you wear this ring.

Ring Slot   225,000 gp

Property

You gain a +4 item bonus to Arcana checks.

Utility Power ✦ Daily (Minor Action)

Requirement: You must be a wizard with a spellbook.

Effect: Choose one unused power that you have prepared from your spellbook. You prepare a different power in its place. The new power must be from your spellbook, of the same type as the replaced power (daily attack power or utility power), and of the same level or lower.

Milestone: If you've reached at least one milestone today, you gain a second use of this power before your next extended rest.

Selection of rings

Ring of X-ray Vision

A Nerathan princeling who had a penchant for peering into the chambers of the court's ladies-in-waiting commissioned the first *ring of X-ray vision*. This fragile-looking band of clear crystal is now highly sought after by adventurers, particularly those who crave the ability to locate hidden treasure. However, using the ring's power comes at a price—its wielder must use it sparingly, or its magic diminishes for a time.

Ring of X-ray Vision — Level 25 Rare

With this crystal ring on, your surroundings come into greater focus. With concentration, you can even see through solid objects.

Ring Slot   625,000 gp

Property

You gain a +4 item bonus to Perception checks, and creatures adjacent to you gain no benefit from concealment against you.

Utility Power ✦ Encounter (Minor Action)

Effect: You can see into and through substances impenetrable to normal sight until the end of your next turn. Your enhanced vision requires no light and has a range of 4 squares. Your enhanced vision can see through 20 feet of cloth, wood, or similar animal or vegetable matter, 10 feet of stone, or 1 foot of iron, steel, silver, and other light metals. Your enhanced vision cannot penetrate lead, gold, platinum, or similar dense metals.

Sustain Minor: The effect persists until the end of your next turn. The first time you sustain this effect, the ring's property is suppressed until the end of your next extended rest.

Milestone: If you've reached at least one milestone today, the ring's property is suppressed only until the end of the encounter.

The lascivious origin story attached to the ring of X-ray vision seems to me an adventurer's fantasy. The great cost of creating such an item makes it much more likely that a king had it crafted for espionage or warfare. The ability to see voids in a battlement's stone or to catch your supposed ally in counsel with enemies provides a value far more in keeping with the cost of the item's creation. That leaded pigments and gilded decorations traditionally cover the walls in the quarters of ladies-in-waiting and other rooms of a castle cannot be taken either as proof or disproof of the ring's original intent, but certainly it might thwart the fancies of an adventurer who found such a ring.

Shadow Band

Thieves, lurkers, and creatures of the Shadowfell particularly covet this smoky obsidian ring. The *shadow band* was created for the renowned warlord Janian as a means to conceal his captive bride's beauty from the world. Aimeth, a half-elf maiden seized as war spoils from her village, was quick to repay her new lord's gift—with a garrote delivered from the darkness he so conveniently provided.

Shadow Band	Level 27 Rare
Shadows leak from this ring to fill the space around you. When needed, you can call upon the ring to fully cover yourself in obscuring shadows.	
Ring Slot 1,625,000 gp	
Property	
You gain partial concealment.	
Utility Power ✦ Daily (Minor Action)	

    Effect: You gain total concealment until the end of your next turn.

    Milestone: If you've reached at least one milestone today, the effect lasts until the end of the encounter.

Waist Slot Items

From the earliest days of magical crafting, belts and other items worn around the torso have been used as repositories for magic that improves the wearer's ability to withstand the rigors of combat.

Baldric of Time

The warlocks of Bael Turath crafted the *baldric of time* to give themselves an edge in combat against the more powerful dragonborn warriors of Arkhosia. Numerous accounts of the ancient battles between those empires describe the ability of these belts to let their wearers seemingly slip the bonds of time to make unexpected and deadly attacks. However, it is said that some of these surviving onyx-studded belts were corrupted when Bael Turath fell.

Baldric of Time			Level 6+ Common
When you slip on this belt, you feel a brief lurch as the march of time seems to skip a beat.			
Lvl 6	1,800 gp	Lvl 16	45,000 gp
Waist Slot			
Property			

Whenever you roll a 20 on your initiative check, you gain an extra move action during your first turn of the encounter.

    Level 16: You instead gain an extra standard action.

Baldric of valor

JIM NELSON

Baldric of Valor

The *baldric of valor* is most often associated with the elite warriors of the Black Steel Guard. Each was given one of these items by their king to help them defend Areya, their ancient homeland. The tales about those guardians also say that none can seize a wearer's belt while he or she lives.

Baldric of Valor	Level 21 Common

You feel the power of this belt inspiring you to hit your foes with everything you have even as its aegis protects you from your enemies' counterattacks.

Waist Slot   225,000 gp

Property

When you spend an action point, you gain a +3 item bonus to saving throws, a +1 item bonus to attack rolls, and a +1 item bonus to all defenses. The bonuses last until the end of your next turn.

Belt of Dwarvenkind

At the height of the dwarves' civilization, one of that race's greatest leaders was not a dwarf but a gnome known as Satsaman. A master wizard and arcane crafter, Satsaman fell in love with the dwarf warrior maiden Jorunna, but found his suit laughingly dismissed by her father the king. Undaunted, Satsaman created the *belt of dwarvenkind* as a means of proving his worth to Jorunna's people—a task he fulfilled as royal son-in-law, and thereafter as trusted advisor to a long line of dwarf kings.

Belt of Dwarvenkind	Level 7 Rare

The delicate metalwork in this belt is unmistakably magical, as is the feeling that courses through you when you lash it on.

Waist Slot   65,000 gp

Properties

✦ You gain a +2 bonus to Diplomacy checks and Intimidate checks against dwarves.

✦ You can speak, read, and write Dwarven.

Utility Power ✦ Encounter (Immediate Interrupt)

Trigger: An attack pushes, pulls, or slides you.

Effect: You ignore 1 square of the forced movement.

Utility Power ✦ Daily (Immediate Reaction)

Trigger: You take ongoing poison damage from an attack.

Effect: You can make a saving throw against the ongoing poison damage.

Cincture of Vivacity

The explorer Katakna the Cautious was known for his use of this heavy damask wrap. A coward by nature, Katakna counted on the power of the *cincture of vivacity* to keep him from ever coming to serious physical harm. His advanced age when he died suggests that it did its job well.

Cincture of Vivacity	Level 14 Common

Where it covers you, this wrap holds you in a firm grip that strengthens your physical resilience.

Waist Slot   21,000 gp

Property

Whenever you spend a healing surge during combat that would grant hit points to you beyond your maximum, you gain the extra hit points as temporary hit points.

Diamond Cincture

The monetary value of this platinum band studded with diamonds is obvious to all, but only someone who can detect its magical nature can determine its true worth. Three of the belt's gems pulse with a faint white light, hinting at the *diamond cincture*'s healing and defensive qualities.

Diamond Cincture		Level 10+ Uncommon	

Each gleaming diamond on this belt is a powerful conduit for healing energy.

Lvl 10	5,000 gp	Lvl 30	3,125,000 gp
Lvl 20	125,000 gp		

Waist Slot

Property

This belt holds one diamond, and you gain a +1 item bonus to Fortitude.

Level 20: Two diamonds, and a +2 item bonus.

Level 30: Three diamonds, and a +3 item bonus.

Utility Power (Healing) **✦ At-Will** (Minor Action)

Effect: You spend a healing surge. One diamond on the belt cracks and darkens, becoming worthless. Each time a diamond is expended in this way, the belt's item bonus is reduced by 1 (to a minimum of 0). If there are no unexpended diamonds on the belt, you can't use this power. After an extended rest, each expended diamond is restored.

Healer's Sash

This rough-looking swath of white homespun is fed through five wooden rings, which serve as a conduit for its healing power. The elves of the haunted Rorawood first crafted the *healer's sash* for use by the brave sentinels who stood against that dark land's undead. By drawing on and channeling the vitality of yourself or another, you can bestow healing upon an ally.

Healer's Sash		Level 11+ Uncommon	

This magic sash resists staining by blood or gore—a testament to its latent restorative power.

Lvl 11	9,000 gp	Lvl 21	225,000 gp

Waist Slot

Utility Power (Healing) **✦ Daily** (Minor Action)

Effect: Close burst 5 (you and one ally in the burst, or two allies in the burst). One of the targets loses a healing surge, and then the other target regains hit points equal to his or her healing surge value.

Level 21: The burst increases to 10, and an additional ally in the burst regains hit points equal to his or her healing surge value.

Survivor's Belt

Fortune favors the halflings, and this well-known example of that race's magical craft imbues its wearer with the benefit of halfling luck when things are at their darkest.

Survivor's Belt	Level 11 Common
This belt lets you demonstrate fortune's favor when you are brought to the brink of death.	
Waist Slot	9,000 gp
Property	
Whenever you make a death saving throw, you can roll twice, using the higher result.	

Wondrous Items

Any form of magic that can be imagined might be found embodied in one of the objects known as wondrous items. The forms of some of these items hint at their function, but in other cases a wondrous item's appearance offers no clue to what it does.

We wizards like to categorize things— no surprise, what with our libraries of books and scrolls and out laboratories of potions and unguents. We separate swords from wands and belts from boots and consider ourselves sensible. Then we take everything else, from broomsticks to drums to lanterns, and lump them all into "wondrous items." That's the same as devoting a bookshelf to "various topics" and then arranging the books by color of the cover. Wondrous items might do anything, might be anything, and so I suppose they deserve to be called wonders, but I shall henceforth endeavor to organize them in a more helpful manner.

Backpack of Concealment

Although many pursue magic in search of the keys to ancient mysteries or to gain great status, others have more mundane goals in mind. *Backpacks of concealment* were first crafted to conceal the activities of a ring of powerful smugglers who dealt in extraplanar goods, rare components, and other magical objects.

Backpack of Concealment	Level 2 Common
This plain leather backpack is covered with pockets big and small.	
Wondrous Item	520 gp
Property	
This backpack can conceal any one object placed within it from a physical search. Any creature other than the one that placed the item in the backpack cannot find the object. If the backpack is destroyed, the object falls from its remains.	

Bottled Smoke

Explorers returning from the fabled City of Brass were the first to introduce *bottled smoke* to the world. Whether one of these bottles was crafted there or traded for in the markets of that metropolis, the magic of the item clearly belongs to the efreet. Some believe that the power of *bottled smoke* serves some secret purpose, explaining why its creators have willingly allowed it to propagate in the mortal realm.

Bottled Smoke			Level 7+ Uncommon
This brass bottle is hot to the touch, and spews forth a cloud of ash and smoke when opened.			
Lvl 7	2,600 gp	Lvl 17	65,000 gp
Wondrous Item			
Utility Power (Fire, Zone) ✦ **Daily** (Standard Action)			

Effect: Close burst 1. The burst creates a zone that lasts until the end of your next turn. Creatures have partial concealment while in the zone. Any creature other than you that starts its turn in the zone takes 1d6 fire damage.
Level 17: Close burst 3; 2d6 fire damage.
Sustain Minor: The zone persists until the end of your next turn. You must be within 10 squares of the zone to sustain it.

Broom of Flying

The dark arcane sect known as the Witches of Blackbriar crafted the first *brooms of flying*, which they employed in raids so brutal that these items became a part of common folklore long after the sect's fall. The few brooms that survived the destruction of the witches are sought by historians, sages, and adventurers.

Broom of Flying	Level 15 Uncommon
This gnarled wicker broom seems to constantly tug at the hand that holds it, seeking to take to the air.	
Wondrous Item	25,000 gp
Property	
While riding the broom, you have a fly speed of 8 and can hover. The broom can carry you and your gear (up to a normal load for you). You take a -2 penalty to attack rolls while riding the broom.	
Utility Power ✦ **Daily** (Standard Action)	

Effect: You call the broom to you from any location within 60 squares of you. As long as the broom is not prevented from moving, it appears in your hand at the start of your next turn. The broom's movement as it moves to you cannot be used to attack or impede any creature.

Chime of Opening

One of the many wonders to disappear with Nerath was the Vaults of Time—great underground repositories of wealth and lore that had been in continuous operation for more than a thousand years. The Keepers of Time used *chimes of opening* to maintain control of their vaults, which were set with locks so impervious that no mortal effort could break them. With the fall of Nerath, the Keepers of Time took the vaults' secret location to their graves, though their precious chimes soon began to turn up in the hands of adventurers. Each chime is a foot-long mithral tube scribed with glyphs from no known language—said by some to be a precious clue to the location of the ruined vaults and the knowledge and treasure that might still be found there.

Chime of Opening	Level 5+ Uncommon
When struck, this chime rings out with a magical tone that opens locks.	
Lvl 5 1,000 gp	Lvl 25 625,000 gp
Lvl 15 25,000 gp	
Wondrous Item	

Utility Power ✦ Daily (Standard Action)

   Effect: When you strike the *chime of opening*, you direct it to open a single locked door, chest, gate, or other object within 5 squares of you and remove any traps upon that object. The chime makes a single Thievery check with a +10 bonus against all the DCs required to open the object and disable any traps on it. Depending on the DCs, it is possible for the chime to unlock an object but not disable the traps on it (or vice versa), or to disable some traps but leave others intact.

   Level 15: +20 bonus.

   Level 25: +30 bonus.

Climber's Rope

Those who brave the Underdark and the ruins of fallen empires keep one of these barbed, spiral-tipped wooden projectiles on hand. When faced with a wall too steep to climb or a gorge that can't be crossed, an archer can fire *climber's rope* deep into a stone, wood, or metal surface, and a thin but strong rope magically unfurls behind it, allowing passage along it.

Climber's Rope	Level 6 Common
When a slope or wall cannot be climbed, this projectile creates an easier path.	
Wondrous Item	1,800 gp

Utility Power ✦ Encounter (Standard Action)

   Requirement: You must be wielding a bow or a crossbow.

   Effect: You fire this projectile from your bow or crossbow at a target within normal range that you can see, either at a wall, ceiling, or similar surface or at a sufficiently heavy unattended object, such as a large statue. A magic rope then trails out behind the projectile, connecting the point of impact to your position. The rope can support up to 500 pounds at one time. The rope remains in place until the end of the encounter or until you dismiss it as a minor action. If fired at a creature, the projectile deals no damage.

Crystal Ball

No magecraft known to Bael Turath, Nerath, or the current age can reproduce the ancient magic of the *crystal ball*, making such items highly valuable to the sages, lords, and magic-wielders who covet their power. It is said that there is no secret safe against the possessor of a *crystal ball*, but the dark rumors of madness inflicted on those not capable of mastering this relic's use are so common that there must be some truth to them.

Crystal Ball	Level 8+ Rare
The vestiges of past, present, and future swirl within this gleaming crystal orb when you view it.	
Lvl 8 3,400 gp	Lvl 28 2,125,000 gp
Lvl 18 85,000 gp	
Wondrous Item	
Property	

While you have the *crystal ball* in your possession, you gain a +4 bonus to Arcana checks for scrying rituals.

Utility Power ✦ Daily (Standard Action)

   Effect: By peering into the *crystal ball*, you can get a glimpse of a creature, object, or location within 100 squares of you. When you view a subject through the *crystal ball*, you see and hear the immediate area around the subject until the end of your next turn as if you were standing beside it. Your perception of the area is with your normal senses and vision, and you might need to make Perception checks to note specific features of the area. If the subject moves, your point of perception moves with it.

   A creature being scried upon, or within 5 squares of the subject being viewed with the *crystal ball*, can make a Perception check opposed by your Arcana check. On a successful Perception check, the creature is aware that it is being magically observed, and it might take steps to thwart your observation. However, it is not automatically aware that you are the one observing it.

   Level 18: The subject of your scrying can be within 100 miles of your location.

   Level 28: The subject of your scrying can be anywhere on your plane.

   Sustain Standard: The effect persists until the end of your next turn.

Daern's Instant Fortress

The artificer and warrior Daern was known as a creator of superior defenses and fortifications, and the seldom-seen wondrous item for which she is most commonly known speaks to the brilliance of her creations. Explorers and adventurers who brave the wilds appreciate this small cube of rust-streaked iron because of the magical fortification it transforms into on command.

A group with one of these rare items in its possession never needs to worry about having a safe place to rest, as long as it's in an area voluminous enough to contain the fortress when it is called forth. In a bit of prudent foresight, Daern made it impossible for the owner to inadvertently collapse the fortress while he or she is inside.

Daern's Instant Fortress	Level 22 Rare

With a touch, you transform this iron cube into a fortress that protects yourself and your friends.

Wondrous Item	325,000 gp

Utility Power ✦ Daily (Standard Action)

Effect: You create a square adamantine tower that occupies a close blast 5. You must create the tower in unoccupied squares. Its walls are 30 feet high, extend 10 feet into the ground, and are impervious to damage. The top 5 feet of the tower is a sealed battlement, and it has windows on all sides that allow a view of the nearby terrain, but which cannot be attacked through in either direction. It has a small door that faces you when the tower is created, and which opens only to your command or a DC 36 Strength check. The door provides the only access to the tower.

The tower provides a safe location for you and your allies. It includes sleeping and living quarters for up to twenty Medium creatures, though it has no sources of food or water. The tower lasts until you dismiss it from the outside as a standard action, returning it to its cube form. Creatures within the tower when you dismiss it are teleported to squares in or adjacent to the tower's area.

Decanter of Endless Water

The great cities of Nerath once featured magically sourced fountains and wells that carried fresh, clear water to all quarters. That same magic imbues the *decanter of endless water*, but this item has even greater usefulness. With its power fully unleashed, the *decanter* spews forth a torrent of water that can batter anything in its path. The force of this flow has been known to catch its user by surprise.

Decanter of Endless Water	Level 7 Uncommon

When you open this always-dripping flask, it will release a steady stream of water, or a torrent that blasts away obstacles.

Wondrous Item	2,600 gp

Utility Power ✦ Encounter (Standard Action)

Effect: You cause the decanter to pour forth fresh or salt water in one of three volumes.
  ✦ Stream: 1 gallon.
  ✦ Fountain: 5 gallons in a 5-foot-long stream.
  ✦ Geyser: 30 gallons in a 20-foot-long stream.
  In addition to filling a container of suitable volume, the fountain function of the decanter can be used to clear dirt or light debris from an area 2 squares on a side.
  The geyser function can be used to break a door or other object. If you do, you gain a +5 power bonus to the check. The area in a burst 1 centered on the door or object is difficult terrain until the end of the encounter. However, the geyser creates considerable pressure, and you must succeed on a DC 16 Strength check when you use it or be knocked prone.

Elven Chain Shirt

Elven chain is forged from mithral and reinforced with arcane magic. A shirt of elven chain is as light as cloth yet provides protection against blade and claw, and can be worn underneath clothes or armor.

Elven Chain Shirt	Level 9+ Uncommon

This fine mesh of mithral links is no more burdensome than a cotton shirt, yet is stronger than steel.

Lvl 9	4,200 gp	Lvl 29	2,625,000 gp
Lvl 19	105,000 gp		

Wondrous Item

Property

You gain a +1 item bonus to AC while wearing this shirt with light armor or no armor.
  Level 19: +2 item bonus
  Level 29: +3 item bonus

Enchanted Reins

The nomadic halflings employ a wide variety of beasts of burden depending on local conditions, climate, and culture. The ancient order of halfling druids known as the Beastmasters first crafted these reins of woven silver and black leather, which have remained in constant use among their many clans. *Enchanted reins* are invaluable in the breaking of wild creatures, from horses and other traditional mounts to large aquatic beasts tamed to draw boats and rafts at speed along the rivers of the frontier.

Enchanted Reins	Level 5 Common

These well-made silver and leather reins make any beast you wish to control more manageable.

Wondrous Item	1,000 gp

Property

Nature checks made to calm or train a natural beast fitted with these reins gain a +2 item bonus.

Enchanted reins might seem an odd thing to an adventurer, but wars have been fought for less potent magic. Just think of this: If you can train mounts and beasts of burden faster and better than others, you can sell them faster too. Add the utility of these reins in battle, and it's little wonder that such simple magic might be considered so valuable.

Endless Quiver

Rangers dedicated to Melora are especially drawn to the *endless quiver*, which they claim was crafted by the god of the wilderness herself. Intricate Rellanic lettering is magically scribed along the quiver's tightly stitched leather, describing deeds done by the heroes who previously carried the item. However, some tales say that the *endless quiver* judges those it serves, and that if its bearer's deeds are not up to the standard of those who came before, it will fail to function at the worst possible time.

Endless Quiver — Level 9 Common

Each time you slip your hand inside this quiver, you find the ammunition you need waiting for you.

Wondrous Item	4,200 gp

Property

When you attack with a bow or a crossbow, you can reach into the quiver, causing the quiver to produce a nonmagical arrow or bolt for the attack. Ammunition created by the quiver that is not used within 1 round of its creation disappears. For all other ammunition, the quiver works like a normal item of its type.

Eternal Chalk

Said to have been created by an apprentice of the great Nolzur, *eternal chalk* became widely known as a tool of the vandalism and public protest that swept through Nerath's outlying regions before the empire's fall. In the current age, this unusual magical tool is more commonly seen in the hands of adventurers, who use it to keep track of their progress in lost ruins and the Underdark's twisting passages.

Eternal Chalk — Level 1 Common

The marks left by this chalk glow briefly as you scribe them, remaining in place to guide you until you choose to erase them.

Wondrous Item	360 gp

Property

A stick of *eternal chalk* never breaks or wears down with normal use. Any writing or drawing made with this chalk cannot be erased for one week by anyone except the original artist or author.

A stick of *eternal chalk* can be created in any color.

Flask of the Veiled Horde

The archmage Evard crafted these items as gifts for his most faithful servants. Made from a strange metal mined in the Shadowfell, a *flask of the veiled horde* collects the stray motes of shadow magic that wend around it, focusing them into a creature of shadow and giving that creature a cruel sentience. By unstoppering the flask and spilling the shadow material within, this item's owner spawns an obedient shadow creature that persists for a few minutes. If the legends are true, Evard tore the souls from his most hated enemies and trapped each one within a flask. The creatures produced by them have, at their core, the trapped, tormented spirits of his enemies.

Flask of the Veiled Horde — Level 10 Uncommon

This flask is wrought from a black metal of unknown origin. It is cold to the touch, and shaking reveals that it is filled with a heavy liquid. A stopper of the same black metal seals it shut.

Wondrous Item	5,000 gp

Utility Power ✦ Daily (Minor Action)

Effect: You pour a mote of darkness from the flask to create a shadow creature that obeys your spoken commands and is allied with you and your allies. The creature appears adjacent to you and takes its turn on your initiative count according to commands you give to it (commanding it is a free action). If you don't command the creature, it takes no actions. The creature disappears at the end of the encounter.

Veiled Horde Shadow — **Level 10 Minion Skirmisher**

Medium shadow animate — XP –

HP 1; a missed attack never damages a minion	**Initiative** +11
AC 24, Fortitude 22, Reflex 24, Will 20	**Perception** +5
Speed 8	Darkvision

STANDARD ACTIONS

⊕ **Shadow Grasp** (necrotic) ✦ At-Will

Attack: Melee 1 (one creature); +13 vs. Reflex

Hit: 9 necrotic damage.

MOVE ACTIONS

Shadow Jaunt (teleportation) ✦ At-Will

Requirement: The shadow must be adjacent to a creature.

Effect: The shadow teleports to a square adjacent to a creature within 6 squares of it.

TRIGGERED ACTIONS

Death Burst (necrotic) ✦ Encounter

Trigger: The shadow drops to 0 hit points.

Effect: The shadow is destroyed, and each creature adjacent to it takes 9 necrotic damage.

Str 10 (+5)	Dex 18 (+9)	Wis 10 (+5)
Con 15 (+7)	Int 3 (+1)	Cha 7 (+3)

Alignment unaligned	**Languages** –

Flask of the veiled horde

Floating Lantern

The archmage and explorer Inora the One-Handed earned her sobriquet as a stripling adventurer, when an altercation with a young black dragon went poorly for her. In later years, she invented a host of magic items designed to ease the rigors of her adventuring career, of which the *floating lantern* remains the best known.

Floating Lantern	Level 3 Common

You hang this lantern on the empty air, where it floats under your command.

Wondrous Item	680 gp

Property

This lantern casts light in a 10-square radius, and it never needs lighting or refilling. When you let go of the lantern, it continues to hang in the air where you leave it. If weight in excess of 1 pound is applied to the lantern, it falls to the ground.

Any creature holding the *floating lantern* or adjacent to it can set its light to be bright (10-square radius), dim (5-square radius), or off as a minor action.

As a move action, the last creature to hold the lantern can mentally command it to move up to 10 squares in any direction, but not more than 10 squares from the commanding creature.

Flying Hook

The greatest cities of Nerath featured magically sculpted spires and towers that stretched toward the heavens, and whose wealthy occupants were a constant target for the thieves' guilds that challenged the empire's law. For decades, the *flying hook* was one of the most prominent and hard-won pieces of sophisticated urban thieves' gear, to the point where these items were stolen as often as the loot whose theft they were meant to facilitate.

Flying Hook	Level 15 Common

When you toss this grappling hook into the air, it soars off under your mental command.

Wondrous Item	25,000 gp

Utility Power ✦ At-Will (Minor Action)

Effect: You command the hook to fly from you to an unattended object within 20 squares of you that you can see, and it magically latches onto the object. Once secured, the hook extends a thin rope back to your hands. Climbing the rope requires an Athletics check, or you can pull the object toward you with a Strength check. The hook and rope can support up to 3,000 pounds before the hook detaches from the surface. The rope cannot be tied or knotted in any way, nor can it be used to attack or affect a creature.

As a minor action, you can command the hook to detach from the object and return to you. This causes the rope to retract.

Gem of Auditory Recollection

Nerath's great halls of justice were the inspiration for the *gem of auditory recollection*, a chunk of rough-cut quartz used to record hearings and evidence as a means of establishing a system of records unparalleled in the history of law. Copies of this relic soon became better known on the other side of the law, making their way into the hands of blackmailers, spies, and kidnappers for whom an unassailable record of events and voices became a dark boon.

Gem of Auditory Recollection	Level 16 Common

This smooth gem records the sounds around it, allowing you to listen to the voices of the past when you wish.

Wondrous Item	45,000 gp

Utility Power ✦ At-Will (Standard Action)

Effect: The gem records all words spoken by one creature within 20 squares of you. You can end the recording as a free action. The gem can record 12 hours of speech before becoming full.

Utility Power ✦ At-Will (Standard Action)

Effect: The gem repeats a section of recorded text aloud in the exact voice and language of the original speaker. The gem continues its recitation until the speech is finished or until you use a free action to stop it.

Utility Power ✦ At-Will (Standard Action)

Effect: You erase all words recorded by the gem.

Gem of Seeing

The first *gem of seeing* was crafted for the minor sovereign King Scarad the Suspicious, whose thirst for murder was matched only by his fear of invisible assassins, cunningly hidden traps, and the ghostly vengeance of those who had died at his hand. In the end, it is said that extensive use of this original gem drove Scarad to distraction and death, and whoever wields one of the copies extant in the world today must be wary of overusing its power.

Gem of Seeing	Level 12 Uncommon

With this translucent stone held to your eye, all things become tantalizingly clear to you.

Wondrous Item	13,000 gp

Property

While you peer through the gem, you gain a +3 item bonus to Perception checks to see things.

Utility Power ✦ Daily (Minor Action)

Effect: Until the end of your next turn, you can see invisible creatures and objects, and you know that any illusion you can see is an illusion.

Greater Flying Carpet

The magical technique that created *greater flying carpets* originated in the rich territories of Nerath's far-flung deserts, and was rigidly controlled by the elite archmages and sultans of those lands. The secret of creating these wondrous items was lost even before the fall of the empire, and thus the few *greater flying carpets* that remain are highly coveted by explorers.

Greater Flying Carpet		Level 20+ Rare
When you unroll this intricately stitched carpet, it floats just above the ground, rippling as if blown by a powerful wind.		
Lvl 20	125,000 gp	Lvl 30	3,125,000 gp
Wondrous Item		
Property		

A *greater flying carpet* carries creatures and objects at a speed of fly 6 and can hover. A character on the carpet can mentally command it to fly as a move action.

Any creature on the carpet takes a –2 penalty to AC and Reflex. The carpet is 1 square by 2 squares and can carry up to two Medium or Small creatures and their gear (up to a normal load for each creature). If additional weight is placed on it, the carpet falls to the ground.

If more than one character on the carpet attempts to mentally command it, the carpet responds to each command in turn according to the characters' initiative order.

If no rider is upon it, a *greater flying carpet* hovers in place 1 foot above the ground if it is unrolled, or sits on the ground if it is rolled up.

Level 30: The carpet is 2 squares by 3 squares and can carry up to six Medium or Small creatures and their gear (up to a normal load for each creature). Riders don't take the penalty to AC and Reflex.

Few things are more entertaining than the sight of two willful adventurers astride a magic carpet, each trying to direct the item. As obliging as a faithful puppy, the carpet flutters this way and that, buckling and rolling, trying to please both masters. Inevitably, the two adventurers come to blows, shoving each other until one falls off and the carpet settles down. All this is amusing when the carpet hovers at a low altitude. When the carpet is soaring through the clouds or crossing a yawning chasm . . . hilarity.

Greater Horn of Blasting

The duergar are thought to have crafted the first *greater horns of blasting*, using them as tools of war in their frequent clashes with the other races of the Underdark. Copied first by the dwarves who came into conflict with their debased kin, then long since spread to the surface world, this horn allows its user to stun foes or break through their fortifications with equal ease. However, the lack of self-preservation typical of the duergar infects this item's design, and its power can affect friends as well as enemies.

Greater Horn of Blasting		Level 17+ Rare
Even as you raise it to your lips, this horn begins to shudder in anticipation of the deadly fury it will unleash.		
Lvl 17	65,000 gp	Lvl 27	1,625,000 gp
Lvl 22	325,000 gp		
Wondrous Item		
Property		

Whenever you make a Strength check to break a door or other object, you can gain a +4 item bonus to the check by blowing the horn as a minor action.
Level 22: +5 item bonus.
Level 27: +6 item bonus.

↤ **Attack Power** (Thunder) ✦ **Daily** (Standard Action)
Attack: Close blast 3 (creatures in the blast); the horn's level + 3 vs. Fortitude
Hit: The target is stunned and takes ongoing 10 thunder damage (save ends both).
Miss: The target is dazed (save ends).
Level 22: Close blast 5, and ongoing 15 thunder damage.
Level 27: Close blast 5, and ongoing 20 thunder damage.

Guardian's Whistle

A *guardian's whistle* is a useful tool crafted by a wizard and granted to a trusted guardian. The whistle creates a burst of magic that winds through the planar firmament, grabs a creature, and pulls it next to the whistle's user. In this manner, a person can be whisked away to safety.

Guardian's Whistle		Level 4 Uncommon
This tin whistle is covered with runes that look like they have been crudely scratched into its surface.		
Wondrous Item		840 gp

↤ **Utility Power** (Teleportation) ✦ **Daily** (Move Action)
Effect: Close burst 10 (one ally in the burst). The target teleports to an unoccupied square adjacent to you.

Hunter's Flint

The rangers who patrolled the now-fallen territories of Nerath's fringe kingdoms crafted the *hunter's flint* as a tool against the harsh climes of those frontier lands. Explorers who spend time in the wilds or the Underdark are often keen to find one of these items, whose benefit can be summoned forth during even the worst weather or inclement conditions.

Hunter's Flint	Level 2 Common
A warm, bright fire quickly erupts from a single spark struck off this magical shard.	
Wondrous Item	520 gp
Utility Power (Illusion) ✦ Daily (Standard Action)	

Effect: You light a campfire using this flint that burns without smoke or sound. The bright light of this magic campfire is invisible from outside its 10-square radius, though creatures and objects within that radius can be seen normally with darkvision or if existing light allows. The campfire is a normal fire in all other respects. The fire lasts for 12 hours (requiring no additional fuel) or until it is extinguished normally. The flint can be used to light lanterns and other fires as normal, but such fires gain no magical qualities.

Instant Campsite

The outlying territories of Nerath were administered according to the laws and social structure of the stronger central kingdoms. The minor nobles and viceroys ordered to patrol these outposts (most of them transferred from the urbanized center of the empire) often found themselves uncomfortable with the more rustic culture and lack of amenities of their subject territories. Widely ridiculed by some when it was first used by these traveling lords, the *instant campsite* has since become part of the gear for many parties of adventurers and explorers.

Instant Campsite	Level 5 Common
This tightly packed satchel expands into a complete campsite that can automatically pack up again.	
Wondrous Item	1,000 gp
Utility Power ✦ Daily (Standard Action)	

Effect: You open this satchel and it magically expands into a complete campsite, including a campfire and four two-person tents with bedrolls. The campfire requires no fuel and lasts up to 12 hours, or until you spend another standard action to pack the campsite back into the satchel once more.

Iron Bands of Bilarro

These seemingly mundane bands were first created to detain powerful warriors and spellcasters without harming them. According to legend, the bands were made by the wizards of a long-lost empire to capture their enemies and carry them into captivity, where they could be forced to reveal their secrets.

Iron Bands of Bilarro		Level 13+ Uncommon	
This rusty iron sphere has a series of shallow grooves that trace concentric circles across its surface.			
Lvl 13	17,000 gp	Lvl 23	425,000 gp
Lvl 18	85,000 gp	Lvl 28	2,125,000 gp
Wondrous Item			
➳ Attack Power ✦ Daily (Standard Action)			

Attack: Ranged 10 (one creature of size Medium or smaller); the bands' level + 3 vs. Reflex

Hit: The target cannot use its arms until it succeeds on an Acrobatics or Athletics check (moderate DC of the bands' level) as a move action. Until the effect ends, the target is prevented from doing anything that requires its arms, such as climbing or making a melee attack. When the effect ends, the bands return to you.

Miss: The bands return to you.

Lens of Discernment

The sage and ritualist Ugundeg crafted a *lens of discernment* for himself to aid his life's work—documenting and cataloging every natural and unnatural creature within the borders of Nerath. The scholar met an early end, however, when he mistook the covering over a deep pit trap for some kind of dormant plant creature. As he crept closer, he peered even more intently through his lens—until he actually stepped on the "creature" and fell to his doom. His assistants claimed the rest of his magical gear (including, presumably, a spare lens or two) and fled for parts unknown. These eyepieces have turned up in the hands of explorers and adventurers ever since.

Lens of Discernment	Level 10 Common
When you look through this lens at an unknown creature, the truth about the creature is suddenly clear to you.	
Wondrous Item	5,000 gp
Utility Power ✦ Encounter (Minor Action)	

Effect: You hold the lens up to a creature that you can see. You gain a +10 power bonus to monster knowledge checks to identify that creature until the start of your next turn.

Even as knowledgeable as I am, a lens of discernment still proves useful. Mad wizards, angry gods, hidden planes, and untouched corners of worlds continue to disgorge new beasts. The lens proves a swift means of knowing crucial facts. Does this creature spit acid? Can that third eye paralyze or blind? Is it beholden to some evil deity? Does it speak a language? All might be revealed by a glimpse through the lens.

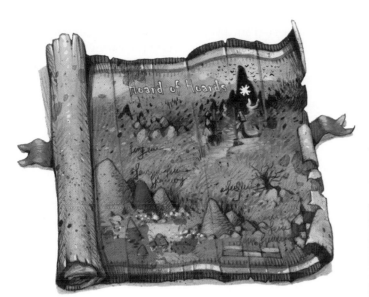

Map of unseen lands

Map of Unseen Lands

Tribes of river-wandering halflings first brought *maps of unseen lands* to the attention of other races, though the origin of these rare relics remains a mystery. Followers of Avandra, the deity of travel and adventure, claim that each map calls upon her knowledge. Others say the maps flow from the memories of all who have ever lived in an area. Many superstitious adventurers are cautious when using one of these maps, fearful of what dark energy it truly taps into.

Map of Unseen Lands	Level 7 Rare

Unseen images glimmer within this mundane-looking sheet of vellum, which erupts with detail as it creates complex maps at your command.

Wondrous Item   2,600 gp
Property
You gain a +2 item bonus to Nature checks and Perception checks to navigate through areas mapped by this item's power.
Utility Power ✦ Daily (Standard Action)
   Effect: You command the map to redraw itself, depicting the surface area in a 10-mile radius around you. The map doesn't go into precise detail, but it is accurate. It shows only aboveground terrain, not underground areas.
   The map displays the following features.
   ✦ General terrain, such as mountains, rivers, and lakes
   ✦ Structures 5,000 square feet or larger in area
   ✦ Structures important for travel, such as bridges and portals
   ✦ Lairs of creatures that are significant threats
   ✦ Names or general descriptions of any of the above features, if such information is well known within the area represented by the map.
   The sketch remains on the map until this power is used again.

Map of Orienteering

The halfling scout Legarri used a *map of orienteering* to great success as a leader of the first imperial survey as it explored the deadliest ruins within the newly forged empire of Nerath. Legarri's final expedition disappeared in the dungeons of Rolonna Tor. A passage in her journal, recovered from one of the dungeon's dark chambers, suggests that Legarri believed that her map secretly retained all the knowledge placed within it, if only a means of accessing that information could be discovered. The ability to temporarily record a user's surroundings has made items of this ilk invaluable to generations of explorers since Legarri's demise, and many have sought her particular copy of the map hoping to learn about all her explorations.

Map of Orienteering	Level 9 Common

As you unfold this sheet of parchment, sepia ink spreads across its surface to depict your immediate surroundings.

Wondrous Item   4,200 gp
Property
While unfolded, this map automatically and continuously produces a rendering of the area within 100 feet of it in all directions. It can display only what you have seen personally, so invisible objects, undiscovered traps or secret doors, and unknown areas around the next corner do not appear on the map. Illusions are faithfully reproduced unless you have previously recognized them as false. Creatures are not shown on the map unless they take the form of objects and have not been recognized for what they are (for example, a gargoyle mistaken for a statue).
   The map shows the area within 100 feet by default, but you can mentally command it to zoom in or out to display any areas explored within the last 24 hours as a minor action.
   The map automatically erases and begins redrawing after you take an extended rest, unless you command it to do otherwise.

Mountebank's Deck

Legend holds that the first of these decks of cards was fashioned by Baalzebul to fulfill a diabolic pact he struck with a wandering gambler. The cards guarantee victory in any game of chance, because they allow their owner to arrange whatever hands he wishes. Most owners of such a deck dole out a few winning hands for other players to begin with, carefully hoarding the deck's power for a decisive victory.

Mountebank's Deck	Level 1 Uncommon

This plain deck of cards looks crisp and new, suggesting that you are likewise new at the game.

Wondrous Item   360 gp
Property
You can attune this deck of cards to yourself by shedding six drops of blood on it during a short rest. From that point forward, whenever you draw or deal a card from this deck, it is of a suit and value of your choice. Anyone else who interacts with the deck finds it to be a normal deck of whatever game it is designed for. Only one creature can be attuned to the deck at a time.

VINCENT DUTRAIT

Nolzur's Inkwell

A useful tool for deterring pursuit, *Nolzur's inkwell* is filled with black ink imbued with the stuff of shadows, illusions, and transmutation. When spilled upon the floor, the ink forms a 20-foot-deep hole within the planar firmament. The hole drops downward, though any creature on a floor below would notice nothing out of the ordinary. The inkwell bends and folds space, creating a hole in space without physically expanding downward. Once the magic of the inkwell is discharged, it slowly replenishes over time, refilling with ink again after several hours.

Nolzur's Inkwell	Level 6 Uncommon
This glass inkwell is stained and battered, as if it has seen much use.	
Wondrous Item	1,800 gp
Utility Power (Zone) ✦ **Daily** (Minor Action)	
Effect: The ink creates a zone in a close blast 2 that lasts until the end of the encounter. The ground of the zone becomes an extradimensional pit that is 20 feet deep. The pit does not extend through the floor, since it warps space to produce its effect. Climbing out of the pit requires a DC 15 Athletics check. A creature in the zone when it is created floats to the bottom of the pit without taking damage. A creature in the pit when the zone ends rises back to the ground safely.	

Pearl of Power

The original *pearls of power* were gifts of the eladrin queen Jillyra to the most devoted members of her arcane guard. Crafted from freshwater pearls plucked from the Moonsheen River in the Feywild, these handy items were brought to the world by eladrin explorers.

Pearl of Power		Level 7+ Uncommon
This pearl grows warm to the touch each time you attack, ready to overcome your enemies' best attempts to thwart you.		
Lvl 7	2,600 gp	Lvl 27 1,625,000 gp
Lvl 17	65,000 gp	
Wondrous Item		
Utility Power ✦ **Daily** (Free Action)		
Trigger: You miss all targets with an encounter attack power of level 3 or lower.		
Effect: You do not expend the use of the power.		
Level 17: You can use the pearl with an encounter attack power of level 13 or lower.		
Level 27: You can use the pearl with an encounter attack power of level 23 or lower.		

Pouches of Shared Acquisition

The twin dwarf rogues Hallfri and Hallger commissioned the crafting of the first *pouches of shared acquisition* for their operations in the nobles' enclaves of Nerath. By magically passing ill-gotten goods back and forth between them, these two master thieves stayed one step ahead of the law for many years. In the end, the twins were victims of their own success, killed by rivals who learned about the special gear and wanted the pouches for their own purposes.

Pouches of Shared Acquisition	Level 15 Common
These matched leather pouches allow you to move items between them.	
Wondrous Item	25,000 gp
Property	
These two matched leather pouches magically share the same interior space. Whatever is placed in one pouch (to a maximum weight of 3 pounds) can be accessed from the other pouch regardless of the distance between them, as long as both pouches are on the same plane. If the pouches are on different planes, neither pouch can access the interior space. Only one pouch can be accessed at a time.	

Do not place money in a pouch of shared acquisition. Even if you can trust your friend not to spend it all, when your pocket gets picked, you both go hungry.

Restful Bedroll

This bedroll appears to be woven of rough wool, though it is soft to the touch and inexplicably comfortable. Though this item is clearly a boon to adventurers and warriors alike, the dwarves of the Black Shakes Mountains crafted the *restful bedroll* for more mundane purposes. The miners who plumbed the mountain's unstable depths worked under the threat of harm at all times, and the vitality granted by this item's magic often meant the difference between mere injury and death.

Restful Bedroll	Level 1 Common
A good long rest in this magic bedroll grants you extra vigor.	
Wondrous Item	360 gp
Property	
Whenever you complete an extended rest in the *restful bedroll*, you gain 1d8 temporary hit points.	

Spymaster's Quill

The Spymaster was the title of the always nameless captain responsible for intelligence operations across ancient Nerath—a position of rank so high that it answered only to the emperor. The *spymaster's quill* was fabricated for the Spymaster and his most trusted operatives, who formed the thieves' guild known as the Unseen Eyes after the empire's fall. Surviving *spymaster's quills* show up from time to time in the hands of adventurers. However, it is said that the Eyes know the location of each of these "misplaced" quills—and that each one is stolen back once it contains valuable lore.

Spymaster's quill

Spymaster's Quill — Level 10 Common

When you set this quill pen to parchment, traces of glowing golden light flare to capture the information you record.

Wondrous Item	5,000 gp

Utility Power ✦ At-Will (Standard Action)

Effect: You pass the quill over an amount of text or an illustration equivalent to a single parchment page. The image or text is magically recorded within the quill for later reproduction. Recording another page with the quill erases the page already recorded.

Utility Power ✦ At-Will (Standard Action)

Effect: You point the quill at a sheet of parchment or paper and mentally command it to reproduce the illustration or text recorded within it. No matter what the medium of the original (charcoal on paper, runes scribed in stone, and so on), the reproduction is rendered in normal ink.

The reproduction created by the quill is identical in appearance to the original, but the quill cannot record magical properties. For example, you cannot perform a ritual from a ritual scroll recorded and reproduced by the quill, nor can the quill copy powers or rituals from a wizard's spellbook.

True Portable Hole

Perhaps the most unusual item to have originated in the Feywild, the *true portable hole* is a circle of magical cloth spun from the webs of the phase spider. Imbued with the power of that otherworldly realm, this item opens up a hole in the world that is under its possessor's control. Most of the similar items that can be found today were crafted by ritualists and artificers from the mortal realm before the secrets of the hole's construction were lost. It is said that the original versions of the *true portable hole* contain a latent connection to the Feywild, and that they are imbued with additional power that can be tapped into only by the creatures of that realm.

True Portable Hole — Level 15 Uncommon

This slip of black cloth lets you safely store items in a hidden space when you unfold it.

Wondrous Item	25,000 gp

Property

A *true portable hole* weighs 1 pound and is 6 inches in diameter in its closed state. It can be enlarged to 6 feet in diameter or shrunk to its smaller size by folding it as one folds a sheet of cloth. When spread upon any surface, a *true portable hole* transforms into the mouth of an extradimensional space 10 feet deep, into which items can be placed for storage. When the hole is picked up from the surface, the entrance disappears and anything inside the space remains there. The hole cannot be closed if any creatures are within it.

The items that can be placed within the *portable hole* are limited only by volume—up to a maximum of 6 feet by 6 feet by 10 feet—not by weight.

Unfettered Thieves' Tools

The half-elf rogue Thalith Three Fingers commissioned this handsome set of thieves' tools shortly after interacting with the trap that earned her that nickname. Even maimed as she was, Thalith's thievery skills became more acute with these tools at her disposal. After she bequeathed her tools to her shiftless son, who then lost them, the secret of their crafting was sold for a paltry sum (some say for beer money), and a few copies began appearing in the world. It is said that Thalith's spirit remains linked to her original set of tools, which will enable even greater feats of thievery and legerdemain when they finally pass into the hands of a thief as skilled as she was.

Unfettered Thieves' Tools — Level 11 Uncommon

The picks, keys, and tongs of this set of thieves' tools appear ordinary—until they rise into the air to move under your mental command.

Wondrous Item	9,000 gp

Property

Like a normal set of thieves' tools, *unfettered thieves' tools* grant a +2 bonus to Thievery checks to open locks or disable traps.

Utility Power ✦ Daily (Standard Action)

Effect: You make a Thievery check on an object you can see within 5 squares of you.

DAVID MARTIN

Consumable Items

Most enchanted items have a special feature that is usable with regularity. Consumable items are different because each one is expended after a single use (and they're priced accordingly). Easy to afford and easy to carry, the potions, elixirs, and other substances in this category can easily be worth more than their weight in gold when they're used at just the right time.

ELIXIRS AND POTIONS

The methods used to create elixirs and potions bear some similarity to alchemical processes, but whereas alchemy relies on the interaction and reaction between substances, an elixir or a potion is directly infused with powerful magic.

Cryptspawn Potion

The necromancers of the Black Scar cult first crafted this foul brew from spider's venom and the blood of the condemned. A hero of good moral bent who comes into possession of a *cryptspawn potion* often feels an almost physical revulsion to it. However, those who overcome this aversion gain a measure of defensive power.

Potions are much like sausages. Far fewer people would consume them if they knew their ingredients: mole hair, bat tongue, spider venom, gorgon blood, even goblin foot fungus—and those are some of the more appetizing ones. Yet much of potion brewing is art and showmanship rather than true formulae. The secrets to creating many potions have been lost because their creators either lacked a true understanding of their process or they deliberately obscured elements in order to preserve their recipes as their personal domains. I know of one brewer who insists upon orphans' tears as the base for his work. I would shudder to think about how he collects that substance in the quantities he requires, except that I'm certain he actually uses well water and a little salt.

Cryptspawn Potion		Level 5+ Common	
Drinking this viscous fluid that smells of decay provides protection against the powers of creatures that live beyond the grave.			
Lvl 5	50 gp	Lvl 25	25,000 gp
Lvl 15	1,000 gp		
Consumable: Potion			
Utility Power ✦ Consumable (Minor Action)			

    Effect: You drink the potion and lose a healing surge. You then gain resist 5 necrotic and resist 5 poison until the end of the encounter. You also gain a +5 power bonus to your next Endurance check against any disease of the potion's level or lower.

    Level 15: Resist 10 necrotic and resist 10 poison.

    Level 25: Resist 15 necrotic and resist 15 poison.

Elixir of Accuracy

The magical laboratories of Nerath turned out countless vials of this sour, azure liquid for use by the scouts and rangers of that realm, who kept the frontiers of the empire safe. Today, bandit chieftains, petty lords, and self-styled heroes all carry this elixir. Many see simply having a flask of this substance as a status symbol and forego using it, even when doing so might tip the balance of combat in their favor.

Elixir of Accuracy		Level 8+ Common	
This crisp draught leaves your senses clear and your aim true.			
Lvl 8	125 gp	Lvl 23	17,000 gp
Lvl 13	650 gp	Lvl 28	85,000 gp
Lvl 18	3,400 gp		
Consumable: Elixir			
Utility Power ✦ Consumable (Minor Action)			

    Requirement: Your level must be equal to or lower than the elixir's level + 4.

    Effect: You drink the elixir. Once before the end of the encounter, you can use a free action when you make an attack roll and dislike the result. You gain a +2 bonus to that attack roll.

Elixir of Aptitude

The wizard-sages of the ancient city of Astigar first crafted the *elixir of aptitude* as a tool to augment their unequaled mastery of research and lore. It wasn't long before the thieves' guild known as the Grayblades stole the crafting process. Their more profitable application of the elixir made it highly sought after by scoundrels and adventurers.

Elixir of Aptitude		Level 5+ Common	
This sweet amber broth enhances your innate talents.			
Lvl 5	50 gp	Lvl 25	25,000 gp
Lvl 15	1,000 gp		
Consumable: Elixir			
Utility Power ✦ Consumable (Minor Action)			

    Effect: You drink the elixir and gain a +1 power bonus to checks using one skill of your choice. This bonus lasts for 1 hour.

    Level 15: +3 power bonus.

    Level 25: +5 power bonus.

Potions on display

Elixir of Chameleon Power

The halfling mage Lohana the Left-Handed first crafted this draught, which the heroes of the ancient clans used to enhance their preferred stealthy fighting style. Lohana traded the formula for the *elixir of chameleon power* to King Paulin of Donostia in exchange for the halfling clans' right to travel freely in the frontier provinces—a pact that set the stage for later compacts between the clans and Nerath.

Elixir of Chameleon Power	Level 8 Uncommon

Once consumed, this clear liquid lets you blend in with your surroundings.

Consumable: Elixir   125 gp

Utility Power (Illusion) ✦ **Consumable** (Minor Action)

Effect: You drink the elixir. Once before the end of the encounter, you can use a minor action to change your color and tone to blend in with your background. You gain total concealment until the end of the encounter, until you attack, or until you are not adjacent to a wall or another object at least as large as you.

While under this power's concealment effect, you do not take the penalty to Stealth checks for moving.

Elixir of Clairvoyance

This substance first came to prominence during the exploits of the adventuring company known as the Band of the Golden Lion. That group made its name in Orhiran, the Dungeon of Endless Doors, whose warren of cells is thought to have once housed a planar prison. Vials of *elixir of clairvoyance* were instrumental in allowing the Golden Lions to best that ruin's deadly traps.

Elixir of Clairvoyance		Level 5+ Uncommon	

As you consume this elixir, a haze of ghostly images fills your sight, focusing finally on the single vision you seek.

Lvl 5	50 gp	Lvl 25	25,000 gp
Lvl 15	1,000 gp		

Consumable: Elixir

Utility Power (Illusion) ✦ **Consumable** (Minor Action)

Effect: You drink the elixir. Until the end of your next turn, you gain the ability to see as if you were standing in a square at any location within 2 squares of you. You do not need line of sight or line of effect to the location, but it must be a place already known to you or clearly defined (for example, a square on the other side of a door that you can see). Your perception of the area is with your normal senses, and you might need to make Perception checks to note specific features of the area.

Level 15: Any location within 5 squares of you.
Level 25: Any location within 10 squares of you.

Sustain Minor: You sustain the effect until the end of your next turn, and you can shift the point of view of your clairvoyance to another square within 2 (or 5 or 10) squares of you.

Elixir of Climbing

The guards of Castle Moonroot, perched high atop the Sanduru Peaks, first commissioned this useful elixir, calling it moonroot juice. Its more common name is prevalent in the wider lands where it can still be found. A creature that imbibes an *elixir of climbing* can cling to sheer slopes of rock with the tenacity of a mountain goat. However, the elixir's power isn't absolute, and those whose climbing is hindered by other factors (such as wearing armor) should still proceed with care.

Elixir of Climbing			Level 6+ Common
This draught smells of clear air and mountain wildflowers. Consuming it allows you to easily move along walls and other sheer surfaces.			
Lvl 6	75 gp	Lvl 26	45,000 gp
Lvl 16	1,800 gp		
Consumable: Elixir			
Utility Power ✦ Consumable (Minor Action)			
Effect: You drink the elixir. Until the end of the encounter, you gain a +4 power bonus to Athletics checks to climb. *Level 16:* +6 power bonus. *Level 26:* +8 power bonus.			

Elixir of Defense

The ancient alchemists of Oihan were said to have crafted enchanted draughts that could protect the imbiber from any attack against body or mind. That craft survives today only in the form of the *elixir of defense*, a viscous fluid set in a weathered vial of wax-sealed bone. Popular legend has it that combining two or more *elixirs of defense* will reproduce the more formidable brew on which these items were modeled. However, countless doses of this draught have been ruined in attempts to achieve that goal.

Elixir of Defense			Level 8+ Uncommon
A flood of protective energy fills you when you drink this bitter draught.			
Lvl 8	125 gp	Lvl 23	17,000 gp
Lvl 13	650 gp	Lvl 28	85,000 gp
Lvl 18	3,400 gp		
Consumable: Elixir			
Special: When this elixir is created, the crafter chooses a defense: Fortitude, Reflex, or Will.			
Utility Power ✦ Consumable (Minor Action)			
Effect: You drink the elixir. Once before the end of the encounter, you can use an immediate interrupt when an attack targeting the chosen defense hits you. Against that attack, your defense equals 17 + the elixir's level.			

Elixir of Flying

This liquid is so clear that it appears almost invisible within its crystal flask. As a result, many an adventurer has inadvertently spilled a precious dose of *elixir of flying* when opening its container. The imbiber of this elixir gains a mastery of flight nearly equal to that of any creature of the air. The benefit is transitory, however, and one must take care not to get too far off the ground.

Elixir of Flying			Level 11+ Uncommon
A moment after imbibing this effervescent draught, your body lifts off the ground and you feel light as a bird.			
Lvl 11	350 gp	Lvl 21	9,000 gp
Consumable: Elixir			
Utility Power ✦ Consumable (Minor Action)			
Effect: You drink the elixir and gain a fly speed of 4 until the end of the encounter. When the effect ends, you float 100 feet toward the ground. If you are not on a horizontal surface sufficient to bear your weight at the end of this distance, you fall to the nearest such surface, taking damage accordingly. *Level 21:* You gain a fly speed of 8 and can hover.			

Elixir of Gaseous Form

The dwarves of the Ingunn Delve are said to have commissioned the first *elixir of gaseous form*, using it as a magical escape route from the constant collapse of that mine's crumbling tunnels. The elixir gives off a noxious odor even when its container is sealed, though the scent is usually detectable only by whoever is carrying it. However, this odor makes the elixir unpalatable to most monsters, and for that reason vials of it are often found scattered loose among the bones of their former owners.

Elixir of Gaseous Form		Level 12 Uncommon
When you drink this elixir, you feel momentarily lightheaded as your body fades to vapor.		
Consumable: Elixir	500 gp	
Utility Power (Polymorph) **✦ Consumable** (Minor Action)		
Effect: You drink the elixir and take on the form of a misty cloud until the end of the encounter or until you end the effect as a standard action. All your gear is absorbed into your gaseous form and is inaccessible. While gaseous, you are insubstantial and gain a fly speed equal to your speed, as well as the ability to hover. You cannot make attacks while in gaseous form, but you can move unhindered through tiny openings that would otherwise prevent movement (such as under a door or through a cracked window).		

Elixir of Giant Strength

An *elixir of giant strength* is usually contained in a hollow stone capsule. When one of these containers falls out of the pack of an unwary or injured adventurer, it blends in with natural stone and can easily be missed by later explorers. When consumed, this elixir enables the imbiber to perform great feats of physical power.

Elixir of Giant Strength		Level 9+ Uncommon	
When you consume this draught, your muscles begin to spasm, but that discomfort ends quickly as you feel great strength rush through your body.			
Lvl 9	160 gp	Lvl 29	105,000 gp
Lvl 19	4,200 gp		
Consumable: Elixir			
Utility Power ✦ Consumable (Minor Action)			

Effect: You drink the elixir. Until the end of the encounter, you gain a +2 power bonus to Strength ability checks and Strength-based skill checks. You also gain a +2 bonus to the damage rolls of melee basic attacks and of ranged basic attacks with thrown weapons. However, if your attack roll for any such attack is a natural 1 or 2, this effect ends.
Level 19: +4 power bonus to checks; +4 bonus to damage rolls.
Level 29: +6 power bonus to checks; +6 bonus to damage rolls.

Elixir of Invisibility

This liquid is appreciated by all adventurers for its use in combat and exploration, but is notoriously hard to find as treasure. Housed in muted vials of cloud-gray glass, these elixirs often go unnoticed among the detritus and shadows of forgotten places.

Elixir of Invisibility		Level 6+ Uncommon	
When you drink this scentless liquid, you fade from view.			
Lvl 6	75 gp	Lvl 16	1,800 gp
Consumable: Elixir			
Utility Power (Illusion) ✦ **Consumable** (Minor Action)			

Effect: You drink the elixir and become invisible until the end of your next turn or until you attack.
Level 16: You become invisible until the end of the encounter or until you attack.

Elixir of Levitation

This flask made from carefully carved and stained black oak feels all but weightless. *Elixirs of levitation* were made famous by the half-elf rogue Almaralin, known as the Thief of Hearts. For years, he scaled the heights of the great towers of Tjunagi, openly taunting that city's noble lords even as he earned his nickname by trysting with their wives.

Elixir of Levitation	Level 8 Uncommon
Drinking this frothy elixir allows you to rise up into the air, in addition to making your feet and hands tingle.	
Consumable: Elixir	125 gp
Utility Power ✦ Consumable (Minor Action)	

Effect: You drink the elixir. Until the end of the encounter, you gain the ability to fly into the air as a move action, moving up to 4 squares vertically and 1 square horizontally. You cannot rise more than 10 squares above the ground directly beneath you. If some effect, such as a pit opening below you, causes you to be more than 10 squares above the ground, you drop the entire distance but do not take falling damage. If you are knocked prone while levitating, you do not fall.
When this power's effect ends, you float safely to the ground.

No small wonder that many potions mimic the effects of wizards' spells, since wizards are so often the potions' creators. And with the many needs placed upon a wizard's prepared spells, you can clearly see the sense of keeping a potion at the ready for some unexpected eventuality. That so many potions can be found in the belongings of folk other than wizards and their friends says something about how well such precautions work.

Elixir of Luck

Elixirs of luck are now rare in the world, due to the scarcity of their key component, orium. In ages long past, such elixirs were produced in the city of Vor Rukoth, where orium was abundant. The city had such a sizable supply of the elixirs that it was forced to impose a recreational ban on the liquid due to excessive use in gambling dens and gladiatorial combat. Many of the surviving elixirs are those that were smuggled out of Vor Rukoth during its final days.

Elixir of Luck	Level 10 Rare
The red-gold liquid contained within this vial shines with its own dim light. When you drink it, you feel as though nothing could go wrong.	
Consumable: Elixir	200 gp
Utility Power ✦ Consumable (Minor Action)	

Effect: You drink the elixir and lose an action point. Once before the end of the encounter, you can reroll a failed skill check, attack roll, or saving throw. You must use the second result.

Elixir of Phasing

This draught grants the unearthly power of the phase spider to whoever drinks it. It is brewed and stored in an enchanted vial crafted from a fang of one of those dread arachnids. The eladrin warrior-princess Ranaeria is credited with first crafting the elixir. She did so to protect her lover, Gaveny, from the dangers of the world when he led their race to a new home after the war that sundered the fey races.

Elixir of Phasing	Level 17 Uncommon
This brackish gray liquid seems to appear and disappear within its vial at short intervals. The effect carries over to you when you consume it.	
Consumable: Elixir	2,600 gp
Utility Power ✦ Consumable (Minor Action)	
Effect: You drink the elixir and are phasing until the end of your next turn.	

Elixir of Protection from Evil

These holy elixirs used to be produced by a small group of monastics residing in Gardmore Abbey in the Nentir Vale. The monastics produced the elixirs for the knights of Bahamut, who guarded the abbey. After the abbey's fall, the recipe for the elixirs was lost for a time. Recent expeditions to the abbey have uncovered the recipe, and a few holy orders have begun to unravel the secrets of crafting the elixir.

Elixir of Protection from Evil		Level 5+ Uncommon	
The pearly white liquid of this potion leaves you with a feeling of righteous zeal against those who would do evil.			
Lvl 5	50 gp	Lvl 25	25,000 gp
Lvl 15	1,000 gp		
Consumable: Elixir			
Utility Power ✦ Consumable (Minor Action)			
Requirement: Your level must be equal to or lower than the elixir's level + 5.			
Effect: You drink the elixir and gain a +1 power bonus to damage rolls against evil creatures and to all defenses against evil creatures' attacks. The bonus lasts until the end of your next turn.			
Level 15: +2 power bonus.			
Level 25: +3 power bonus.			

Elixir of Treasure Finding

The adventuring group known as the Fists of Kord is remembered for its exploration of the Nerath frontier. Much of the group's early work was underwritten by the early emperors, who found it easier to hire out the task of searching and mapping the more dangerous corners of their realm. After some time, however, the keepers of the imperial treasury grew dissatisfied with the expense of this operation when they learned how little wealth the Fists were bringing back. The group's wizard crafted the first *elixirs of treasure finding* in response, enabling the Fists of Kord to locate valuable objects that might otherwise have been overlooked—prompting the empire to give the Fists of Kord a lifetime contract. The method of the elixir's creation eventually spread throughout the empire, and the number of undiscovered treasure hoards diminished accordingly.

Elixir of Treasure Finding		Level 5+ Uncommon	
A hint of exotic spices fills your senses as you drink this draught, which produces a faint tingling in the back of your mind when treasure is close by.			
Lvl 5	50 gp	Lvl 25	25,000 gp
Lvl 15	1,000 gp		
Consumable: Elixir			
Utility Power ✦ Consumable (Minor Action)			
Effect: You drink the elixir. Until the end of your next turn, you gain an innate sense of the direction to the nearest treasure worth at least 100 gp within 10 squares of you (ignoring treasure carried by you and your allies). This power functions through any intervening barrier except special magical wards or barriers lined entirely with lead. You are not aware of the distance to the treasure, nor do you gain any hint of the route to it or any physical features at its location.			
Level 15: Within 20 squares.			
Level 25: Within 40 squares.			

The elixir of treasure finding must be one of the most fiendish pranks played upon greedy folk. My one-time adventuring companion, Robilar, once purchased one for a hefty sum and used it in a dungeon to find a gem worth roughly fifty gold more than he paid for the potion. He then "invested" in a dozen more potions. Needless to say, without having a very good idea that a princely sum lies nearby, the investment often fails to pay off.

Elixir of Water Breathing

The ancient king Kelemen is said to have commissioned the first *elixir of water breathing* to help him plunder the lost sahuagin ruins known as the Mouth of Darkness. These draughts offer great benefit to explorers plumbing the depths, but the effect is far from permanent. Sahuagin, kuo-toas, and other intelligent aquatic predators use this fact to their advantage when facing enemies from the surface, intentionally prolonging conflicts in the hope that the defilers of their realms would end up dying there.

Elixir of Water Breathing	Level 8+ Common

The shortness of breath you feel when quaffing this potion is offset by its ability to allow you to breathe easily underwater.

Lvl 8	125 gp	Lvl 18	3,400 gp

Consumable: Elixir

Utility Power ✦ Consumable (Minor Action)

> *Effect:* You drink the elixir and can breathe underwater for 1 hour.
> *Level 18:* You can breathe underwater until your next extended rest.

Lesser Elixir of Dragon Breath

This elixir was first crafted by the warlocks of Bael Turath during that empire's bitter conflict with Arkhosia. Tiefling shock troops took great delight in blasting their dragonborn foes with an attack that matched the dragonborns' innate power. However, when the Turathi spread the rumor among their enemies that this draught was crafted from the blood and bile of fallen dragonborn warriors, the *elixir of dragon breath* proved even more effective as a psychological weapon.

Lesser Elixir of Dragon Breath	Level 6+ Common

You drink this syrupy elixir, and a surge of energy courses through your body, waiting to be released in an explosion of breath.

Lvl 6	75 gp	Lvl 26	45,000 gp
Lvl 16	1,800 gp		

Consumable: Elixir

Special: When this elixir is created, the crafter chooses acid, cold, fire, lightning, or poison. The elixir gains that keyword, and all damage dealt by it is of that damage type.

← Attack Power (Varies) ✦ Consumable (Minor Action)

> *Effect:* You drink the elixir. Once before the end of the encounter, you can use a minor action to make the following attack.
> *Attack:* Close blast 3 (creatures in the blast); the elixir's level + 5 vs. Reflex
> *Hit:* 2d6 + 3 damage of the chosen type.
> *Level 16:* 3d8 + 7 damage.
> *Level 26:* 4d6 + 12 damage.

Lesser Elixir of Speed

The war couriers of Nerath were protected by decrees of imperial law that promised death to anyone who interfered with the communications of the state. In practice, however, these expertly trained runners and riders trusted less in such statecraft than they did in the *lesser elixirs of speed* crafted for them in the empire's arcane laboratories.

Lesser Elixir of Speed	Level 10 Common

Your heartbeat races as you drink this elixir, which sends energy surging through your nerves and limbs.

Consumable: Elixir	200 gp

Utility Power ✦ Consumable (Minor Action)

> *Effect:* You drink the elixir and lose a healing surge. You then gain a +2 power bonus to speed until the end of the encounter.

Potion of Clarity

All present-day examples of these crystal flasks of cyan liquid are said to be derived from a single cache of ancient drow treasure, dating from the conflict that sundered that race from the elves and eladrin. The dark elves' belief in the superiority of their race drove them to create these potions, which drastically (and secretly) improve the imbiber's chance of success in combat.

Potion of Clarity	Level 5+ Uncommon

This cool draught hones your physical and mental acuity at a critical moment, allowing you to strike true.

Lvl 5	50 gp	Lvl 20	5,000 gp
Lvl 10	200 gp	Lvl 25	25,000 gp
Lvl 15	1,000 gp	Lvl 30	125,000 gp

Consumable: Potion

Utility Power ✦ Consumable (Minor Action)

> *Effect:* You drink the potion. Once before the end of the encounter, when you make an attack roll for an encounter or a daily attack power and dislike the result, you can reroll the attack roll, but you must use the second result. The power's level must be equal to or lower than the potion's level.

Potion of Cure Critical Wounds

This curative draught was once favored by combat medics, who would wear a bandolier of the potions during wartime. They would save the potions for the most grievously wounded soldiers, who would be fed the potions and then helped off the battlefield. Although such wars are scarce now, the potions have lost none of their utility.

Potion of Cure Critical Wounds	Level 20 Uncommon

This potion covers your deep wounds in bright silver light, causing them to mend.

Consumable: Potion	5,000 gp

Utility Power (Healing) ✦ Consumable (Minor Action)

> *Effect:* You drink the potion. If you have a healing surge, you must spend one. Instead of the hit points you would normally regain, you regain 3d8 + 20 hit points. If you are bloodied and don't have any healing surges, you still regain the hit points. If neither of these things is true, there is no effect.

Potion of Cure Light Wounds

Adventurers heading out into the wilderness or plumbing the depths of dungeons keep a plentiful supply of these potions in their satchels, in case of emergency. Scholars believe that this variety of curative potions was one of the first types of potions to be created. In the days of the Dawn War, the gods saw how their mortal allies suffered on the battlefield, and they devised a way to bottle up the healing powers of clerics in a small flask. The *potion of cure light wounds* represents the most basic variety of the potion, though more powerful versions exist as well.

Potion of Cure Light Wounds	Level 1 Uncommon

This potion covers your small cuts and minor bruises in dim silver light, causing them to heal over.

Consumable: Potion   20 gp
Utility Power (Healing) ✦ **Consumable** (Minor Action)
  Effect: You drink the potion. If you have a healing surge, you must spend one. Instead of the hit points you would normally regain, you regain 1d8 + 1 hit points. If you are bloodied and don't have any healing surges, you still regain the hit points. If neither of these things is true, there is no effect.

Potion of Cure Moderate Wounds

Along with other vast stores of lore, the knowledge of how to brew these curative potions was lost after the fall of Nerath. Only in recent years did the potions start appearing across the world again. The origin of the potions was tracked to a peddler south of the Nentir Vale, who had purchased a recipe from adventurers who had been exploring Nera, the ancient capital of Nerath.

Potion of Cure Moderate Wounds	Level 10 Uncommon

This potion covers your wounds in silver light, helping them heal.

Consumable: Potion   200 gp
Utility Power (Healing) ✦ **Consumable** (Minor Action)
  Effect: You drink the potion. If you have a healing surge, you must spend one. Instead of the hit points you would normally regain, you regain 2d8 + 10 hit points. If you are bloodied and don't have any healing surges, you still regain the hit points. If neither of these things is true, there is no effect.

Potion of Heal

This powerful healing potion is among the most sought after consumables in the world. Alchemists have tried for centuries to master the recipe. Some claim it requires tears of joy shed from an angel of good. Others say the potion cannot be created, but rather, it comes from water captured from a magical fountain hidden deep within the Astral Sea. The few creatures that have the knowledge and power to craft this astonishing brew keep the secret close, lest it fall into the wrong hands.

Potion of Heal	Level 30 Uncommon

This potion covers your most grievous wounds in brilliant silver light, restoring your body.

Consumable: Potion 125,000 gp
Utility Power (Healing) ✦ **Consumable** (Minor Action)
  Effect: You drink the potion. If you have a healing surge, you must spend one. Instead of the hit points you would normally regain, you regain 4d8 + 30 hit points. If you are bloodied and don't have any healing surges, you still regain the hit points. In addition, you can make a saving throw against each effect on you that a save can end. If neither of these things is true, there is no effect.

Potion of Heroism

The mage known as Mad Mikolas popularized the *potion of heroism*, though it remains unknown whether he actually created it or merely improved upon the work of other crafters. The physically frail Mikolas was fond of challenging the burliest warriors to barroom grudge fights, and almost inevitably cleaning up in the wagering when his magical handiwork left him the last one standing.

Potion of Heroism		Level 16+ Uncommon

This bitter potion gives you a surge of vitality and resilience.

Lvl 16	1,800 gp	Lvl 26	45,000 gp

Consumable: Potion
Utility Power ✦ **Consumable** (Minor Action)
  Effect: You drink the potion and gain 20 temporary hit points. In addition, you gain a +2 power bonus to saving throws until the end of the encounter.
  Level 26: 50 temporary hit points.

Potions carry strange names. The potion of heroism, while useful, grants you none of the courage of a true hero. And the potion of invulnerability is disastrously misnamed; though it can protect you from a great many dangers, its benefit is exceptionally brief. Of course, if the elixir of giant strength were called the "elixir of somewhat greater strength than you had before," its name would neither roll off the tongue nor inspire confidence in whoever drank it. That the potion of heroism is called such might be enough to make one act like a hero upon drinking it, and that in itself has value.

Potion of Invulnerability

The tart draught in this iron flask confers tremendous defensive strength to its imbiber, though the efficacy of the *potion of invulnerability* is only a pale reflection of its legend. Crafted for the celebrated King Thorkat, the original potion is said to have rendered its imbiber immune to all damage dealt by any mortal creature—a latent feature that some believe might yet be found in the oldest examples of this substance.

Potion of Invulnerability		Level 10+ Common	
A sense of unyielding resolve floods through you when you drink this sweet draught.			
Lvl 10	200 gp	Lvl 30	125,000 gp
Lvl 20	5,000 gp		
Consumable: Potion			
Utility Power ✦ Consumable (Minor Action)			
Effect: You drink the potion and gain resist 25 to all damage until the end of your next turn.			
Level 20: Resist 35 to all damage.			
Level 30: Resist 45 to all damage.			

Potion of Lesser Haste

Although the recipe for a true potion of haste has eluded potion makers, this imitation has earned respect among warriors for its versatility. Thieves' guilds often hire alchemists specifically to brew *potions of lesser haste*. Beneath cities, they brew huge vats of the silvery liquid, which are distributed among the guilds' members so they can make quick getaways.

Potion of Lesser Haste		Level 10 Uncommon
When you consume the silvery liquid of this elixir, your body begins to blur as your movement quickens.		
Consumable: Potion		200 gp
Utility Power ✦ Consumable (Minor Action)		
Effect: You drink the potion and spend a healing surge. You gain an extra move action to use either during your current turn or your next turn.		

Potion of Regeneration

Sages and others who are knowledgeable about such things claim that the original versions of this draught were distilled from the blood of lycanthropes. Arcane craft quickly reworked those original formulas to use ingredients whose collection was less life-threatening. Original versions of this copper-scented potion do show up from time to time, however, and rumors suggest that those potions infect whoever drinks them with the curse of lycanthropy.

Potion of Regeneration		Level 9+ Uncommon	
The most grievous wounds trigger this potion's remarkable restorative power.			
Lvl 9	160 gp	Lvl 29	105,000 gp
Lvl 19	4,200 gp		
Consumable: Potion			
Utility Power (Healing) ✦ Consumable (Minor Action)			
Effect: You drink this potion and lose a healing surge. You then gain regeneration 5 while you're bloodied until the end of the encounter.			
Level 19: Regeneration 10.			
Level 29: Regeneration 15.			

Potion of Shadow's Essence

By carefully collecting the essence of a monstrous shadow as it dies, a skilled potion maker can craft a *potion of shadow's essence*. When the potion is ingested, the imbiber's skin turns an ashen gray as lines of darkness rise beneath his skin like bulging veins. In a moment, those lines exude an inky, black fluid that covers the drinker and turns him into a creature of shadow.

Potion of Shadow's Essence	Level 17 Uncommon
The liquid in this vial is black and viscous, absorbing the light around it.	
Consumable: Potion	2,600 gp
Utility Power ✦ Consumable (Minor Action)	
Effect: You drink the potion. Until the end of the encounter, you gain darkvision and are insubstantial and phasing, but you are weakened. You can end this effect as a minor action.	

It should be no surprise given the ingredients in a typical potion, but drinking a potion is rarely a pleasant experience. Taste is only half the problem. Some potions are viscous and sticky, leading to a sensation akin to swallowing a slug. Others are thin but oily, leaving the drinker with a lingering sensation that even wine can't wash away. Many are grainy, some contain chunks that seem to demand chewing, and a few actively move in the mouth. Usually, the magical effects are worth the unpleasantness.

OTHER CONSUMABLES

Not all consumable items are meant to be ingested. The selection that follows here is as diverse as any group of wondrous items, ranging from a sprinkling of powder or a vial of oil to a fantastic feather that changes form on command.

Bead of Force

A *bead of force* is the distilled, physical form of force energy twisted, focused, and forged into a solid object. The energy within the bead seethes and roars, ready to explode upon any stout, physical contact. Stories abound of adventurers being blown to pieces when an unlucky blow landed on a belt pouch carrying several of these items.

Bead of Force			Level 15+ Uncommon
This lusterless black pearl seems mundane, but as you grasp it you feel the force magic contained within it reverberate up and down your arm.			
Lvl 15	1,000 gp	Lvl 25	25,000 gp
Lvl 20	5,000 gp	Lvl 30	125,000 gp
Consumable			

⤢ **Attack Power** (Force) ✦ **Consumable** (Standard Action)

Attack: Ranged 10 (one creature of size Medium or smaller); the bead's level + 3 vs. Reflex

Hit: The target is restrained, cannot teleport, and takes ongoing 10 force damage (save ends all). Until the effect ends, line of effect cannot be traced into or out of the target's space, and attacks cannot enter or exit it.

Miss: The target is slowed and takes ongoing 5 force damage (save ends both).

Level 25 or 30: Ongoing 15 force damage, and ongoing 10 force damage on a miss.

Dust of Disappearance

Dust of disappearance makes the individual over which it is shaken invisible. The downside is that only an observer's vision is affected; the person using it still emits sounds and smells. It also doesn't negate physical effects such as splashing water or a sprinkling of flour from revealing the user's location.

Some ancient tomes suggest that early versions of what is now known as *dust of disappearance* were viscid salves that had to be laboriously applied to skin and equipment to render it invisible, and that any inadvertent gaps in coverage resulted in gaps in the invisibility as well.

Dust of Disappearance	Level 8 Uncommon
When you sprinkle this dust over yourself, you disappear from sight until you do something to shake it loose.	
Consumable	125 gp

Utility Power (Illusion) ✦ **Consumable** (Minor Action)

Effect: You sprinkle this dust over yourself or an adjacent ally. That character becomes invisible until he or she moves or attacks, or until the end of the encounter.

Nolzur's marvelous pigments

Nolzur's Marvelous Pigments

This fantastic set of paints can create solid objects where none were before. However, it is the strength and accuracy of the painter's observation and imagination that determine the objects' appearance, beauty, and utility, rather than his or her skill with a brush.

Nearly any nonmagical item can be conjured into being with *Nolzur's marvelous pigments*, from armor to weaponry, tools to gears, patchwork hose to royal robes. Created items act as expected—painted food is nourishing, painted axes cut wood and flesh, and a painted shield turns back the slings and arrows of invaders.

The painter cannot subtract volumes of space from existing objects, such as painting a hole in the ground, or drawing a (functional) door on a wall. The pigments also cannot conjure living plants or creatures, whether magical, mundane, or simulated (such as golems).

Nolzur's Marvelous Pigments	Level 7 Uncommon
You smear a glob of this paint on a wall or floor, creating any object you desire.	
Consumable	100 gp
Utility Power ✦ Consumable (Standard Action)	
Effect: You create a nonmagical object that is up to 1 square in volume and weighs up to 200 pounds. The object must be created in an unoccupied square and on a solid surface, such as a floor, a wall, or a tree. The object disappears at the end of the encounter.	

Oil of Lasting Flame

This enchanted oil is sometimes used by the wealthy to keep their homes or estates warm. Any fire made with *oil of lasting flame* burns much longer than usual, unless something puts it out aside from want of fuel. Both mundane and magical methods of extinguishing the flames work as expected: water, sand, a strong gust of wind, or even a cantrip. For this reason, *oil of lasting flame* is not often employed in combat or turbulent situations. Its best use is to keep a campfire burning all night in areas where natural fuel is difficult to find.

Oil of Lasting Flame	Level 2 Common
A vial of this oil provides heat and flame for a long time.	
Consumable	25 gp
Property	
When you use this oil to start a fire or light a torch, it burns for 8 hours using its existing fuel. The fire can be put out by normal means.	

Oil of Red Flame

This oil gives any weapon coated with it the ability to burst with crimson fire when its wielder lands a strike in combat. This capability does not fade over time, persisting until the weapon is used to make a successful attack. Once the flame is invoked, it can sear its victim continuously for a short time before burning out.

An ancient legend tells of an entire army that maintained their blades every day using this oil over the course of a decade-long campaign. Some scholars think that many of these blades still exist, their scarlet flames still waiting to be ignited because their wielders fell in battle before they could strike a blow.

Oil of Red Flame	Level 8+ Uncommon
You coat your weapon's blade with this oil, knowing that you will be able to call flame to your weapon thereafter.	

Lvl 8	125 gp	Lvl 28	85,000 gp
Lvl 18	3,400 gp		

Consumable	
Utility Power (Fire) **✦ Consumable (Minor Action)**	
Effect: You coat a weapon with this oil. The next time you hit a creature with that weapon before the end of the encounter, that creature also takes ongoing 5 fire damage (save ends).
Level 18: Ongoing 10 fire damage (save ends).
Level 28: Ongoing 15 fire damage (save ends).	

Powder of Appearance

The sentiment that an unknown warrior expressed more than a millennia ago is so universal among martial heroes bedeviled by magic that it has become a catchphrase among their kind everywhere: "If I could see it, it'd be dead!"

It's not clear whether the equally anonymous enchanter who first crafted *powder of appearance* was a traveling companion of that original frustrated combatant, or whether he or she simply sought to solve the same problem. In any case, when this dust is scattered around an area, it makes visible that which is hidden, whether from invisibility or simple obscurement.

Powder of Appearance	Level 8 Common
As this dust settles over a creature, it reveals that which was hidden.	
Consumable	125 gp
⟵ **Utility Power ✦ Consumable** (Minor Action)	
Effect: Close blast 3 (creatures in the blast). Each target loses invisibility and any concealment, and it cannot become invisible or gain concealment (save ends).	

Quaal's Feather Tokens

The master wizard who created the original *feather tokens*, and whose name is still attached to those being crafted today, appreciated magic that was both spectacular and innocuous. Each of these seemingly nondescript feathers turns into something entirely different when the user commands its magic to come forth.

To do so, the wielder holds a feather in hand and announces in a firm voice, "The peerless magic of Grand Archwizard Quaal commands your obedience!" The feather instantly transforms into whatever item it was created to embody.

Among the known kinds of original feather tokens are enchanted anchors that cannot be moved, carrier pigeons that unerringly deliver messages over any distance, and sails that can move a ship even in a dead calm.

Numerous other versions of this item exist, and no doubt others are being researched. There is no apparent relationship between certain kinds of feathers and their effects, so that it takes either studious investigation or actual use to determine what a particular *Quaal's feather token* does.

Quaal's Feather Anchor	Level 12 Uncommon
You produce a heavy iron anchor that is immobile and sturdy.	
Consumable	500 gp
Utility Power ✦ Consumable (Minor Action)	
Effect: You produce an anchor that cannot be moved from the location where it comes into being. The anchor persists for one year.	

Quaal's Feather Pigeon	Level 16 Uncommon
This feather turns into a messenger pigeon that awaits your instruction.	
Consumable	1,800 gp
Utility Power ✦ Consumable (Minor Action)	
Effect: You produce a small bird that can travel 50 miles a day to unerringly reach any location or individual you name, carrying with it a small written message. The bird disappears after delivering its message.	

Quaal's Feather Sail	Level 12 Uncommon
With a wave of this feather, a sail unfurls from its tip, ready to be lashed to mast and ropes.	
Consumable	500 gp
Utility Power ✦ Consumable (Minor Action)	
Effect: You produce a sail that, once installed on a ship, can move it at a normal sailing speed even in the absence of wind. The sail persists for 24 hours.	

Sands of Restored Opportunity

It is said that every grain of the *sands of restored opportunity* originated in an hourglass stolen by an exarch of Sehanine from Ioun's own chambers. One of these deity-scale grains of sand—the size of a small pebble—is able to negate an event that just transpired when it is cast into the air at just the right moment. As the cast pebble disappears in a flash of light, a missed blow instead lands, an ill-timed stumble is corrected, or a mispronounced word of arcane might rings true.

If the tales about the sands are true, these specks will one day be exhausted, and the world will be left without recourse for misfortune. At least one cult that reveres Ioun believes that the expenditure of the last grain of the *sands of restored opportunity* will presage the end of the world.

Sands of Restored Opportunity	Level 29 Uncommon
You fling this pebble into the air. As it flashes and is consumed, time rewinds slightly, allowing events to take a new course.	
Consumable	105,000 gp
Utility Power ✦ Consumable (Free Action)	
Trigger: The result (success or failure) of any check or roll that affects you is determined (for example, a check that you make or an attack that will damage you).	
Effect: Reroll that die roll, and use the second result.	

Scroll of Protection

Many kinds of protective scrolls are known among the learned, but all function similarly. Upon reading such a scroll, the reader and the area around him or her become inviolate to some category of creature, as determined when the scroll was scribed and enchanted.

When the first of these scrolls was made, it was easy to determine how large an area each one would protect, and it was easy to understand why the one who used the scroll had to refrain from making any attacks. Not so obvious, though, was the fact that allies of the scroll's user could attack from within the shielded area without causing the scroll's aura to vanish. The first warrior who inadvertently

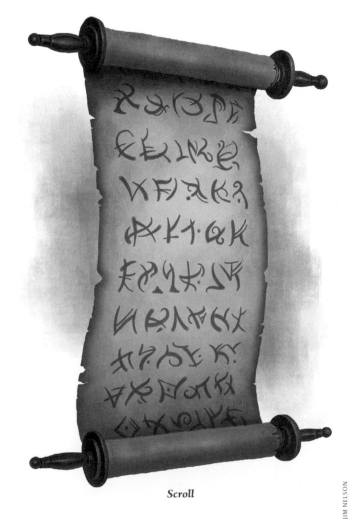

Scroll

JIM NELSON

discovered that fact will be forever appreciated by those who have taken full advantage of that knowledge.

A more scarce version of these scrolls also exists, offering protection against magic. This protection is inviolate against spells and similar effects, but does not physically repel wizards and their kin.

Scroll of Protection				Level 5+ Uncommon

You read words of power from this scroll that repel your enemies and prevent them from attacking.

Lvl 5	+1	1,000 gp	Lvl 20	+4	125,000 gp
Lvl 10	+2	5,000 gp	Lvl 25	+5	625,000 gp
Lvl 15	+3	25,000 gp	Lvl 30	+6	3,125,000 gp

Consumable

Special: When the scroll is created, it is tied to a creature type of the creator's choice: angels; demons; devils; dragons; elementals that have the air, earth, fire, or water keyword; or undead.

Utility Power (Aura) ✦ Consumable (Standard Action)

Effect: You activate an aura 2 that lasts until the end of the encounter or until you make an attack. The aura affects any creature of the type chosen at the scroll's creation, as long as the creature's level is equal to or lower than the scroll's level. An affected creature takes a –4 penalty to attack rolls against targets in the aura, and the creature cannot enter the aura willingly. If the creature starts its turn in the aura, it must use its first action to leave the aura by the shortest route possible, unless no route exists.

Trackless Ashes

When mixed into the debris of a dying campfire, a single portion of *trackless ashes* renders the tracks of all those who were encamped around the fire (including mounts) undiscoverable.

A general in ancient times once experimented with the magic of *trackless ashes*, trying to keep the activities of his entire legion secret by mixing the ashes into the bonfire of the legion's main encampment, but every attempt at such broad effect failed. His supply of the ash ran out before he was able to learn anything conclusive about the maximum number of soldiers and mounts that could be affected.

Nowadays, this item is available in one size only—an amount sufficient for a typical group of adventurers, plus any mounts or pack animals traveling with them. Using more than one container of trackless ashes on the same campfire has no apparent additional benefit (but that hasn't kept people from giving it a try from time to time).

Trackless Ashes	Level 6 Common

You dump these ashes into your campfire, removing all signs of the camp and of your passage from it.

Consumable	75 gp

Utility Power ✦ Consumable (Standard Action)

Effect: You pour the ashes into a dying campfire. After 5 minutes, the remains of the campfire as well as all tracks within 20 squares of it vanish.

Unreadable Ink

In both its liquid and scribed forms, *unreadable ink* is invisible. Although difficult to write with because of this characteristic, it is the perfect medium for communicating messages that must remain safe from prying eyes and curious minds.

Any message scribed with *unreadable ink* must begin with the name, title, or description of the intended recipient. Only that individual can decipher the message, or even realize that a message exists on the material used to scribe it. That individual can be identified specifically ("Lord Blackwood") or generically ("the burgomaster of Watershed") or even by a broad statement ("the first half-elf who finds this parchment").

Unreadable Ink	Level 5 Common

You look at a blank folio, seeing the hidden message written there while others see nothing.

Consumable	50 gp

Property

When used, the ink is invisible to everyone but its intended recipient. The message's recipient need not be able to read the inscription, or even be literate. Due to the magic of the ink, the recipient understands the message as soon as he or she touches whatever material it was scribed upon.

Vial of Darkness

When the wax used to seal a *vial of darkness* is broken, the stuff of shadow trapped within it bursts forth to fill the area around the vial with impenetrable darkness. Although the darkness lasts only a moment, that is time enough for a clever thief to escape, hide, or launch a deadly attack.

Vial of Darkness	Level 5 Uncommon

This glass vial is filled to the brim with a black liquid and stoppered with a thick gob of dried black wax.

Consumable	50 gp

✦ Utility Power (Zone) ✦ Consumable (Minor Action)

Effect: Breaking the vial creates a zone in a close burst 1. The zone is totally obscured, and it lasts until the end of your next turn.

CHAPTER 5

Artifacts and Curses

SURELY THE *most dangerous items are those designed to deceive. Adrift in the world, they lurk like icebergs in frigid seas. One might see a bright axe or a fine cloak, never suspecting the danger that lies beneath such surface beauty.*

Artifacts are liars by their nature. They often do not appear to have much power at all, and yet they contain magic of devastating strength. I have encountered too many in my time, and never has the confrontation ended well. Any artifact puts the scales out of balance.

War leaders scour the world with their armies, fighting over the ownership of artifacts. Planes disgorge their demons or belch genies or unleash angels to claim them. Friends and family turn on one another just for a chance at gaining the power of an artifact. Yet when has anyone who gained such a prize died happy? Unfortunately, destroying artifacts has proven . . . inefficient. Better that they remain unfound and inaccessible.

I would say the same thing of cursed items, but curses have proved themselves useful on occasion. Curses can afflict the innocent, of course, but rarely has a great entity contrived a cursed item for such a shallow purpose, nor does fate tie itself in knots to twist dark magic about an everyday object or person. No, every cursed item has its own story. It exists because someone sought to punish another.

Like artifacts, cursed items usually do not reveal themselves to superficial investigation. This is because those who create cursed items often act under the mistaken assumption that those who covet a magic item would not use it if they knew it was cursed. Had they any sense about them, those who craft curses would realize that an obvious curse can be more effective. Even the most avaricious learn to look askance at good fortune, but bad fortune seems as normal to them as clouds in the sky. When a gift or a discovered treasure carries an apparent danger, a more insidious and hidden second curse proves most efficacious.

> —Mordenkainen, from a treatise in his master copy of the *Magnificent Emporium*

For the DM: This chapter is meant for the eyes of the Dungeon Master. Players are encouraged to avoid reading this material so that their characters can discover it through seeing how the DM incorporates artifacts and curses into the campaign.

JIM NELSON

Artifacts

Legends swirl about them. Kingdoms go to war over their possession. Generations of heroes die in their pursuit. Artifacts are the most powerful items in existence, essential parts of the world's weave and pieces of the story of the universe.

ARTIFACT RULES

Artifacts break the rules.

They aren't normal items that you account for in treasure distribution, and you don't need to worry about play balance. They exist to help you tell the stories you want to tell in your game.

An artifact can't typically be created, disenchanted, or destroyed by any of the normal means available with other magic items. The characters' access to artifacts and their retention of recovered artifacts is entirely within your control. A character can quest after a particular artifact whose existence is known or suspected, but even then the character acquires an artifact only if you say so.

Similarly, a character can research a specific method to destroy a known artifact, if destroying it fits with your plans for the campaign. Destroying an artifact should require an extraordinary effort—artifacts are normally immune to all forms of damage or unwanted alterations to their form—and each artifact might have a unique means of destroying it. For instance, you might decide that to destroy the *Book of Infinite Spells*, one must cross out each of its pages with ink made from the memory-stealing water of the River Lethe.

ARTIFACTS IN YOUR GAME

At a fundamental level, artifacts are magic items whose role in the game has far more to do with the story of your adventure or campaign than it does with the actual game effects of the item. Characters might buy, sell, enchant, and disenchant any of the hundreds of magic items. They might even quest after those items. But when an artifact enters the characters' lives, the story of the campaign revolves around it for a time.

Remember that artifacts are always completely under your control. It's up to you when you introduce an artifact to your game, and it's up to you when the artifact leaves the characters' hands. Possession of an artifact is the one element of a character's capabilities that the character's player has no control over—it rests in your hands. Use that power for good—the good of your campaign story.

Use Artifacts at Any Level: Each artifacts is associated with a tier at which its powers are on a par with the powers of other items available to the PCs, but that doesn't mean you can't introduce even an epic tier item at an earlier level. The amazing power of an artifact is precisely why it is wondrous. So, go ahead and use artifacts even in a heroic tier game. Introducing an artifact at low levels can help the players see the grand scope of the story they're involved in.

By the same token, an artifact for a lower tier can still be an interesting element of higher-level stories. Artifacts are significantly different from ordinary magic items of roughly the same level.

Allow Artifacts to Do More: Artifacts will be more magical and mysterious if they do more than their rules describe. Allow players to experiment with an artifact and try to use it in new ways. There might not be a wizard spell to repair a hole in a ship's hull, and the *Book of Infinite Spells* might normally require an extended rest to gain such a spell even if it did exist, but when the PCs' ship is sinking, it's a great moment if they can frantically search through the *Book* to find the spell and cast it.

When and how such additional effects operate is up to you. Perhaps an artifact can exhibit such unusual effects only once per day, and then it becomes inert until it regains its power. Maybe instead such a use simply takes the place of a normal encounter or daily power of the item. Alternatively, unconstrained use of invented powers might be possible, but each use might have a chance of unleashing some disastrous effect.

Tie Artifacts to Campaign Themes: Use artifacts to reinforce the story you want to tell with your campaign. If you want to explore themes of how power corrupts those who wield it, introducing an evil artifact that the PCs are tempted to use can help reinforce that story.

Recast Stories and Goals: Add details from your campaign to the origin story for an artifact or alter its goals to strengthen its ties with the themes of your campaign. If restoring the lost glory of the eladrin is a goal of your campaign, you can use the *Jacinth of Inestimable Beauty* as a prize the characters seek to aid in that effort. This goal is in concert with the original intent of the artifact, which was to keep the eladrin realm strong and far-reaching.

Wait Until Players Have Bought In: Hold off on introducing an artifact to your campaign until after the characters have completed an adventure or two and the players are fully invested in the story of the campaign. They should already know what's at stake and have at least a hint of the nature of the major villain in the story. With that groundwork laid, the artifact's arrival carries the appropriate weight.

SENTIENT ARTIFACTS

You can treat artifacts as sentient items that have goals and emotions, if not an actual voice. Perhaps an artifact in the characters' possession speaks telepathically to whoever holds it. Maybe instead it tugs upon a character's conscience or it causes someone to have emotions or visions.

If you decide an artifact is sentient, you can play it however you like, but if you want a system for how that works in the game, consider using the rules below.

Goals

As a sentient object, an artifact should have one or more goals related to the reason for its creation. A sentient lance made by a deity for the purpose of slaying Tiamat would obviously want to accomplish that goal, but it might also drive its wielder to slay all chromatic dragons, or even every dragon the character encounters regardless of kind or alignment.

Concordance

A sentient artifact's concordance score measures the artifact's attitude toward its wielder based upon the wielder's actions in relation to its goals. The scale ranges from 0 (angered) to 20 (most pleased).

When a character takes possession of an artifact, it starts with a concordance of 5. (The owner's race, class, outlook, or other characteristics might adjust this starting concordance.) When the artifact is pleased with its wielder's actions, its concordance increases. When the wielder acts contrary to the artifact's desires, its concordance decreases. Other factors might influence concordance as you see fit.

Concordance	Artifact's Attitude
16-20	Pleased
12-15	Satisfied
5-11	Normal
1-4	Unsatisfied
0 or lower	Angered

Concordance Effects

A sentient artifact should have properties and powers that function no matter what its concordance with its wielder is, but you can alter or add to some features of an artifact depending on its concordance. An artifact that is satisfied or pleased with the character who wields it might grant a new power, impart some lore, warn the character of danger, or otherwise aid the character. An item that is unsatisfied or angered might impose a penalty on the character, not allow itself to be put down or put away, lie to the character, or otherwise manipulate the situation so that the character does what the artifact wants, or so that the artifact can find a more fitting wielder.

Moving On

A sentient artifact moves on when you decide it does. A particularly mighty quest might provide a great finale for the artifact's presence—perhaps it must be sacrificed to complete the quest, or the final act of slaying the evil champion drains the artifact of its power, or the artifact just decides that it has other places to be and other things to do. Of course, not all exit points are heroic—a villain might steal the artifact for his own use, the artifact's evil might move the characters to seek its destruction, or it might move on when its concordance reaches 0.

An artifact that is happy with its wielder might choose a quiet time to go, leaving a more mundane but still powerful item in its wake. If the artifact's concordance is not high, it could disappear at the end of an encounter, communicating its disappointment in its wielder as it departs. An artifact that is displeased or angry with its wielder might choose to vanish at a most inopportune moment.

In all my travels, I have never encountered any magic so pernicious as that of artifacts. Why the gods allow such items to exist escapes me, but mayhaps they are as powerless against them as we mortals are. Indeed, it is not uncommon for creations to escape the control of their creators. Ask any parent— or any who have an apprentice.

ARTIFACT DESCRIPTIONS

Artifacts vary widely in appearance and the degree to which they hide or reveal their true nature. Some artifacts, such as *Zax, Cloak of Kings*, are clearly examples of extraordinary craftsmanship; anyone can tell at a glance that they're something special. Other artifacts such as the *Shield of Prator* present a relatively ordinary—or even defective—appearance. Beyond their physical characteristics, artifacts might reek of magical power, or the extent of their enchantments might be deeply hidden. However, fate often takes a hand in the winding paths that artifacts follow down through history; through seeming accidents or coincidences, those heroes and villains who are meant to find artifacts usually do so, even if someone else might easily overlook an ordinary-looking object with deeply dormant powers.

Book of Infinite Spells

Legend has it that this tome is the spellbook of the goddess Ioun, dropped from the heavens into the world, and that it is the source of all arcane knowledge. Others say Vecna used the *Book of Infinite Spells* as his spellbook during his lifetime, and that he knows how any spell cast from it is used. Perhaps both bits of lore are true.

The *Book of Infinite Spells* is a hefty tome that shows signs of its great age. Scars of battle mar its weather-beaten cover, and the edges of its yellowed pages are blotched with every sort of stain from blood to wine to strange reagents. Yet no wound can ever do great harm to the book, and nothing can obscure the arcane scribbles and runes that describe its spells. Liquids spilled upon the pages bead and slide away from words and diagrams toward the margins. Anything written in the book vanishes unless it pertains to the spells inside. Fire cannot harm it, nor can even the mightiest titan tear out its pages.

The volume's original title, if it had one, is long lost to antiquity. The name it is known by today, *Book of Infinite Spells,* is seemingly not a misnomer: Even a newly created piece of wizardly magic appears instantly in the book, its ink still slightly moist as if the spell had been penned just an hour before. What many—including wizards—don't know is that the book proves powerful in anyone's hands, allowing whoever studies it to cast spells.

Book of Infinite Spells	Paragon Level
Opening this thick spellbook, bound in strange leather, causes its pages to flip in rapid succession.	

Artifact: Implement (tome)
Enhancement Bonus: +3 to attack rolls and damage rolls
Critical: +3d8 damage
Properties

✦ At the end of an extended rest, a character who studied the book for at least an hour of the rest can replace any attack power that he or she knows with a wizard attack power that is the same level or lower and of the same usage (at-will, encounter, or daily). Similarly, the character can replace any utility power with a wizard utility power of the same level or lower. The replacement lasts until the end of the character's next extended rest.

✦ When preparing powers from a spellbook at the end of an extended rest, a wizard can use the *Book of Infinite Spells* to retrain any number of powers in his or her spellbook, choosing from all wizard powers available and following the normal rules for retraining.

Special: A character can draw a particular wizard power from the book only once, regardless of which property the character uses.

Codex of Infinite Planes

This enormous book, the size of a small table, seems fit more for the hands of gods than mortals. Its obsidian covers enclose pages made from thin sheets of dull gray metal. Embossed upon or etched into the surface of every page are images both beautiful and horrific, and words in languages both rare and unknown. No matter how many pages its owner turns, another and another still remains, because the number of scenes that the book can depict from throughout the multiverse is truly without limit.

The origin of the *Codex of the Infinite Planes* seems to be somehow entwined with the formation of the planes themselves. Certainly the book contains writing that cannot now be deciphered, but particular symbols in the book use the language of creation—those mysterious figures that runepriests now use to make their magic. Regardless of its origin, the codex appears in legend as an object upon which empires are founded—and one that brings them to utter ruin. Its powers seem to shift each time it comes to the fore in history, but it is said to have been used in eons past to transport whole armies from one plane to another. At one point a careless or inept user ended up bringing Garniax, the Indestructible Fiend, into the world—whereupon the codex had to be used again to send the demon back to the Abyss.

Codex of Infinite Planes	Epic Level
Sandwiched between the heavy covers of this outsized volume are uncountable pages of metal with a dizzying array of images of symbols inscribed upon them.	

Artifact: Wondrous item
Utility Power ✦ Daily (Standard Action)

Effect: Choose a location on any plane, even a location that you have never visited or seen. You and each willing ally within 5 squares of the codex is transported to that location. You could choose "a king's treasure room," and you would appear in a king's treasure room somewhere. You could choose "a safe place," and you would appear somewhere safe, although it might be surrounded by dangers.

When you choose the location, make an Arcana check against a hard DC of your level. If the check succeeds, the transport occurs without incident. If the check fails, the transport occurs, but disaster follows you. The disaster could be anything: an earthquake, a disease, demons appearing with you when you arrive, years of winter, or worse.

Nothing can stop the transport, short of the will of a deity or a primordial, and even that might be surmounted by sufficient arcane skill (at the DM's option).

Utility Power (Psychic) ✦ Daily (Standard Action)

Effect: Make a Charisma, Intelligence, or Wisdom ranged attack against the Will of a target from another plane. On a hit, the target is sent back to its home plane and cannot return to the plane you are in for 100 years or until the codex's other power is used. On a miss, you and the target take 6d10 psychic damage, and you are stunned until the end of your next turn.

Hammer of Thunderbolts

The *Hammer of Thunderbolts* has found its way into many hands over the millennia of its existence. Many dwarves believe that Moradin crafted the *Hammer* as his original weapon of choice. Yet the legends of most other races attribute the artifact to the ambition of Kord, who gained his power over storms by slaying a primordial of tempests. According to such stories, the *Hammer* is the primordial's heart, ripped free from its body and twisted into its present shape by Kord's bare hands.

If Moradin or Kord did create the *Hammer of Thunderbolts*, neither seems to miss it. Instead, the weapon has cascaded through history from the possession of one great hero or villain to the next. Though it is certainly a weapon of nearly inestimable value in melee, the true power of the hammer manifests only when it is hurled at foes. Then the roar of the storm echoes about it, and some of these throws culminate in a radiating wave of thunder that flattens every creature nearby.

Hammer of Thunderbolts	Epic Level

This mighty weapon seems made of mithral and adamantine swirled together, and lightninglike lines of platinum crawl over its surface. When you heft it, all your hair stands on end as if you sense the coming of a great storm.

Artifact: Weapon (warhammer)
Enhancement Bonus: +5 to attack rolls and damage rolls
Critical: +5d10 thunder damage, or +10d10 if the target is a giant.

Properties

✦ You gain resist 20 lightning and resist 20 thunder.
✦ You can throw the hammer as a heavy thrown weapon (range 10/20). It returns to your hand after being thrown as normal for a magic thrown weapon.
✦ This weapon deals 2d10 extra lightning and thunder damage when used as a thrown weapon as part of a weapon attack. Each time you throw it, a peal of thunder explodes around you.

⚡ Attack Power (Thunder) ✦ **Encounter** (No Action)

Trigger: You hit or miss with a ranged weapon attack using the hammer as a thrown weapon.

Effect: Make the following attack.

Attack: Close burst 2 (creatures in the burst); Strength vs. Fortitude

Hit: 5d10 thunder damage, the target falls prone, and the target is deafened until the end of your next turn.

Miss: Half damage.

Jacinth of Inestimable Beauty

A famous eladrin heirloom, the *Jacinth of Inestimable Beauty* is a large orange jewel cut in the shape of a flower and mounted in a brooch of gold.

Long ago, an eladrin master jewelsmith named Immeral Silverleaf invented a way to use high elven magic to enhance the beauty and durability of natural gemstones. The magic gems he created were the wonder of the realm, and with each one he made, his skill and confidence grew. One day the dwarves of a neighboring realm unearthed a striking gemstone of perfect orange corundum—a blazing sapphire the color of fire. Immeral acquired the great gemstone from the dwarves in exchange for lavish gifts of his earlier work and promises of more to come, and then set about the task of creating his masterwork. Utterly devoted to his queen, he crafted a piece for her that would capture and reflect her beauty forever, which he dubbed the *Jacinth of Inestimable Beauty*.

When the eladrin queen donned Immeral's jewel, all who stood before her fell under the influence of her beauty. Her realm flourished for many years, and she was famed far and wide for the aid and comfort that she provided for her subjects through the power of the artifact. Yet finally the long golden afternoon of her realm faded into dusk; her enemies grew strong, and the untold value of the jewel incited avarice in the hearts of the wicked. One dark day the queen was murdered by her husband, who was half-mad with jealousy because of the love so many nobles and courtiers held for his queen. The prince-consort was put to death, but the deed was done. The jacinth was sequestered away in the royal vaults, only to disappear when evil forces sacked the kingdom a few years later. As for Immeral, he never made another jewel after the jacinth.

Since the days of the ancient eladrin kingdoms, the jacinth has appeared now and again in the possession of a series of monarchs. It is associated with gracefulness, justice, and prosperity . . . but also with vanity and avarice. Any monarch in the world would be strengthened by mere possession of the jacinth, and yet all too often the owners who have come after the queen have become obsessed with continuing to add to their own splendor, seeking to gain ever more objects of art and other items treasured for their beauty. Scholars speculate that the jacinth began planting this objective in the minds of its owners after leaving the queen's care. It prompts this greedy behavior in them precisely for the reason of making them vulnerable to others who envy their exquisite treasures. In such a way do these items of utmost value change hands from time to time, perhaps destined to land ultimately in the possession of a great ruler whose appreciation of their beauty knows no bounds, and whose ability to hold onto them despite threats is just as great. So it is with the jacinth itself, which is said to gravitate from owner to owner in a search for one who can truly replace the queen.

Jacinth of Inestimable Beauty — Paragon Level

A fiery orange-red gemstone cut in the shape of an exotic flower, this dazzling jewel is set in a graceful necklace of purest gold.

Artifact: Neck slot item

Enhancement Bonus: +3 to Fortitude, Reflex, and Will

Properties

✦ You gain a +5 item bonus to Charisma-based skill checks.

✦ Enemies take a -2 penalty to saving throws against your charm powers and effects.

Utility Power (Healing) ✦ **Encounter** (Minor Action)

Effect: Melee 1 (one creature). The target can make a saving throw against each effect on it that a save can end, and can spend a healing surge (or two healing surges if the target is bloodied).

☼ **Utility Power** (Aura, Charm) ✦ **Daily** (Standard Action)

Effect: You activate an aura 5 that lasts until the end of the encounter or until you make an attack or are hit by an attack. While in the aura, creatures take a -4 penalty to the attack rolls of powers that include you as a target.

Goals of the Jacinth

✦ Be treasured and worn by the most beautiful, graceful, and noble owner; urge an owner lacking in these traits to improve himself or herself.

✦ Reign in splendor and magnificence, adored by all.

✦ Celebrate and protect works of art and those who create and cherish them.

Concordance

Starting score	5
Owner gains a level	+1d6
Owner gains rank, title, or nobility	+1d4
Owner has a Charisma score of 16 or higher	+2
Owner does not wear the *Jacinth* for a month	-1
Owner has a Charisma score of 10 or lower	-4

Pleased (16–20) The jacinth is enchanted with the personal majesty of its owner, and gladly reflects and magnifies its owner's glory for all to see.

The jacinth's enhancement bonus becomes +5, and its owner gains the use of the item's attack power for as long as the jacinth remains at this concordance.

➹ **Attack Power** ✦ **Daily** (Standard Action)

Attack: Ranged 5 (one creature in range); your level + 5 vs. Will.

Hit: The target is dominated (save ends). While the target is affected by this domination, you can direct it to make an attack as normal, but only against a creature that has attacked you.

Satisfied (12–15) The jacinth is content that its owner is providing opportunities for all to see and admire its beauty.

The jacinth's enhancement bonus becomes +4, and its owner gains the use of the following property for as long as the jacinth remains at this concordance or higher.

Property

You gain a +2 bonus to any skill check associated with ruling, governing, or leading a realm.

Normal (5–11) The jacinth sees potential in its owner, but is not prepared to give him or her its full allegiance yet.

At this concordance, the jacinth has the properties, powers, and other characteristics included in its description at left.

Unsatisfied (1–4) The jacinth believes that its owner is behaving in an ugly, grasping, or ungracious manner. It might entertain some small hope that he or she is a diamond in the rough, and if so it begins to make its prodding more and more obvious. If the owner doesn't show signs of improvement, the jacinth soon leaves.

The jacinth's enhancement bonus becomes +3, and its owner loses the use of the item's aura power, until the jacinth's concordance again increases to 5 or higher.

Angered (0 or lower) The owner refuses to behave in a manner befitting the jacinth's owner. The artifact seeks to abandon him or her at the first opportunity, and it incites greed and jealousy in those nearby.

The jacinth's enhancement bonus becomes +2, and its owner loses the use of the item's healing power, for as long as the jacinth remains at this concordance.

Moving On

The jacinth is eternally compelled to search for the quintessential site of beauty, splendor, and wealth in the world. When the prospects of a monarch or some other rich individual exceed its current owner's prospects, the jacinth finds its way into the custody of a new owner.

If the jacinth is pleased when it moves on, the previous owner gains a permanent +2 increase to his or her Charisma score.

The Shadowstaff

Made from strands of congealed shadow, the *Shadowstaff* is the handiwork of a long-dead shadar-kai warlock prince named Amarethydd. One of the most powerful of his race, he is said to have entered into a pact with the very essence of shadow in order to forge a suitable implement for himself.

Armed with the *Shadowstaff*, Amarethydd ruled over his people for centuries and exacted tribute from many realms. But in time, the deadly ennui that afflicts the shadar-kai overcame Amarethydd as well, and he faded away after bequeathing his staff to his foremost apprentice. That young individual was soon killed by her rivals, and various shadar-kai wizards and warlocks murdered each other over the staff for many years before a band of human adventurers carried it back to the mortal world—where it has again changed hands several times.

The infamous wizard Evard is the last known owner of the *Shadowstaff*. He seems to have been parted from it under mysterious circumstances, and who or what owns the *Shadowstaff* now is a matter of speculation. Some believe that the staff abandoned Evard, and that the wizard is looking for the artifact and will deal harshly with anyone who tries to keep it from him. Others say that Evard bargained away the *Shadowstaff* to a powerful drow prince, who intends to use the device to further his evil designs against the surface world.

The Shadowstaff	Heroic Level

This staff appears to be made from twisted strands of smoky black glass, but it's harder than steel.

Artifact: Implement (staff)
Enhancement Bonus: +2 to attack rolls and damage rolls, or +3 if the wielder is 11th level or higher
Critical: The target takes ongoing 10 necrotic damage and is slowed (save ends both).

Property
While holding the staff, you have partial concealment and resist 10 necrotic.

⌁ **Attack Power** (Implement, Necrotic) ✦ **Encounter** (Standard Action)
Attack: Ranged 10 (one creature in range); Intelligence or Charisma vs. Fortitude.
Hit: 3d8 + Intelligence or Charisma modifier necrotic damage, and the target is slowed and weakened (save ends both).
Miss: Half damage.

Utility Power (Summoning) ✦ **Daily** (Minor Action)
Effect: You summon three servants of the staff in unoccupied squares within 5 squares of you. The servants are allies to you and your allies, and act on your turn. When a servant makes a check, you make the roll using your game statistics. Unlike most summoned creatures, the servants of the staff act independently to attack your enemies, and do not require your actions. The servants must remain within 10 squares of the staff.

Servant of the Staff	Summoned Creature (minion)
Medium shadow humanoid	

HP 1; a missed attack never damages a minion.
Defenses your defenses, not including any temporary bonuses or penalties
Speed 6; phasing

TRAITS
Shadowy Invisibility
The servant is invisible in dim light.

STANDARD ACTIONS
✦ **Shadow Touch** (necrotic) ✦ **At-Will**
Attack: Melee 1 (one creature); your level + 5 vs. Reflex
Hit: 3 + your Charisma modifier necrotic damage, and the target is slowed until the end of your next turn.

Shield of Prator

The paladin Prator was a mighty hero of old, famed as a slayer of evil dragons and a champion of justice. The shield he carried through his many battles is imbued with the memory of his courage and selflessness. Prator fell during a desperate fight in Minauros, third of the Nine Hells, and his famous shield disappeared for many years, presumably taken as a trophy by some archdevil or pit fiend. About two centuries ago, the *Shield of Prator* turned up in the clutches of a githyanki pirate defeated by a band of mortal heroes. In the time since, it has been reported in the hands of a different hero or villain every few years.

From tales of its ancient history, the shield is renowned as a formidable defense against the threat of evil. In point of practical application, its powers and properties are equally effective against enemies of any alignment. As with almost all enchanted items, how the *Shield of Prator* is used depends greatly on the mindset and desires of its current owner.

Shield of Prator	Heroic Level

Creased and dented, this large steel shield is emblazoned with the symbol of Pelor. Despite its appearance, it weighs lightly on the arm and almost seems to anticipate the next strike.

Artifact: Arms slot item (heavy shield)
Properties
✦ You gain resist 10 to the following damage types: acid, cold, fire, lightning, and thunder.
✦ You gain a +1 bonus to AC and Reflex while using the shield.

☼ **Utility Power** (Aura, Healing, Radiant) ✦ **Encounter** (Minor Action)
Effect: You activate an aura 2 that lasts until the end of your next turn. Any ally who starts his or her turn in the aura regains 5 hit points. Any enemy that ends its turn in the aura takes 5 radiant damage, and until the end of its next turn it takes a -2 penalty to attack rolls against targets other than you.

Utility Power (Healing) ✦ **Daily** (No Action)
Effect: All effects that a save can end immediately end on you, and you can spend a healing surge.

Zax, Cloak of Kings

The *Cloak of Kings* looks spun entirely from gold, and its hem and edges glitter with gemstones. It would be counted among the most beautiful objects in the world even without its intricate embroidery that depicts scenes of great castles in settings of natural beauty, and crowned and enthroned figures seated before their bowing subjects.

The origin of the cloak is shrouded in conflicting claims. Dwarf scholars say that only one of their race could have spun the gold so finely. Elven legends tell of a star that fell from the sky, leaving a crater in which the cloak was found. Humans attribute its creation to various deities, including Erathis and Pelor.

Regardless of its history, the *Cloak of Kings* has become a dynastic relic to several empires. It has served a host of kings, empresses, dukes, marchionesses, and others of less noble title. Wars have been fought over its possession, and legends formed about those who sought and won it from great dangers.

The cloak knows itself as Zax, a garment of great power that deigns itself to be worn by someone of equally great importance. When worn by a leader, Zax communicates mentally to help settle disputes, warn of danger, and educate its wearer on the exploits of earlier rulers who bore the cloak.

Zax, Cloak of Kings	Paragon Level

This brilliant cloak of spun gold is bedecked with gems and delicately embroidered with scenes of great beauty.

Artifact: Neck slot item
Enhancement Bonus: +4 to Fortitude, Reflex, and Will
Properties
+ You gain a +5 item bonus to Diplomacy checks, History checks, and Insight checks.
+ When worn, the cloak sheds dim light in a radius of 5 squares. Invisible creatures and objects are rendered visible while in this light.

Goals of Zax, the Cloak of Kings
+ Maintain its status as an object of renown by being worn or sought by a great ruler.
+ Make its wearer a ruler of ever greater importance.
+ Avoid obscurity at all costs.

Concordance

Starting score	5
Owner gains a level	+1d10
Owner is considered a leader of many people	+2
Owner gains more political power (1/day)	+1
Owner kills a rival for leadership (1/day)	+1
Owner uses stealth against an enemy (1/encounter)	-2
Owner disobeys a directive from the cloak	-2

Pleased (16–20) Zax enjoys sharing the power and accolades of its wearer, and it offers greater protection in order to maintain that position.

The cloak's enhancement bonus increases to +6, and its owner gains the use of the following property and power for as long as the cloak remains at this concordance.

Property
Enemies that score a critical hit against you are blinded (save ends).
Utility Power ✦ Daily (No Action)
Trigger: An attack hits you while you are surprised.
Effect: The attack misses you instead.

Satisfied (12–15) The wearer has proved worthy of Zax, and the cloak becomes a loquacious companion, offering counsel on many topics.

The cloak's owner gains the use of the following property for as long as the cloak remains at this concordance or higher.

Property
You gain a +10 item bonus to Diplomacy checks, History checks, and Insight checks.

Normal (5–11) The cloak is reserved and cautious with its wearer until the character proves or reaffirms his or her leadership potential.

At this concordance, the cloak has the properties and other characteristics included in its description at left.

Unsatisfied (1–4) Zax dislikes the wearer's attitude or believes the wearer is a weak leader. If the wearer doesn't change, Zax soon leaves.

For as long as the cloak remains at this concordance or lower, it does not shed dim light when its owner wears it.

Angered (0 or lower) The wearer is not meeting Zax's expectations, and it looks to leave unless a dramatic turnaround occurs soon.

The cloak's enhancement bonus becomes +3, and its owner gains the use of the following properties for as long as the cloak remains at this concordance.

Properties
+ You gain a +2 item bonus to Diplomacy checks, History checks, and Insight checks.
+ You take a -2 penalty to attack rolls and damage rolls against any creatures that have the leader role or that are leaders of others.

Moving On
Zax desires fame and to be borne upon the shoulders of greatness, and now it seeks those objectives elsewhere. If Zax is at least satisfied, it leaves behind a normal +4 *cloak* for its former wearer.

Item Curses

Cursed magic items were a mainstay of older editions of the DUNGEONS & DRAGONS game, much to Dungeon Masters' delight and players' occasional frustration. Items that hold curses seem just like normal magic items. They are, in fact, perfectly useful magic items in their own right. Under certain conditions, however, the dark magic of an item's curse causes the item to fail or malfunction in some spectacular way.

Cursed items should never be placed maliciously in a game or treated simply as a way to thwart the players. Such items can be a useful tool for the Dungeon Master, leading to interesting roleplaying opportunities and adventure hooks.

ITEM CURSES IN THE GAME

Each item curse described here is a quality that makes a cursed item of that kind seem as though it's another magic item of the same general sort. For example, a character might don a *ring of the ram* that turns out to be a *ring of weakness,* or purchase *hero's gauntlets* that are actually *gauntlets of fumbling.*

A cursed item functions normally until its curse is triggered, and it becomes a fully functioning beneficial magic item after its curse is lifted. When its curse is triggered, a cursed item imposes penalties or effects upon its wielder that run the gamut from irritating to deadly.

A cursed item looks and functions like a normal magic item, and it is the same level as the item on which the curse has been placed. Cursed items cannot be detected by any means; a character can use a cursed item normally—sometimes for weeks—until its curse is triggered.

REMOVING AN ITEM CURSE

A character can use expertise in magical lore to try to remove the curse on an item, but first the character must know that the item is cursed. Normally this knowledge is gained only when the curse is triggered, for there is no tried-and-true way of detecting curses.

To remove an item curse, a character must spend 1 hour in study while the cursed item is within arm's reach. At the end of the hour, the character makes an Arcana check (hard DC of the item's level). If the check succeeds, the curse is broken, and the magic item functions normally. If the check fails, the magic of the curse lashes out, causing the character to lose a healing surge, and everyone must wait 24 hours before trying to remove the curse again using Arcana in this way.

Once the curse on a cursed item has been triggered and identified, the curse can be removed. Most curses can be lifted with a successful Arcana check (see the sidebar). You might also assign alternative methods of lifting the curse (which become known to an item's wielder when the curse is studied). They could range from bathing the item in the breath of a red dragon, to completing a skill challenge in the arcane foundry where the item was crafted, to taking the item to a powerful magical nexus where its curse will be cleansed. When a party undertakes a specific activity to lift a curse from an item, you should make lifting the curse a minor or a major quest.

A cursed magic item can be destroyed with the Disenchant Magic Item ritual, but the curse's presence halves the amount of *residuum* collected. A cursed item can be destroyed by other effects that would destroy a normal magic item, including the attack of a rust monster, powers that specifically target items (such as *disintegrate*), and so on.

Using Cursed Items

Cursed items can be placed in a campaign as an ad hoc additional challenge. A cursed item does not create the same degree of challenge as an entire encounter or even a single creature, but any encounter in which an item's curse is activated might have an additional XP reward based on how much the curse increases the challenge of the encounter.

Each item curse has a statistics block, just like a normal magic item. This statistics block explains the trigger and the effect of the curse, which functions in addition to the item's base powers and properties. When an item's curse is triggered, the curse typically stays in effect until the end of the encounter.

Once an item's curse is triggered for the first time, the item's owner cannot be rid of the item until the curse is broken. A cursed item that is being worn cannot be physically removed. A cursed item that is being wielded (including an implement, a shield, or a weapon) can be put away on the owner's person, but it cannot be discarded.

If a cursed item is removed by extraordinary means (such as by an unusual ritual), the item magically reappears in its owner's possession in 1d4 days.

The owner of a cursed weapon or implement can choose not to wield the item, but if the item's curse has been triggered, he or she must succeed on a saving throw in order to attack with a different item. If the saving throw fails, he or she must use the cursed item and must do so for the rest of the encounter.

Curses are typically named for their most commonly found form. Many of them can be imposed on other items. The *berserker's axe* curse, for instance, might be applied to a greatsword or a scimitar. The *periapt of foul rotting* curse can be embodied in an *Ioun stone,* an amulet, a scarab crafted from a single gem, and so on.

CURSE DESCRIPTIONS

Any of the curses described here can be used "off the shelf" or as inspiration for others of the DM's devising.

Armor of Powerlessness

This curse was first named in the lore of the fallen King Firah, who is said to have crafted *armor of powerlessness* as gifts and punishments for overly ambitious court wizards and priests. All masters of magic fear such items, and many attempt to destroy one when it is found, regardless of its worth.

In addition to its normal properties and powers, a set of armor that has this curse siphons away its wielder's powers.

Armor of Powerlessness	Item Curse
You feel a sudden wrenching as your mind and soul are laid open by the malicious magic of this armor.	
Armor: Any	
Utility Power ✦ Encounter (No Action)	
Trigger: The wearer misses with a daily attack power that has a power source other than martial.	
Effect: Until the end of the encounter, the wearer cannot use daily attack powers that have a power source other than martial. In addition, when the wearer misses with an at-will attack power that has a power source other than martial, he or she loses the ability to use that power again until the end of the encounter.	

Armor of Vulnerability

Enchanted armor is one of the most common forms of magic item craft, the oldest examples of which have been passed from fallen hero to hero for uncounted generations. But the rigors of combat—especially when other magic is involved—can taint and corrupt the protective enchantment on a suit of magic armor. Although some examples of *armor of vulnerability* are specifically crafted with the intent of tricking enemies into using them, most versions of this curse are found in ancient relics whose magic has become warped over time.

In addition to its normal properties and powers, a set of armor that has this curse loses its defensive properties at the worst possible time.

Armor of Vulnerability	Item Curse
As your enemies make their deadliest attacks against you, you feel the protective ability of this armor suddenly flag.	
Armor: Any	
Utility Power ✦ Encounter (No Action)	
Trigger: While bloodied, the wearer takes damage from an attack equal to 5 + the level of the armor.	
Effect: Until the end of the encounter, the armor loses its enhancement bonus, and the wearer takes a -2 penalty to all defenses.	

Backbiter Spear

The shamans of the hobgoblin empire of Ushakak crafted the first spears bearing this curse with specific intent, designing them to deliver a nonharmful warning to anyone wielding such a weapon whose attacks were not forceful enough. Over time, the magic of the curse has been warped so that the consequences to an unskilled or unlucky wielder can be deadly.

Backbiter Spear	Item Curse
In response to your botched attack, this weapon lurches in your hands, striking you instead of your foe.	
Weapon: Spear	
Utility Power ✦ Encounter (No Action)	
Trigger: The wielder rolls a 1 through 5 on an attack roll with this weapon.	
Effect: The attack ignores the intended target, and it targets the wielder instead, hitting automatically. Until the end of the encounter, whenever the wielder rolls a 1 or 2 on an attack roll with this weapon, the attack ignores the intended target and targets the wielder instead, hitting automatically.	

Berserker's Weapon

It is said that the primal power of the Rashena barbarians is imbued in this curse, though those people saw such power as a boon, not a thing to be avoided. Most warriors who inadvertently pick up a weapon bearing this curse have a different opinion—particularly those whose own companions fall to their accursed bloodlust.

In addition to its normal properties and powers, a weapon that has this curse harms its wielder when an enemy scores a critical hit on him or her.

Berserker's Weapon	Item Curse
A sudden frenzy overtakes you, blinding you to everything but battle.	
Weapon: Axe or heavy blade	
Utility Power (Charm) **✦ Encounter** (No Action)	
Trigger: While bloodied, the wielder is subject to a critical hit.	
Effect: Until the end of the encounter, the wielder gains a +2 bonus to attack rolls and takes a -4 penalty to all defenses. All the wielder's attacks using this weapon must be melee basic attacks or charge attacks. Additionally, the wielder chooses a random creature as the target of his or her attack each round. If the wielder cannot attack, he or she takes 1d10 damage, and the penalty to all defenses worsens to -6 until the start of his or her next turn.	

Blood-Crazed Weapon

The clerics of the noble god-king Garakun were poised to take their final vengeance on the crumbling forces of the necromancer Haylah when that dark wizard unleashed his revenge. The curse of the *blood-crazed weapon* infected the weapons of Garakun's servants, setting off a barrage of brutality that eventually sundered the god-king's faith.

In addition to its normal properties and powers, a weapon that has this curse must be routinely appeased by the death of an enemy.

Blood-Crazed Weapon	Item Curse

Each attack with this weapon fills you with a thirst for vengeance that can be slaked only by blood.

Weapon: Any

Utility Power (Charm) ✦ **Encounter** (No Action)

Trigger: The wielder scores a critical hit or deals maximum damage with this weapon.

Effect: If the weapon is not used in an attack that slays an enemy before the end of the encounter, the encounter continues, and the wielder must attack the nearest ally before the end of each of his or her turns or else take damage equal to his or her healing surge value (save ends).

Boots of Uncontrollable Dancing

The crazed archmage Tigla created the first *boots of uncontrollable dancing* as a means of torturing servants who lost his favor, driving them to exhaustion and death. Lesser versions of this curse (such as the one described here) continue to plague enchanted footwear. Though these versions are less potent, many adventurers have suffered greatly from them.

In addition to its normal properties and powers, magic footwear that has this curse forces the wearer to perform an irresistible dance.

Boots of Uncontrollable Dancing	Item Curse

Even as you skid to a stop, your feet begin to move against your will.

Feet Slot

Utility Power ✦ **Encounter** (No Action)

Trigger: An enemy's attack pulls, pushes, or slides the wearer 2 or more squares.

Effect: Until the end of the encounter, the wearer takes a -2 penalty to speed, AC, and Reflex, and he or she must spend a minor action each round to dance uncontrollably.

Bracers of Defenselessness

Many of the learned believe that this curse originated during ancient times when the rites for creating magical protective items were first crafted. The mispronunciation of a single word during those rites created the curse effect, and the incorrect ceremony is still used by some to craft protective items. The curse is most disadvantageous to warriors who fight in the thick of combat.

In addition to its normal properties and powers, a set of bracers that has this curse depletes its wearer's defenses.

Bracers of Defenselessness	Item Curse

As your shrug off a hard blow in the heat of battle, a feeling of weakness overcomes you. Your enemies rush forward to test your lagging defenses.

Arms Slot

Utility Power ✦ **Encounter** (No Action)

Trigger: The wearer takes damage from a single attack greater than 5 + his or her level.

Effect: Until the end of the encounter, the wearer takes a -2 penalty to all defenses and grants combat advantage.

Gauntlets of Fumbling

The mage Fedhari of Kiza was said to have developed the means to attach vicious curses to the magic items worn by his enemies. The *gauntlets of fumbling* curse is one remaining example of his legacy of dark magic, but it is rumored that even more devious examples of his craft still linger in the world.

In addition to its normal properties and powers, an item that has this curse undermines its wearer's manual dexterity.

Gauntlets of Fumbling	Item Curse

Your grip suddenly falters as your feel these gauntlets tighten, sending tremors through your hands and arms.

Hands Slot

Utility Power ✦ **Encounter** (No Action)

Trigger: The wearer rolls a 1 or a 2 on a weapon attack roll or a Thievery check.

Effect: Until the end of the encounter, the character takes a -2 penalty to weapon attack rolls and Thievery checks. In addition, whenever the character hits with a weapon attack, he or she must make a successful Dexterity check against a DC equal to the attack roll result or drop the weapon. It takes a minor action for the wearer to pick up a weapon dropped in this way.

5

Necklace of Strangulation

Though the origin of the curse remains unknown, the *necklace of strangulation* appears time and again in history and lore, and it has played a dark part in the deaths of countless heroes and monarchs.

In addition to its normal properties and powers, an item that has this curse strangles its wearer during combat.

Necklace of Strangulation	Item Curse

The chain at your neck suddenly tightens, resisting all your attempts to tear it off as it chokes the life from you.

Neck Slot
Utility Power ✦ Encounter (No Action)
Trigger: While bloodied, the wearer takes ongoing damage.
Effect: The ongoing damage increases by 5, and the wearer takes a -2 penalty to saving throws. In addition, whenever the wearer takes a standard action while being subjected to ongoing damage, he or she takes 10 damage. This effect lasts until the end of the encounter.

Periapt of Foul Rotting

This curse was first seen in the spoils taken from Itimish, the Tower of Tombs, but its tenebrous essence has long since spread. A *periapt of foul rotting* curse inflicts a deadly plague upon its wearer—a horrific scourge that few survive.

In addition to its normal properties and powers, an item that has this curse infects its wearer with a flesh-eating disease.

Periapt of Foul Rotting	Item Curse

A stinging pain suddenly lances into you from this periapt, and the stench of death staggers you as your body begins to rot away.

Neck Slot
Utility Power ✦ Encounter (No Action)
Trigger: The wearer takes damage from a single attack equal to 5 + the periapt's level.
Effect: The wearer contracts the disease foul rotting (stage 1).

Foul Rotting	Variable Level Disease

Grotesque lesions form on your skin as your flesh begins to loosen and your bones soften.

Stage 0: The target recovers from the disease.
Stage 1: While affected by this stage, the target takes a -2 penalty to Fortitude and loses a healing surge.
Stage 2: While affected by this stage, the target takes a -2 penalty to Fortitude, loses a healing surge, and grants combat advantage.
Stage 3: The target dies, collapsing into a pool of noxious slime.
Check: At the end of each extended rest, the target makes an Endurance check if it is at stage 1 or 2.
Lower than Easy DC: The stage of the disease increases by 1.
Easy DC: No change.
Moderate DC: The stage of the disease decreases by 1.
Special: The level of the disease equals the target's level.

Ring of Weakness

When Bael Turath fought Arkhosia, magic rings imbued with this sinister curse were seeded among the tieflings, who would carry but not wear them. The dragonborn claimed the rings from the tieflings who fell in battle, realizing only too late the price of their looting.

In addition to its normal properties and powers, a ring that has this curse inflicts a crippling weakness on its wearer.

Ring of Weakness	Item Curse

Sudden and searing pain courses through your body from this ring, making your every movement require great strength of will.

Ring Slot
Utility Power ✦ Encounter (No Action)
Trigger: One of the item's other powers is used.
Effect: Until the end of the encounter, the wearer takes a -2 penalty to Strength-, Dexterity-, or Constitution-based attack rolls, damage rolls, skill checks, and ability checks.

Scarab of Death

The warlocks of Bael Turath first crafted items bearing this curse. They were originally given out as "awards" to those who had been discovered to be traitors of the empire. Later, such items became highly sought after for use in assassinations. Rival nobles, jilted lovers, and outright enemies would give or send one of these objects as a gift, making it more likely that a hired assassin's subsequent strike would be fatal.

In addition to its normal properties and powers, an item that has this curse hastens the demise of its wearer when that creature is at death's door.

Scarab of Death	Item Curse

With a shudder, this scarab transforms into a horrible demonic beetle that tears through armor, cloth, and flesh as it burrows toward your heart.

Neck Slot
Property
The wearer takes a -10 penalty to death saving throws.

A necklace of strangulation makes for a gruesome death, but it proves relatively quick. Similarly, the subtle scarab of death does you little harm until it suddenly slams death's door behind you. But the slow wasting and ultimate fate of the curse of foul rotting . . . a truly twisted mind devised this blight.

Shield of Arrow Attraction

It is said that the elves of Chelwood first crafted this curse, placing it on the shields of their hated orc enemies through the use of stealth and dangerous magical practices. Items bearing the *shield of arrow attraction* curse are most commonly found in uncivilized lands, where people lack the magical skill to identify and destroy these treacherous relics.

In addition to its normal properties and powers, a shield that has this curse attracts ranged attacks to the wearer with fatal effect.

Shield of Arrow Attraction	Item Curse

This shield begins to tremble on your arm, loosing a near-silent cry that draws your enemies' ranged attacks.

Arms Slot: Any shield

Utility Power ✦ Encounter (No Action)

Activation: The wearer is the subject of a critical hit or takes damage greater than 5 + the shield's level from a ranged attack.

Effect: Until the end of the encounter, the wearer takes a -5 penalty to AC and Reflex against ranged attacks.

The shield of arrow attraction does not actually attract arrows. That would be too useful. Imagine wielding a shield that drew arrows into it when they were aimed in your direction. That seems far preferable to, say, the helmet of arrow attraction—to say nothing of the codpiece of sword attraction. I mean, where would you rather have arrows land? Unfortunately for those who wield such a shield, it merely makes you a more attractive target for those who attack from range. That effectively turns your whole body into the arrow attractor.

Worse, the magic compels no one to shoot at you. So even if you wanted to draw the attention of your enemies, such as in some foolhardy and misguided effort to save a companion, your foes can simply ignore you. However, if you can get a hated foe to wield such a shield . . .

Stone of Weight

This subtle curse was first seen in amulets and jewelry crafted by the royal mages of the tyrannical city-state of Rathay. Some believe the curse of the *stone of weight* to be indicative of deep flaws in the Rathayan mages' magical art, but others swear that this curse was originally designed for remote triggering, as a way to hinder the movements of enemies of the state.

In addition to its normal properties and powers, an item that has this curse imposes a magical weight on its owner that slows that creature's movement.

Stone of Weight	Item Curse

A great weight suddenly presses down on you, threatening to hold you fast.

Neck Slot

Utility Power ✦ Encounter (No Action)

Trigger: The wearer makes an attack that hits.

Effect: The wearer's speed is halved until the end of the encounter.

Sword of the Fallen

First spoken of in the annals of the martyred King Hargawa, the *sword of the fallen* curse can strip away the combat prowess of even the most seasoned warrior. Whether a weapon bearing this curse has been corrupted by the lingering magic of ancient treasure troves or was crafted intentionally as a ruinous gift for would be thieves, every such item has been the bane of countless heroes.

In addition to its normal properties and powers, a weapon that has this curse loses its magic while its wielder is in combat.

Sword of the Fallen	Item Curse

When you need it the most, this weapon's power suddenly fails, leaving you at the mercy of your foe, unable to break away.

Weapon: Any melee

Utility Power ✦ Encounter (No Action)

Trigger: While bloodied, the wielder scores a critical hit or deals maximum damage.

Effect: Until the end of the encounter, this weapon loses its enhancement bonus and all its properties and powers (except this one). The wielder can use a minor action to reactivate the weapon's properties (but not its other powers) until the start of his or her next turn.

5

Story Items

Story items are unique, named magic items whose creation or existence cannot be explained by the normal laws of magic. They are the province of myths, legends, and fairy tales, functioning as key components in the most fantastical of stories. Unlike traditional magic items, story items do not have levels and employ few game mechanics.

Story items enable you to use fantasy effects that fall outside the normal mechanics of the game and allow for scenarios that might otherwise be impossible within the rules. A story item is designed to unlock one part of an adventure's saga and then pass out of the characters' ownership.

HOW THEY WORK

A story item requires a story obstacle—a challenge or condition within the adventure that would be difficult to overcome without the story item that fits with it, just as a key fits a lock. Invulnerable monsters, impassable portals, and dangerous spellcasters whose magic imposes permanent effects exemplify story obstacles that might require a story item to resist or overcome.

A heart-shaped silver stone that grows warm and pulsates whenever Bloodreaver the werewolf lord draws near is a story item. It interacts only with Bloodreaver (the story obstacle) and isn't generally useful beyond the current adventure or set of adventures, but it adds an element of suspense when the powerful lycanthrope lurks nearby. The stone doesn't give the characters any mechanical bonuses, or even necessarily require an area of effect beyond what is appropriate in a given scene. It simply alerts the characters to events unfolding in their vicinity when it's important for them to know.

Adding this kind of item to a standard treasure trove gives the characters something to think about and investigate. The discovery of a story item acts as a hook, encouraging the characters to solve the mystery

JACK AND THE BEANSTALK

The magic beans in the story of Jack and the Beanstalk are one kind of story item. Their purpose in the classic story was to grow the beanstalk that Jack climbed to reach the giant's castle in the clouds. Although the beanstalk might require game mechanics (Athletics DC to climb, resistances, hit points), the magic beans do not; they exist only to transport Jack to the giants' cloud castle. Once the characters find or acquire the beans and use them to overcome the story obstacle (getting to the castle), the item's role in the story is complete.

of the item's true purpose—smoothly drawing them into the heart of the adventure.

Story items aren't meant to last forever—an adventure or two, a campaign arc, or even a tier of play, and they move on—although, at your discretion, a fun or compelling story item that does not unbalance play might last longer.

Designing a Story Item

When designing a story item for your game, consider the following questions.

What does it look like? A story item should have a recognizable shape, but what it does might not be obvious from its appearance. If you want the characters to readily discern what the item is for, use its appearance as a clue. If you want the item's nature to be less obvious, put a spin on the "form follows function" principle. For example, a dimensional gateway (page 118) in the shape of a key tells the characters something straightforward about how the item is employed. The same item in the form of a stick of chalk (for drawing the outline of a door) might not be as easy to figure out, but it'll be rewarding and fun when the characters do get the hang of it.

What does it do? A story item needs to accomplish something fantastic within the story. In fable, myth, and saga, fey spells can put creatures to sleep for hundreds of years, genies can grant wishes, straw is spun into gold, an enchanted arrow slays a mighty dragon, a bucket of water destroys a witch, and so on. How is your story item meant to interact with its obstacle?

What are its limitations? The characters should be curious about a story item and will try to find ways to use it, perhaps in a manner you did not anticipate. Although story items can be fun, make sure their lack of precise mechanics doesn't cause them to be abused. Reward clever thinking by expanding an item's utility, but if you're uncomfortable with the characters using the object for something other than its intended purpose, don't be afraid to say no. Always keep in mind that story items and obstacles exist

NO ROADBLOCKS

A story item should be the easiest and most efficient way to overcome a story obstacle, but it might not be the only way. Similar to failing a skill challenge, losing a story item or failing to obtain it is an opportunity to place complications in the heroes' path; it should not stop the adventure. However, in case the characters don't obtain a story item required for the adventure's completion, you might present an alternate—perhaps indirect—game solution two or three levels higher than the party's level that does not require the use of the story item for success.

only to make the game more colorful; they should stop short of granting the characters or the monsters unfair mechanical advantages.

What happens once it has accomplished its purpose? Invent an exit strategy for a story item before you introduce it. Ultimately, a story item should exist until it has fulfilled its purpose and then move on. If the characters fail to use it, it will leave their ownership one way or another. This removal can be as simple as the individual who gave them the item asking for it back once it has achieved its purpose. Or perhaps the item's magic is spent, or it just vanishes. A character could even retire the object by placing it on his or her mantel as a memento of the adventure. Story items are as difficult or as easy to destroy as you want them to be.

ITEM DESCRIPTIONS

Each story item description consists of three elements.

Story Obstacle: The challenge the item ties into or overcomes.

Property: The manner in which the obstacle and the item interact.

Form: Although a story item can take any physical form you desire, this entry offers some suitable examples.

Blessed Weapon

Story Obstacle: A unique creature cannot be slain until someone wielding the item harms it.

Property: When struck with the story item, the associated creature can then be slain.

Form: Blessed crossbow bolt, rune-carved sword, wooden stake.

Box of the Seven Demons

Story Obstacle: At the dawn of time, the god Tharizdun created a golden box containing physical embodiments of the greatest mortal evils. Before the other gods chained him, he used the box to unleash chaos and misery upon all that they created. Now the box travels randomly throughout the planes, its beautiful exterior tempting mortals' curiosity, and leaving horrors in its wake. Only one creature can own the box at a time. When its owner opens the box, a level-appropriate demon emerges and attempts to possess a creature other than the owner. If the demon succeeds, it forces the creature to exemplify one of the evils embodied by the box to horrible extremes, or else the demon simply engages in brutal violence. If the demon drops to 0 hit points, it immediately possesses a different body or re-forms within a day and continues its spree. Each time a demon drops to 0 hit points, the owner can open the box again to release another demon into the world (maximum seven).

Property: When a demon from the box drops to 0 hit points, any creature holding the box can command the demon back inside as a minor action. As long as this is done within 7 rounds of the demon's defeat, the demon is bound within the box once more. The instant all seven demons are bound within the box, it vanishes.

Form: A beautiful golden box engraved with seven scenes of mortals enjoying romance, food, wealth, leisure, righteousness, friendship, and fame.

Consecrating Altar

Story Obstacle: A magical plague is spreading through the land, and a forgotten ritual of a long-dead deity is the only way to stop it.

Property: Once the deity's last holy relic is recovered and placed upon this altar, the god's voice will recite the words to the ritual that will destroy the plague. The altar lies in a warded area, and the characters must overcome the three deadly trials of the dead deity before they can gain access to it.

Form: Large carving of a forgotten holy symbol, statue of the deity's likeness, worn stone plinth.

Curse Carrier

Story Obstacle: An evil wizard or warlock either uses an item to place a curse upon one of the characters (or a nonplayer character the heroes know), or places a curse upon an item, which is delivered to a character. As the curse grows within the character, it brings on many harmful and horrific effects, and eventually causes death or some other terrible effect. The curse cannot be removed by normal means, and the characters must either kill whoever placed the curse, or find the item that caused the curse and destroy it.

Property: If the curse was delivered through an item, then the item is no longer special (though it might yield clues to whoever sent it), and the only way to break the curse is to kill the one who enchanted the item. Otherwise, finding and destroying the item will remove the curse. As the curse takes hold, the cursed person has dreams that reveal details about the item and its location. The cursed character's personality also changes as the curse progresses, making that person work against the group in secret.

Form: Enchanted fruit, poison garment, spinning wheel.

Demonic Tome

Story Obstacle: Demon-worshipers have discovered a profane tome and are using a ritual within it to open a portal to the Abyss, allowing demons to freely enter the world to sow chaos. The worshipers must be stopped, and the tome must be destroyed so this can't happen again.

Property: The ritual the demon-worshipers are attempting is powerful and takes time to complete. It requires the sacrifice of many innocents. To help acquire victims, the demon-worshipers used the tome to summon some minor demons, who have been kidnapping youths from the local area for those sacrifices. The characters can follow the clues of the missing youths and magical emanations of the powerful ritual back to the tome's location.

Form: Codex, grimoire, libram, scrolls written on humanoid skin.

Dimensional Gateway

Story Obstacle: The characters must travel quickly between planes to complete their quest.

Property: Whenever the item is placed upon a door, or used to draw the outline of one, the door opens upon a plane of the user's choice. When the door closes, it reverts to a normal door (or no door at all, if the item was used to draw one). This item is either usable once and then its power is expended, or it is usable within a certain time period (usually the course of the adventure).

Form: Chalk (for drawing), doorknob, key.

Fannigan's Dream Ale

Story Obstacle: The characters seek hidden knowledge or they need to reach a distant location, yet they lack the means to make such a discovery or journey.

Property: No one knows just who or what Fannigan was—a powerful wizard, or perhaps an immortal fey who walked in the guise of a human—but he left small casks of this special ale behind before he left this world. Those who drink of the heady brew pass into a deep, dream-filled slumber that transports them to any place or time they desire for eight hours. While they inhabit this place, they can gather information and speak to the dreaming forms of other creatures, but events and items do not carry over into the waking world—only information and communication. Dreaming characters might become idealized versions of themselves in their travels; this could be an opportunity for the players to try out their characters at a different level of play, perhaps raising them to paragon or epic tier for the adventure (although experience is always awarded as though the challenges match the characters' true level).

Form: Fannigan branded the casks of his dream ale with the symbol of a closed eye. The ale is thick and dark, and it appears to glitter with tiny motes of color when it is disturbed.

Instrument of Planar Passage

Story Obstacle: The only planar gate to a location the characters must travel to stands closed and is guarded by a powerful fey creature. To open the portal, the characters must find a special magic instrument and challenge the fey creature that guards the portal to a duel of music, outplaying the guardian.

Property: The fey guardian is very talented, and those who lose the musical competition pay a heavy price. (Some stories claim that a powerful item must be wagered, while others say that the loser must serve the guardian for a decade.) Only someone playing the instrument has a chance of beating the guardian. Any attempt at harming the guardian results in a fight against the former losers of musical duels who are serving the guardian.

Form: Flute, harp, music box, scroll of musical notes.

Invulnerable Armor

Story Obstacle: A unique creature has a deadly melee or ranged attack that instantly kills or causes a permanent condition. Examples include a medusa, a basilisk, or a catoblepas that has an enhanced gaze attack, or a serpent whose venom instantly slays living creatures.

Property: The armor's wearer can resist the special attack of this creature; that attack is instead treated as one that does not instantly kill or cause a permanent condition.

Form: Armor, brooch, shield, protective salve.

Magical Simulacrum

Story Obstacle: A character must brave tremendous peril, or needs to appear in two places at once.

Property: A simulacrum looks, speaks, and acts exactly like the character it is modeled on, perfectly replicating all the character's personality traits and quirks. It has the same defenses, skills, and abilities, but cannot attack or defend itself, and has 1 hit point. As with a minion, any damage destroys it, but a character trained in Heal can heal the simulacrum by making a Heal check (hard DC) as a standard action. Only characters trained in Heal can aid this check. A character who fails this check can try again, but only after 24 hours have passed. After three such failures, the simulacrum is destroyed permanently. The simulacrum can operate independently from the character and recount its adventures at a later date.

Form: When first discovered or employed, a simulacrum is an unassuming humanoid shape, white and featureless. When activated by a character, the simulacrum's fragile exterior instantly mirrors that character's appearance, but its interior is hollow, like a drained eggshell. Mechanical simulacra with innards constructed of delicate moving parts are also rumored to exist.

Marut Warden's Token

Story Obstacle: Maruts have established a domain in the Astral Sea where they imprison the bodies and souls of creatures that have broken contracts with them. The characters need access to someone held within this fortress, but a Huge construct guards its massive mechanical gates, and this guardian requires a special token from anyone seeking access.

Combating the guardian is not a wise choice, because defeating it causes it to consume the life force of an imprisoned creature—perhaps the one the characters seek—and then it reanimates at full health on the same initiative count during the following round. Only the guardian knows the secret to opening the mechanical gates.

Property: The guardian will not harm the token's bearer unless it is provoked. The guardian places a proffered token into a slot in its head. Machine parts whir and click as the massive gates unlock and open. Whoever presents the token can remove one creature (or soul) from the prison without resistance from the guardian.

Form: The token is a 1-foot-diameter round bronze disc, divided into four quadrants by a cross. Each quadrant is inscribed with strange reliefs that seem to follow a pattern.

Messenger of the Gods

Story Obstacle: A problem of grave import captures the attention of the gods, who have a stake in the way the conflict resolves. One or more of the gods become aware of a world-ending threat, or of something that poses danger to their own existence. Due to the nature of the threat, or to the rules that govern the deities' interactions with the world, they cannot take direct action to fix the problem and need the help of mortals, preferably worshipers, to do so.

Property: One of the gods communicates with a devoted follower among the characters through an item that they acquire (or an item that the worshiper owns that didn't previously have any direct connection to the deity). The god uses the item to instruct, command, and guide his or her worshiper on how to defeat the threat. However, this communication isn't direct, requiring the characters to read portents, puzzle out obscure references, or seek out other agents who can decipher the clues imparted through the item.

Form: Brooch, sacred chest, talisman.

Miraculous Item

Story Obstacle: Reality has become a twisted nightmare or a hostile setting for the heroes, who require great support to survive or to defeat their mighty adversaries.

Property: This item holds the captive spirit of a powerful entity (such as a genie) or puts the characters in contact with an immortal creature that bestows a single wish. This creature is not required to grant wishes, and does not grant selfish wishes, except possibly those that would punish an unwary wisher. The entity refuses to kill for the characters, but it will aid them in a single endeavor on their quest, such as transporting them to a desired destination or lending them an item that will help them defeat their foe. This item yields story results, not mechanical results. At your discretion, a wish can provide temporary boosts, items, status, or anything else the players can dream up, but all of this fades once the adventure ends and reality returns.

Form: Bottle, holy relic, magic lamp, ornate box, ring.

Oracular Glass

Story Obstacle: The heroes are searching for a missing person, a lost treasure, or some form of guidance on their current quest.

Property: This reflective item shows the heroes what they seek, hinting with cryptic words or visions at a grave danger they must overcome to succeed. However, before the item can be used, the characters must fight past a guardian or face a series of trials to reach or acquire the item. Additionally, to use the item, the characters might have to pay a price, perhaps giving up an item, revealing a hidden secret, or accepting a limitation upon their abilities.

Form: Crystal sphere, mirror, scrying pool.

Pathfinder

Story Obstacle: A torturous labyrinth, a deadly dungeon, or a trackless wilderness stands between the characters and their hidden destination.

Property: This item reveals an invisible path through or past the obstacle. It could constantly reveal the path to its bearer, or it could show the way once per hour or once per day.

Form: Amulet, goggles, helm, lantern.

Restorer of the Earth

Story Obstacle: The land has been ravaged by unnatural famine, or by the tainted energy of a portal to the Abyss. The fields have been laid barren and the people sickened.

Property: This item restores the soil, driving out the curse that besets the land, or healing a particular region of blight. Afterward, the land thrives and bears healing fruit.

Form: Enchanted tilling tools, fey seeds, magical soil.

Ring of Mortal Delights

Story Obstacle: Some desperate need drives a character and, in answer to fervent prayers, a stranger gives this ring as a gift, or it is found unattended somewhere. This ring could also be found upon the hand of a powerful devil, which seemingly (though falsely) accounts for the ring's power.

Property: The first three times a creature bearing this ring makes a wish—usually an offhand desire mentioned in passing—the desire is realized. Wishes granted in this manner come to pass only if something terrible occurs in their fulfillment. The wishes affect neither powerfully evil creatures (so a character cannot wish Demogorgon dead) nor significant characters in the campaign. For example, a character can wish for and receive a magic longsword, but the sword's previous owner might resent him or her for the theft. If the character wishes for the death of some creature, that creature might die choking on the bones of one of the character's friends.

Once three desires have been voiced and fulfilled, the item disappears. It cannot be destroyed by any known means, and the ring always finds another greedy mortal to ruin, even if it is hidden away or secured. This item requires shrewd adjudication, but keeping its nature secret should give you enough opportunity to think of ways to make negative story effects occur.

Form: A golden ring encrusted with rubies.

Sacred Charm of Warding

Story Obstacle: A unique creature is stalking people in their sleep, feeding on them while they dream. The victims remember the attacks, but can't recall anything about what is stalking them or why. Within a few days of the first attack, each victim is found dead, apparently having expired in his or her sleep. No normal means has been found to stop the creature, and people are trying to keep themselves awake in order to keep themselves alive.

Property: To fight the nighttime terror, the characters must acquire this item and then use it to enter the world of dreams during their sleep so they can find and stop whatever is preying on people. In addition, the charm protects those sleeping near it from the creature's attacks within their dreams.

Form: Blessed oil, holy symbol, special herbs or incense.

Scales of Power

Story Obstacle: The party's enemy waxes and wanes in strength. When this foe is at its strongest, it is impossible to defeat.

Property: When activated, this item measures the strength of a single powerful creature and compares the party's strength to the current strength of that creature. By being able to determine when their enemy is at its weakest, the characters can plot when to strike.

Form: Abacus, balance, dowsing rod, knotted measuring cord.

Soul Vessel

Story Obstacle: A unique creature conceals its life force inside a vessel. As long as the creature's life force is tied to the vessel, the creature cannot truly be destroyed; when slain, it uses the vessel to quickly return to life and power.

Property: Destroying the vessel negates the creature's immortality and causes it to become a mortal creature of its kind.

Form: Amulet, earth-filled coffin, jar, piece of bone.

Summoning Instrument

Story Obstacle: The characters must cross a boundary between worlds, and they need a mystical creature or vessel to transport them from one realm to the next. This transport might inhabit the watery depths or soar at dizzying heights; it might sail the Astral Sea or the ether of the Far Realm.

Property: This instrument calls a creature or a vessel to the characters' location at a boundary between planes or worlds. The summoned conveyance might require a price for transport. After the characters move aboard, on, or in it (and any agreement is made), it carries the characters to their destination.

Form: Gong, horn, scroll of mystic poetry, coin.

Talking Object

Story Obstacle: The heroes need outside aid, clues, or specific knowledge to help them with a problem in their current adventure.

Property: This item is native to the area the characters are exploring. It represents an inanimate but sentient entity that the characters can pick up and carry with them. The item might reflect the characteristics of its surroundings (for example, a pure voice and a radiant glow if found in a temple of good, or oozing blood and spewing curses during conversation if found in a necromancer's lair). The item provides helpful advice and guides the characters toward clues that allow them to succeed on their quest. Depending on the nature of the item, it might direct the characters to follow a difficult or painful path, possibly causing them to unwittingly cause mischief that comes back on

Talking lantern

them later. The item might also intend to deceive the characters, revealing enough clues to keep the heroes on the right track before finally betraying them.

Form: Amulet, lantern, skull, statuette.

True Name

Story Obstacle: A unique creature has unusually powerful abilities or is more than five levels higher than a normal creature of its kind.

Property: Intoning the creature's true name compels the creature to obey the speaker's commands, or weakens it by lowering its level to that of a normal creature of its kind.

Form: Oracular knowledge, scroll, tablet.

Ward of Protection

Story Obstacle: A horde of demons, a host of barbarian raiders, or some other large destructive force descends on a nation or a key population center. The characters must stop it from destroying the area.

Property: This item must be acquired, possibly from a dangerous location, and placed in front of the approaching horde, or the item must be found and activated before the horde arrives. Doing so will protect the region from the opposing force, causing it to be unable to approach (either physically, or by hiding the population center in a place the horde can't reach). Only small groups of the enemy that were already within the protected region when the item was placed, or those few enemies strong enough to force their way past the ward, can bypass this protection.

Form: Monument, obelisk, standard, statue, totem.

JIM NELSON

CHAPTER 6

Adventuring Gear

I WOULD be remiss if I did not provide at least some slight guidance on certain ordinary topics. Though wizards and other spellcasters might not think much about items that do not rely upon enchantment, we live in a world full of individuals who spend most of their lives relying upon such mundane objects for their livelihood and their survival.

I will limit the discussion to those items most useful to ourselves and our hirelings: adventuring tools, architectural constructions, and alchemical items.

Alchemy is of some interest to one of our number, and I'll leave it to him to provide a more in-depth treatise of the topic. For my part, I shall merely observe that the process by which the reagents produce effects warrants closer observation. The system of interactions between ingredients bears a certain resemblance to the complexity of the systems through which we practice magic. As I noted earlier in the introduction to the chapter about magical equipment, such systems are ultimately false. Thus, keen observation of alchemy's "nonmagical" systems could lead to illuminating insights on the nature of the universe in which we exist.

And of course hirelings themselves warrant a certain amount of discussion. As we all know, a dependable hireling can make even the most complex plan feasible, whereas an untrustworthy mercenary can cause even the simplest endeavor to come crashing down around us. When assessing the reliability of a hireling, you should look not only for fidelity and earnestness, but for predictability of behavior. For example, a disloyal hireling can be a boon if you can surmise under what circumstances you will be betrayed.

—Mordenkainen, from his master copy
of the *Magnificent Emporium*

Scholar's Note: The last sentence of this passage has always been unnerving to me. I do not doubt that Mordenkainen would consider my copying of a text he eradicated from existence to be a betrayal. And the manner in which I left his service can leave no doubt. Did he know that I would create this extra copy of the work? If so, did he predict that I would kill the other seven apprentices to protect my secret? I would not put such a callous calculation past the old scoundrel. But if he knew I would act this way, am I being allowed to live out my part in his plans, or shall I be eliminated now that my part is done?

—Qort

TYLER JACOBSON

ADVENTURING GEAR

Most of the adventuring gear presented here has a specific application that makes it useful. Many of these items also lend temselves to being used in other creative ways.

Ball Bearings: As a standard action, you can drop these smooth metal spheres into an adjacent square (or gather them back up). Any creature moving on the ball bearings must either treat the square as difficult terrain or succeed on a saving throw to avoid falling prone. Creatures that are running can use only the latter option.

Bell and Whistle: A bell is useful for setting an alarm, while blowing a whistle lets you alert comrades at a greater distance.

Bestiary: Each of these books offers lore about a single combination of creature origin and type, such as fey humanoids. When you fail a monster knowledge check related to a creature with this origin and type, you can reroll the check by spending one hour studying the bestiary. You must use the second result.

Block, Tackle, and Winch: After you attach this set of simple machines to a solid surface, you can pass a rope through it to triple the weight you can lift, pull, or drag on the other end of the rope.

Caltrops: You can drop these pyramid-shaped metal spikes into a square adjacent to you (or gather them back up) as a standard action. Any creature moving on the caltrops must either treat the square as difficult terrain or become slowed (save ends). Creatures that are running can use only the latter option.

Camouflaged Clothing: While you are not moving, these garments allow you to blend into your surroundings by granting you a +2 bonus to Stealth checks.

Candle Clock: Lighting one of these wax tapers allows you to count hours by observing how far the candle has burned down against marks made in the wax. Each clock lasts for 8 hours and is consumed after use. Candle clocks are typically sold in pairs to help synchronize timing between separate groups.

Chalk and Slate: Use chalk to write on dungeon walls to help find your way back out or to leave messages for those who follow. Drawing on a slate lets you communicate simple ideas when you need to remain silent or work around a language barrier.

Charlatan's Kit: This kit includes caltrops, a crook-eye, disguise kit, gambler's gear, gambling

KITS

Purchasing a kit is a good way to make sure you have all the adventuring gear you need. A standard adventurer's kit covers the basics, while the kits described here provide specialized equipment for different character concepts.

cheats, and a glass cutter. Many purchasers supplement this kit with *goodnight tincture* (page 132).

Chirurgeon's Tools: This surgical gear includes brass wedges that can be heated to cauterize wounds and jars of leeches for bleeding patients. When you use these tools to treat an ally who has contracted a disease caused by an attack from a creature, that ally gains a +2 bonus to the next check he or she makes against the disease.

Cold-Weather Clothing: Wearing these furs gives you a +2 bonus to Endurance checks against cold weather. Wearing the snowshoes included in

ADVENTURING GEAR

Item	Price	Weight
Ball bearings	10 gp	1 lb.
Bell and whistle	1 gp	–
Block, tackle, and winch	10 gp	10 lb.
Charlatan's kit	136 gp	13 lb.
Caltrops	10 gp	1 lb.
Crook-eye	50 gp	2 lb.
Disguise kit	30 gp	5 lb.
Gambler's gear	1 gp	–
Gambling cheats	20 gp	–
Glass cutter	25 gp	5 lb.
Dagger boots	2 gp	4 lb.
Delver's kit	40 gp	28 lb.
Crowbar	2 gp	4 lb.
Iron spikes (10)	1 gp	5 lb.
Manacles, iron	10 gp	2 lb.
Miner's helmet	10 gp	3 lb.
Sacks (2)	1 gp	1 lb.
Surveyor's gear	15 gp	5 lb.
Ten-foot pole	1 gp	8 lb.
Devotee's kit	146 gp	14 lb.
Candle clocks (2)	1 gp	1 lb.
Chalk and slate	5 sp	–
Chirurgeon's tools	20 gp	4 lb.
Doctrinal book	25 gp	3 lb.
Regalia	100 gp	6 lb.
Footpads	5 gp	–
Harness	5 gp	1 lb.
Manacles, adamantine	650 gp	2 lb.
Sage's kit	135 gp	12 lb.
Bestiary	25 gp	3 lb.
Hidden item compartment	40 gp	2 lb.
Investigation gear	40 gp	4 lb.
Iron filings and lodestone	15 gp	–
Jar of glowworms	5 gp	1 lb.
Writing case	10 gp	2 lb.
Traveler's kit		
Camouflaged clothing	30 gp	6 lb.
Cold-weather clothing	10 gp	10 lb.
Desert clothing	5 gp	4 lb.
Map case	15 gp	2 lb.
Signal ammunition (5)	15 gp	5 lb.
Snares	5 gp	4 lb.

this gear allows you to ignore difficult terrain caused by snow and ice, but reduces your speed by 2.

Crook-Eye: You can look around corners with the angled mirrors in this leather-bound wooden tube. You grant combat advantage and take a –2 penalty to Perception checks while using a crook-eye, but you can trace your line of sight from a square adjacent to you.

Crowbar: Wielding this metal pry bar gives you a +2 bonus to Strength checks to break open locked doors or containers.

Dagger Boots: These spike-toed footwear help you kick notches into a surface you are climbing. While wearing dagger boots, you gain +2 bonus to Athletics checks to climb but take a –2 penalty to Stealth checks to move silently.

Delver's Kit: This kit includes a crowbar, ten iron spikes, iron manacles, a miner's helmet, two sacks, surveyor's gear, and a ten-foot pole. Many purchasers supplement this kit with *clinging essence of fire* (page 130).

Desert Clothing: Wearing this mask and loose-fitting robes gives you a +2 bonus to Endurance checks to resist heat or to avoid the effects of persistent dust or sun glare.

Devotee's Kit: This kit includes two candle clocks, chalk and slate, chirurgeon's tools, a doctrinal book, and regalia. Many purchasers supplement this kit with *holy water* (page 132).

Disguise Kit: Using these cosmetics and prosthetics gives you a +2 bonus to Bluff checks to pass off your disguises.

GAMBLING

Although a particular high-stakes wager might be the subject of a skill challenge, gambling is usually resolved by opposed checks. Each gambler chooses to make either a Bluff check or an Insight check. The gambler with the highest result wins the stakes; the others share the loss.

If you choose to cheat while gambling, make a Bluff check or an Insight check as usual. If you dislike the result, you can make a Thievery check and use that result instead. You are exposed as a cheater if your Thievery check does not exceed the passive Perception checks of the other participants, or their active Perception checks if they suspect you are cheating and are watching for it.

Introducing marked gambling gear (gambling cheats) into the game makes it easier to cheat. At the start of a wager, the process of deciding whose gambling gear will be used is typically resolved by an opposed Diplomacy check. To substitute marked gear once the gambling is under way, you must succeed on two opposed checks against the highest-level opponent: Bluff against Insight, and Thievery against Perception.

Doctrinal Book: Each of these volumes holds lore pertaining to a certain deity. After a failed Religion check associated with this deity or its followers, you can attempt the check again after spending 1 hour studying the doctrinal book. You must use the second result.

Footpads: While wearing these felt soles over your normal footwear, you gain a +1 bonus to Stealth checks to move quietly.

Gambler's Gear: These dice, cards, knuckle-bones, or diviner's sticks are necessary equipment for games of chance.

Gambling Cheats: This marked gambling gear gives you a +2 bonus to Thievery checks to cheat while gambling.

Glass Cutter: By affixing this tool to a piece of glass, you can quickly and silently etch the surface and create a round hole large enough to fit your arm through.

Hidden Item Compartment: While wearing this cunningly crafted piece of apparel, you can conceal an object on yourself that weighs 1 pound or less. You gain a +2 bonus to Stealth checks against Perception checks to notice the item.

Investigation Gear: This bag of equipment includes containers made from different materials, brushes, dusts, tweezers, picks, probes, a magnifying glass, ink and quills, parchment, and a small journal. You gain a +2 bonus to Perception checks when you use the kit to search an area for specific details.

Iron Filings and Lodestone: Watching for disruptions in the patterns that iron filings normally form around a lodestone can help you perceive strong magical forces. When you fail an Arcana check to detect magic on an object or a location, you can attempt the check again after spending 1 hour spreading and studying the iron filings. You must use the second result.

Iron Spikes: Hammering one of these blunt, wide metal wedges between a door and its frame requires a standard action and adds 5 to the DC of checks to open the door. If nothing but a spike is holding a door shut, the base DC to open it is 15. Spiking a door is noisy; each time you drive in a spike, creatures within 20 squares can make a Perception check with a +5 bonus to hear you.

Jar of Glowworms: The tiny insects in the jar create dim light in the jar's square.

THINGS TO DO WITH A JAR OF GLOWWORMS

The worms give off just enough light to read by, and the jar can be covered to avoid revealing your position in the darkness. You can use a ten-foot pole to push the jar into an ominous-looking area, sometimes revealing danger if the light goes out. This method of using the jar is also a good way to spring traps that are triggered by the presence of living things.

FOR THE DM: IMPROVISED EQUIPMENT

Sooner or later, someone in your game is sure to think of a new mundane item that's not mentioned in the rules, or a new use for one that is. These guidelines are meant to help you decide how to handle such situations.

Specific: If you have the right tool for the job, you might bypass the need for a skill check altogether. But if something gives a bonus to every possible use of a skill, it's a magic item. Mundane gear provides bonuses only in specific circumstances.

Tradeoffs: Gear sometimes gives a bonus when you're trying to do one thing but a penalty when doing something else. Using equipment can also create challenges for adventurers—using a grappling hook to swing across a chasm could enable someone to avoid making an Athletics check to jump, but it also might mean that an enemy can cut the rope when that person is halfway across.

Detailed: Bringing equipment into a scene establishes facts that both the players and you can use to make action happen. Visualizing the details is essential to making common-sense rulings about what mundane items can do.

Hefty: Adventuring gear is limited by weight in the same way that slots limit magic items. Players need to track whether the amount their characters are carrying exceeds their normal load (Strength × 10 in pounds) and pay attention to where the character keeps the items (in hand or stowed). You have the right to establish reasonable limits on the bulkiness of what a character can carry (*Rules Compendium*, page 265).

Flexible: When a character wants to take an improvised action that falls outside the standard rules, use a check if possible, keying the DC to the difficulty of the action. For example, if a character wants to jam an iron spike into an iron golem's knee joint to slow it, the act might require a hard Athletics check. However, if the action might deal damage, such as using a ten-foot pole to push a statue over onto a foe, set the DC for the check and establish an appropriate amount of damage if the check succeeds (perhaps equating it to a basic attack).

Always Possible: Arguments about what equipment is or isn't capable of can go on for a long time. Let everyone have a brief say, set the odds that something will work—for example, "It's a good plan, but there's still a 1 in 4 chance it will fail"—and then let the dice decide. Even if the plan seems impossible or a sure thing, the fact that the group has been arguing about it means that it's reasonable and fun to allow a 1 in 20 chance of miraculous success or failure.

BEN WOOTTEN

Manacles: When you put these shackles on a helpless or otherwise incapacitated creature, that creature is restrained until it escapes or is freed. The Acrobatics check to escape from these restraints is against a hard DC of the creature's level.

The Strength check to break the manacles is against a DC that depends on the quality of the manacles, whether iron (DC 24) or adamantine (DC 31).

Map Case: This waterproof leather tube can be unrolled to form a writing surface. The maps you make with the tools inside, which include parchment, charcoal, ink, and strings with distance markings, can be sold to others interested in your discoveries.

Miner's Helmet: You can attach a lantern, a sunrod, or some other lighting device to the forehead reflector of this headgear to provide hands-free illumination.

Regalia: In social situations where appearances and wealth matter, wearing regalia gives you a +2 bonus to Bluff, Diplomacy, and Intimidate checks.

Sack: You can carry up to 100 pounds in one of these leather or canvas drawstring bags.

Sage's Kit: This kit includes a bestiary, a hidden item compartment, investigation gear, iron filings and lodestone, a jar of glowworms, and a writing case.

Many purchasers supplement this kit with *tracking dust* (page 135).

Snares: When you use these baited tripwire traps, you gain a +2 bonus to Nature checks or Dungeoneering checks to forage, but each check requires 2 hours instead of 1 hour.

Signal Ammunition: These arrows, sling bullets, or crossbow bolts incorporate sunrod materials that ignite when the ammunition is fired, and are useful for coordinating maneuvers or signaling for help.

Surveyor's Gear: With this plumb line, measuring chain with pins, and slate for recording notes, you gain a +2 bonus to Perception checks to search for secret doors or hidden rooms, but using the gear takes at least 5 minutes.

Ten-Foot Pole: Prodding dangerous-looking things with a ten-foot pole lets you trigger many traps from the safety of 2 squares away.

Traveler's Kit: This kit includes camouflaged clothing, cold-weather clothing, desert clothing, a map case, five pieces of signal ammunition, and snares. Many purchasers supplement this kit with *icening* (page 132).

Writing Case: This leather case holds a blank journal, loose sheets of parchment, an ink stone and ink brushes, a blotter, quills, and penknives.

POCKET CHANGE

It's sometimes useful to know how much money a character might typically have on hand. The table below gives minor and major purchase values (in gp) for a character of a given level. A character can make a minor purchase with the monetary treasure he or she might earn in a single combat encounter, skill challenge, or minor quest. Major purchases are those the character would have to save up for an entire level's worth of adventuring to afford. A mage's tower (priced at 10,000 gp) is a major purchase when you're level 15, but a minor expense when you're level 22.

MINOR AND MAJOR PURCHASE VALUES

Level	Minor	Major	Level	Minor	Major
1	10	144	16	1,800	18,000
2	20	208	17	2,600	26,000
3	30	271	18	3,400	34,000
4	40	336	19	4,200	42,000
5	50	400	20	5,000	50,000
6	75	720	21	9,000	90,000
7	100	1,040	22	13,000	130,000
8	125	1,360	23	17,000	170,000
9	150	1,680	24	21,000	210,000
10	200	2,000	25	25,000	250,000
11	350	3,600	26	45,000	450,000
12	500	5,200	27	65,000	650,000
13	650	6,800	28	85,000	850,000
14	800	8,400	29	105,000	1,050,000
15	1,000	10,000	30	125,000	1,250,000

BUILDINGS

The prices in this section apply to creating a new structure or purchasing an existing one. A single-room dwelling in a desirable city neighborhood can cost as much as a castle overlooking a backwater province, and characters who take over a fort will not necessarily be able to find a buyer willing to purchase property in a monster-infested wilderness.

Castle: Hundreds or thousands of people live and work in safety between the curtain wall and keep of one of these massive stone structures.

Castle with Dungeon: The excavations below this structure are as extensive as the towers that crown it.

Cottage: This single-room hut typically has walls of wood or sod and a thatched roof.

Floating Castle: For those who want to travel without leaving home.

Gatehouse: This building has reinforced walls, its own gate and portcullis, and quarters for five guards.

Keep: This heavy stone fortification is built to withstand a siege.

Mansion: This stately edifice has multiple wings, making it a good guildhouse or residence in which to entertain guests in style.

Palace: The architecture and ornamentation of this immense complex is designed to impress.

Palisade Fort: Surrounded by a wall of sharpened logs, this wooden fort can be constructed quickly and garrisons up to fifty troops and their families.

Private Island: From beaches, docks, and sea caves to towers, villas, and observatories, it's all yours.

Quarters: These three small rooms might be a single-story wooden house, or an apartment within a larger building.

Stone Building: The stone walls of this building make it an ideal workshop or townhouse. It can be two stories tall and is typically 30 feet wide by 40 feet long.

Tower: A favorite residence for mages, this stone spire rises 30 feet high and is 20 feet in diameter.

Wood Building: This two-story structure is typically 30 feet wide by 40 feet long and makes a good tavern or farmhouse. However, its wooden walls make it susceptible to fire.

BUILDINGS

Item	Price
Castle	250,000 gp
Castle with dungeon	1,000,000 gp
Cottage	400 gp
Floating castle	1,250,000 gp
Gatehouse	6,500 gp
Keep	75,000 gp
Mansion	40,000 gp
Palace	175,000 gp
Palisade fort	25,000 gp
Private island	650,000 gp
Quarters	1,000 gp
Stone building	3,000 gp
Tower	10,000 gp
Wood building	1,500 gp

TRADE GOODS

Whether someone is a trapper bringing a cart full of furs to market or a ship captain pulling into port with a hold full of astral cloth, it is important to know the relationship between the amount of the goods one hopes to sell and the price one expects to earn. The table below presents this information for some of the most important valuables in the DUNGEONS & DRAGONS game, as well as the unit of finished goods in which each is typically encountered.

A seller might need to seek out a buyer for items such as rare wines or artwork, whose value is not always obvious to the untrained eye. Someone who wants to buy such items might need to worry about counterfeits.

Buying and Selling: To perform either of these transactions, establish the total value of the trade goods in question. Use the major purchase column on the table in the Pocket Change sidebar (page 127) to figure out the level of this transaction. For example, unloading a rare book worth 10,000 gp—or a forged copy of the same—would be a 15th-level transaction. Use this information with the Difficulty Class by Level table (*Rules Compendium*, page 126) to determine the DC to sell or buy a trade good, or to recognize or pass off a fake item.

Then make a check (usually Streetwise) to find either a buyer or a seller. Use the moderate DC for the level of the transaction in a location with a good-sized marketplace or population. Use the easy DC in major trading hubs such as the City of Brass, and the hard DC if the value of the items far exceeds the locals' wealth. A successful check indicates that the transaction has been completed.

Counterfeits and Forgeries: In the case of a counterfeit, the buyer has a chance to recognize the fake before purchasing it, and the check is based on how much the forger invested in the item. Use the easy DC if the forger spent one-tenth of the item's true value on the forgery, the moderate DC if one-fifth the value was spent, or the hard DC if one-half the value was spent.

TRADE GOODS

Item	Finished Unit	Weight per Unit	Value per Unit	Value per Pound
Artwork, epic	statuette	5 lb.	5,000,000 gp	1,000,000 gp
Artwork, fine	statuette	5 lb.	500 gp	100 gp
Book, rare	volume	5 lb.	10,000 gp	2,000 gp
Cloth, astral	outfit	2 lb.	125,000 gp	25,000 gp
Cloth, fine	outfit	5 lb.	30 gp	6 gp
Cloth, shadow	outfit	3 lb.	5,000 gp	1,000 gp
Fur	coat	15 lb.	3,000 gp	200 gp
Stone, precious	gem	1/500 lb.	1,000 gp	500,000 gp
Stone, semiprecious	gem	1/500 lb.	20 gp	10,000 gp
Mithral	bar	1 lb.	250,000 gp	250,000 gp
Perfume	vial	1/10 lb.	100 gp	1,000 gp
Residuum	grain	1/5000 lb.	1 gp	5,000 gp
Silk	square	5 lb.	5 gp	1 gp
Spice	jar	5 lb.	50 gp	10 gp
Tapestry	square	45 lb.	15 gp	1/3 gp
Wine, common	bottle	1 lb.	5 gp	5 gp
Wine, rare	bottle	1 lb.	500 gp	500 gp

Alchemical Items

In a fantasy setting where magic is real, how does alchemy fit in? In our own history, alchemy was a precursor to science, but you can avoid many arguments by not applying scientific reasoning to fantasy concepts. Here are some guidelines for thinking about alchemy.

Alchemy is formulaic. Much like wizardry or ritual magic, alchemy relies on following certain steps in a particular order. Alchemy will reliably produce a desired result, but its effects are less flexible than a wizard's spells or an artificer's creations because it does not directly channel a power source.

Alchemy is earthy. Alchemy uses the traces of magic left in the world when power is channeled through base matter. Alchemists seek to collect the parts of exotic beasts, such as a unicorn's horn or a dragon's blood, because such objects are a rich source of these magical remnants.

Alchemy is risky. Alchemy makes no distinctions between friend and foe. Its effects are often long lasting and can do more harm to the party than good. Be careful when using alchemy against enemies with forced movement powers that can push you into the area of your own alchemical effects.

USING ALCHEMY

The craft of creating alchemical items is more accessible to most characters than creating full-fledged magic items or learning and performing rituals. If you have the Alchemist feat (below), you can concoct items for which you have the formula and the necessary skill training.

All alchemical items are consumable. An item is expended when put into use, although its effects might last well beyond the time when it is applied or otherwise employed.

Alchemist If you are equipped with the proper formula and sufficient talent, you can concoct alchemical items for the use of yourself or others.

Benefit: You can make alchemical items of your level or lower. You must have the correct formula and training in an appropriate skill.

Special: If you receive the Ritual Caster feat as a class feature, you can take the Alchemist feat instead.

Reading the Table

The alchemical formulas used to create the items in this section have three common characteristics, all summarized on the table below.

Key Skills: You must have training in at least one of the indicated skills to use a particular formula.

Market Price: This is what you pay to purchase the formula (which can also be thought of as the recipe).

Creation Time: How long it takes to produce one dose or application of the alchemical item of the same name.

Item Categories

Each alchemical item in the following section has a category that defines how the item is used or its general effect.

ALCHEMICAL FORMULAS

Name	Key Skills	Market Price	Creation Time
Alchemist's essence	Arcana, Thievery	70 gp	30 minutes
Chartreuse gas	Nature, Thievery	250 gp	1 hour
Clinging essence	Arcana, Nature, Thievery	120 gp	1 hour
Corpseburster	Arcana, Thievery	200 gp	30 minutes
Elemental accelerant	Arcana	70 gp	1 hour
Foaming plaster	Arcana, Thievery	70 gp	30 minutes
Goodnight tincture	Nature, Thievery	750 gp	1 hour
Greater sovereign glue	Arcana, Thievery	120 gp	2 hours
Holy water	Religion	50 gp	1 hour
Icening	Arcana	100 gp	1 hour
Oil of etherealness	Arcana	6,750 gp	1 hour
Oil of slipperiness	Nature, Thievery	375 gp	1 hour
Ossip wax	Arcana, Nature, Thievery	600 gp	30 minutes
Precarious crystal	Arcana, Thievery	120 gp	30 minutes
Protean silk	Arcana, Nature, Thievery	450 gp	1 hour
Smoke snake	Arcana, Nature	800 gp	30 minutes
Sweet water	Arcana, Nature, Religion	100 gp	30 minutes
Tracking dust	Nature. Thievery	160 gp	1 hour
Twinned flames	Arcana, Nature	120 gp	30 minutes
Universal solvent	Arcana, Thievery	600 gp	30 minutes

Oil: Oils are applied to other objects (typically weapons), granting those objects temporary properties or powers.

Volatile: An item of this category explodes or expands when shattered or broken, often dealing damage by the creation of a specific type of energy, such as acid, cold, fire, or lightning.

Poison: A poison is a toxin that hampers or harms a creature.

Other: Some items create miscellaneous effects that don't fall into one of the above categories. These have no designation aside from "Alchemical Item."

ITEM DESCRIPTIONS

For convenience, the formula cost of each of the alchemical items in this section is repeated in its statistics block. The other gold piece values represent the cost of the components (or ingredients) needed to create the substance. For instance, the formula for chartreuse gas will set you back 250 gp as a one-time purchase, and if you want to brew a level 9 version of that item it'll cost another 320 gp for the ingredients for that dose.

Alchemist's Essence

All agree that fire was the first element to be distilled into a pure essence whose destructive energy could be safely contained. Some say Vol Tomo created alchemist's fire to give common people a weapon against the young empire of Bael Turath, and that the tieflings' rise to imperial power was hastened because only they could survive when peasants threw a flask of the fiery stuff through a noble's carriage window. The variant essences that were later developed are often called alchemist's frost, alchemist's acid, alchemist's spark, and alchemist's venom.

Alchemist's Essence		Level 1+ Common	
When this flask is shattered, its contents fill an area with a deadly distilled element.			
Lvl 1	20 gp	Lvl 16	1,800 gp
Lvl 6	75 gp	Lvl 21	9,000 gp
Lvl 11	350 gp	Lvl 26	45,000 gp
Alchemical Item: Volatile		**Formula Cost:** 70 gp	
Key Skill: Arcana or Thievery		**Time:** 30 min.	

Special: When this item is created, the alchemist chooses acid, cold, fire, lightning, or poison. The item gains that keyword, and all damage dealt by the item is of that damage type.

✳ **Attack Power (Varies) ✦ Consumable (Standard Action)**
Attack: Area burst 1 within 10 (creatures in the burst); the item's level + 3 vs. Reflex
Hit: The target takes 1d6 damage of the chosen type.
Level 6: 2d6 damage of the chosen type.
Level 11 or 16: 3d6 damage of the chosen type.
Level 21 or 26: 4d6 damage of the chosen type.
Miss: Half damage.

Chartreuse Gas

Inhaling these green vapors, which are usually contained within a glass sphere, causes the victim to mistake memories and fantasies for reality, experiencing them as if they were truly unfolding. In some disreputable quarters of decadent cities, customers pay to be tied down and exposed to chartreuse gas. The proprietors of these establishments often turn a secondary profit by tricking their clients into revealing valuable secrets during their reveries.

Chartreuse Gas		Level 4+ Common	
The green mist contained in this glass globe can make dreams and memories seem real.			
Lvl 4	80 gp	Lvl 19	8,400 gp
Lvl 9	320 gp	Lvl 24	42,000 gp
Lvl 14	1,600 gp	Lvl 29	210,000 gp
Alchemical Item: Poison		**Formula Cost:** 250 gp	
Key Skill: Nature or Thievery		**Time:** 1 hour	

➶ **Attack Power (Poison) ✦ Consumable (Standard Action)**
Attack: Ranged 2/5 (one creature); the item's level + 3 vs. Will
Hit: The target is dazed until the end of your next turn. While dazed, the target takes a –5 penalty to Insight checks to resist Bluff attempts or to recognize effects as illusory, and the target is not aware that this attack has been made against it.

Clinging Essence

One of the most successful new formulas that followed the development of alchemist's fire and its diversification into different elements added a caustic tar that allowed the essence to stick to a target or a weapon. Because many magic weapons are enchanted to repel grime, gore, and other foreign agents, the sophistication of the alchemy required is proportional to the power of the weapon.

Clinging Essence		Level 3+ Common	
This vial holds enough sticky essence of a distilled element to apply to one weapon or to douse one enemy.			
Lvl 3	30 gp	Lvl 18	3,400 gp
Lvl 8	125 gp	Lvl 23	17,000 gp
Lvl 13	650 gp	Lvl 28	85,000 gp
Alchemical Item: Oil		**Formula Cost:** 120 gp	
Key Skill: Arcana, Nature, or Thievery		**Time:** 1 hour	

Special: When this item is created, the alchemist chooses acid, cold, fire, lightning, or poison. The item gains that keyword, and all damage dealt by the item is of that type.

Utility Power ✦ Consumable (Minor Action)
Effect: You apply the essence to a weapon or ammunition. The level of the *clinging essence* must be equal to or higher than the level of the weapon or ammunition. Until the end of your next turn, damage dealt by a weapon attack using that weapon or ammunition is of the chosen type instead of any other type.

Corpseburster

Few remember that the original version of this unpleasant toxin was made by alchemists of the fallen empire of Zannad for use by rat catchers. A single rat would be poisoned and then allowed to return to its nest before it expired, at which point its life force would be explosively converted to necrotic energy. The toxin's subsequent battlefield use depended on the ability of the yuan-ti wizards using it to time its release so that an enemy was among its own forces when it was hit by the fluid.

Corpseburster			Level 5+ Common

Death is the trigger for the true virulence of this poisonous purplish fluid.

Lvl 5	50 gp	Lvl 20	5,000 gp
Lvl 10	200 gp	Lvl 25	25,000 gp
Lvl 15	1,000 gp	Lvl 30	125,000 gp
Alchemical Item: Volatile		**Formula Cost:** 200 gp	
Key Skill: Arcana or Thievery		**Time:** 30 min.	

Attack Power (Necrotic, Poison) ✦ **Consumable** (Standard Action)

Attack: Ranged 5/10 (one creature); the item's level + 3 vs. Fortitude

Hit: The target takes ongoing 5 poison damage (save ends).

Aftereffect: The target takes ongoing 1 poison damage (save ends).

Level 15 or 20: Ongoing 10 poison damage (save ends); aftereffect ongoing 2 poison damage (save ends).

Level 25 or 30: Ongoing 15 poison damage (save ends); aftereffect ongoing 3 poison damage (save ends).

Effect: If the target drops below 1 hit point while still taking ongoing damage from this power, make a secondary attack.

Secondary Attack: Close burst 1 centered on the primary target (each creature in the burst); the item's level + 3 vs. Reflex

Hit: 1d8 necrotic damage.

Level 15 or 20: 2d8 necrotic damage.

Level 25 or 30: 3d8 necrotic damage.

Elemental Accelerant

One principle of alchemy is that every reaction has an associated fuel. For example, because adding wood to a fire heightens the blaze, alchemists hold that wood contains the latent essence of fire.

At the time of the creation of the Elemental Chaos, matter had not yet been separated into different essences. This formula recreates that early protomatter to produce a powder that blankets an area and fuels whatever type of reaction first gives it form.

Elemental Accelerant			Level 3+ Common

This pouch is designed to break apart when thrown, coating everything around it with a dust that intensifies the next reaction in its area.

Lvl 3	30 gp	Lvl 23	17,000 gp
Lvl 13	650 gp		
Alchemical Item: Volatile		**Formula Cost:** 70 gp	
Key Skill: Arcana		**Time:** 1 hour	

Utility Power (Zone) ✦ **Consumable** (Standard Action)

Effect: Area burst 1 within 10 squares. The burst creates a zone that lasts until the end of the encounter. The first time a creature in the zone takes cold, fire, lightning, radiant, or thunder damage, the following effect is triggered: Attacks against creatures in the zone gain a +2 power bonus to damage rolls that include the triggering damage type. In addition, creatures in the zone take a -2 penalty to saving throws against ongoing damage of that type. These effects last until the end of the triggering creature's next turn, at which point the zone ends.

Level 13: +4 power bonus.

Level 23: +6 power bonus.

Foaming Plaster

The utility of this alchemical item is limited only by the volume of the shape it can be used to simulate. Some people have tried to combine multiple batches of foaming plaster in an attempt to capture an impression of an exceedingly large object (such as a bas relief carved into a wall). The problem they encountered was that as the amount of each reagent is increased, the length of time the plaster stays wet decreases. Whoever came up with the original formula seems to have found the right balance between the volume of the plaster and how long it remains malleable.

Foaming Plaster		Level 1 Common

When you combine these two reagents, one chalky and one viscous, a billow of expanding foam quickly forms in the area and then soon afterward hardens.

Lvl 1	20 gp	
Alchemical Item		**Formula Cost:** 70 gp
Key Skill: Arcana or Thievery		**Time:** 30 min.

Utility Power ✦ **Consumable** (Standard Action)

Effect: You mix the plaster. Once before the end of the encounter, you can use a minor action to create an impression in the wet plaster of a footprint, a key, or a similar small object. Giving the hardened plaster to someone else allows that person to identify the footprint, duplicate the key, and so on as if he or she had the original item.

If the plaster is not used by the end of the encounter, it hardens into a lump.

Goodnight Tincture

This liquid is dissolved into the food or drink of an unsuspecting victim to knock the subject unconscious. It is said that street vendors in the City of Brass spread fearful tales about how the city's taverns dose their patrons with goodnight tincture to sell sweet water to visitors.

Goodnight Tincture		Level 6+ Common	
This odorless, tasteless elixir can incapacitate a foe without harming it.			
Lvl 6	75 gp	Lvl 21	9,000 gp
Lvl 11	350 gp	Lvl 26	45,000 gp
Lvl 16	1,800 gp		
Alchemical Item: Poison		**Formula Cost:** 750 gp	
Key Skill: Nature or Thievery		**Time:** 1 hour	
Utility Power ✦ Consumable (Minor Action)			
Effect: You apply the *goodnight tincture* to an item of food or drink you are holding or that is adjacent to you. A creature that consumes the food or drink is subject to the following attack 1 minute later: the tincture's level + 6 vs. Fortitude; on a hit, the creature falls unconscious for 1 hour, or until it is subject to an attack or to violent motion.			

Greater Sovereign Glue

This ultimate adhesive is stored in a special vial. *Greater sovereign glue* can be applied directly to bond two objects together, or thrown at an enemy to keep that creature stuck in place.

Greater Sovereign Glue		Level 3+ Common	
This vial of gray paste creates a virtually unbreakable bond between the objects it glues together.			
Lvl 3	30 gp	Lvl 18	3,400 gp
Lvl 8	125 gp	Lvl 23	17,000 gp
Lvl 13	650 gp	Lvl 28	85,000 gp
Alchemical Item		**Formula Cost:** 120 gp	
Key Skill: Arcana or Thievery		**Time:** 2 hours	
↗ Attack Power ✦ Consumable (Standard Action)			
Attack: Ranged 5/10 (one creature); the item's level + 3 vs. Reflex			
Hit: The target is slowed (save ends).			
Effect: The item is consumed.			
Utility Power ✦ Consumable (Standard Action)			
Effect: You apply this glue to an object and affix that object to another object within 1 square of you. Doing so consumes this item. If the two objects remain affixed to one another until the end of your next turn (which might require you to hold them together), the items are adhered, and separating them requires a Strength check against a hard DC of the glue's level. A successful Strength check deals 2d10 damage to each adhered object.			

Holy Water

It is thought that the secret of making holy water was given to mortals by the gods. Most members of good and unaligned faiths see holy water as a symbol of the deities' common origin in the Astral Sea, despite the many differences in religious iconography that have emerged since the deities carved out their individual dominions. Adventurers who have little time for devotion still value holy water for its effectiveness in harming the traditional enemies of the non-evil gods.

Aside from its effect on undead and demons, holy water acts as normal water in all ways. It can be distinguished from normal water with a successful Arcana check or Religion check.

Holy Water		Level 1+ Common	
Undead and demons react poorly to the touch of this liquid.			
Lvl 1	20 gp	Lvl 16	1,800 gp
Lvl 6	75 gp	Lvl 21	9,000 gp
Lvl 11	350 gp	Lvl 26	45,000 gp
Alchemical Item: Volatile		**Formula Cost:** 50 gp	
Key Skill: Religion		**Time:** 1 hour	
↗ Attack Power (Radiant) ✦ Consumable (Minor Action)			
Attack: Ranged 3/6 (one undead creature or demon); the item's level + 3 vs. Reflex			
Hit: 1d10 radiant damage.			
Level 11 or 16: 2d10 radiant damage.			
Level 21 or 26: 3d10 radiant damage.			

Icening

A now-deceased deity of winter carved her dominion from the Astral Sea with a single snowflake—when she exposed it to the formless stuff of creation, the silvery material took on the snowflake's rigid perfection, forming a crystalline structure. This alchemical formula creates a seed crystal whose shape resembles that primal snowflake, and it can influence normal water in the same way.

Icening		Level 5+ Common	
When you toss this crystal into water, it freezes that liquid solid.			
Lvl 5	50 gp	Lvl 20	5,000 gp
Lvl 10	200 gp	Lvl 25	25,000 gp
Lvl 15	1,000 gp	Lvl 30	125,000 gp
Alchemical Item: Volatile		**Formula Cost:** 100 gp	
Key Skill: Arcana		**Time:** 1 hour	
❄ Attack Power (Zone) ✦ Consumable (Standard Action)			
Attack: Area burst 1 within 10 (each creature at least partially submerged in water); the item's level + 3 vs. Fortitude			
Hit: The target is immobilized until the end of its next turn.			
Effect: The burst creates a zone that lasts until the end of the encounter. Water in the zone is difficult terrain. However, if no creatures are in the zone when it is created, water in the zone turns to solid ice.			

Alchemist at work

Oil of Etherealness

Delvers report that a mad wizard's dungeon holds a fountain that seems empty but actually brims with this invisible oil. Expeditions intending to grow rich from bottling it have fallen prey to the dungeon's denizens, who coat themselves in the oil and rise through the floor in ambush. Groups still make the attempt, however, because spending too much time in ethereal form weakens a creature's physical health and many believe all those guardians will eventually be slain.

Oil of Etherealness	Level 20 Common

When you apply this oil to yourself or an object, it is momentarily removed from the physical world.

Lvl 20	5,000 gp	
Alchemical Item: Oil		**Formula Cost:** 6,750 gp
Key Skill: Arcana		**Time:** 1 hour

Utility Power ✦ Consumable (Minor Action)

Effect: You apply the oil to yourself or to an adjacent creature or object. That creature or object becomes insubstantial and gains phasing until the end of your next turn. As a minor action, a creature benefiting from this power can lose a healing surge to sustain this power until the end of its next turn.

Oil of Slipperiness

The original impetus for the development of this alchemical item was the search for an agent that would allow sovereign glue to be poured from a vial without bonding to the glass. This greenish-black fluid soon found other industrial uses, such as lubricating iron golem gears. After burglars stole the formula, oil of slipperiness became popular among adventurers, who anticipated needing to squirm free from a choker's grasp or slip away from a pursuing band of bugbears.

Oil of Slipperiness	Level 8 Common

The oily gel in this vial quickly spreads to make your body or a patch of ground very slick.

Lvl 8	125 gp	
Alchemical Item: Oil		**Formula Cost:** 375 gp
Key Skill: Nature or Thievery		**Time:** 1 hour

Utility Power (Zone) **✦ Consumable** (Standard Action)

Effect: Area burst 1 within 10. The burst creates a zone that lasts until the end of the encounter. Whenever a creature on the ground enters the zone, it must succeed on a saving throw or fall prone. When forced movement moves a creature into the zone, that forced movement increases by 1 square, and creatures in the zone take a –2 penalty to saving throws to avoid entering hindering terrain.

Special: Recognizing the zone requires a hard Perception check.

Ossip Wax

Records from the Anauli Empire suggest that this wax, which induces weightlessness, was originally harvested directly from a now-extinct creature of the beholder family called an ossip. The reconstruction of this formula used by contemporary alchemists is a compound created by a sage who was a noted expert on both beholder anatomy and the Ruined Realms.

Ossip Wax	Level 10 Common
This stiff yellow wax makes anything it's spread on lighter.	
Lvl 10 200 gp	
Alchemical Item	**Formula Cost:** 600 gp
Key Skill: Arcana, Nature, or Thievery	**Time:** 30 min.
Utility Power ✦ Consumable (Standard Action)	

Effect: You smear the wax on one adjacent object of Large or smaller size. The object's weight is reduced by 500 pounds. If this reduction causes the object to become weightless, it floats 5 feet above the ground. Pushing a floating object causes it to continue moving in the direction of the push, at an initial speed of 10. At the end of each round of movement, the object's speed is reduced by 1. This power lasts for 5 minutes or until the end of the encounter.

Precarious Crystal

This item is a favorite of trap makers who want to ward an area against flying creatures. The item has two parts—a bag of chemical salts and a small glass flask of *alchemist's essence* (fire). In preparing the crystal, the salts are dropped into the flask, and the fire fuses them into a highly unstable crystal in a short amount of time. Thereafter, any major movement near the crystal will cause it to collapse, releasing the fire to trigger another alchemical item or sound an alarm.

Precarious Crystal		Level 3+ Common	
This small, clear crystal collapses into a tiny flame in response to motion, activating another nearby alchemical item.			
Lvl 5	50 gp	Lvl 20	5,000 gp
Lvl 10	200 gp	Lvl 25	25,000 gp
Lvl 15	1,000 gp	Lvl 30	125,000 gp
Alchemical Item		**Formula Cost:** 120 gp	
Key Skill: Arcana or Thievery		**Time:** 30 min.	
Utility Power (Zone) **✦ Consumable** (Standard Action)			

Effect: You place the crystal in a square adjacent to you, along with a volatile alchemical item that the crystal will activate. The level of that item must be the same as or lower than the crystal's level. At the end of your next turn, the crystal creates a zone in a burst 1 centered on its square. The first time a creature enters the zone, the crystal vanishes in a bright flash, the volatile alchemical item activates, and the zone ends.

Special: Recognizing the zone requires a Perception check. Disarming it requires an Arcana check or a Thievery check as a standard action. All of these checks are against a hard DC of the crystal's level.

Protean Silk

Some believe that the drow first developed the formula for protean silk. Drow raiders certainly appreciate its ability to form a lightweight rope that can be retracted without leaving a trace, as well as its association with spiders. Having the glands and spinneret extracted from a spider is useful when preparing this item, but not necessary.

Protean Silk	Level 6 Common
You draw forth a long, thin filament from this viscous glob that you can turn into a strong rope that lasts for a short time.	
Lvl 6 75 gp	
Alchemical Item	**Formula Cost:** 450 gp
Key Skill: Arcana, Nature, or Thievery	**Time:** 1 hour
Utility Power ✦ Consumable (Minor Action)	

Effect: You extract a silk strand that can stretch up to 40 squares away. The strand does not move on its own, but it can be carried or attached to an arrow, a bolt, or some other ammunition. As a second minor action, you can turn the strand into a silk rope. As a third minor action, you can cause the rope to dissolve, leaving no trace of it.

Smoke Snake

When lit, this twist of tightly compressed powder leaves a growing tail of ash, creating a cloud of dark, caustic smoke that obscures the area around it.

Smoke Snake	Level 10 Common
You throw this tab of compacted black powder to the ground and it ignites, releasing a cloud of foul-smelling smoke.	
Lvl 10 200 gp	
Alchemical Item	**Formula Cost:** 800 gp
Key Skill: Arcana or Nature	**Time:** 30 min.
Utility Power (Zone) **✦ Consumable** (Standard Action)	

Effect: Area burst 1 within 10. The burst creates a zone of lightly obscured squares that lasts until the end of the encounter.

Sweet Water

Mixing sweet water into food provides protection against poisoned meals, making it a favorite among wealthy nobles.

Sweet Water	Level 1 Common
This small glob of white jelly purifies even the most toxic food and drink, from poisons to dwarven spirits.	
Lvl 1 20 gp	
Alchemical Item	**Formula Cost:** 100 gp
Key Skill: Arcana, Nature, or Religion	**Time:** 30 min.
Utility Power ✦ Consumable (Minor Action)	

Effect: You apply the *sweet water* to a portion of food equivalent to a light meal for one person or to a single serving of a beverage. The sweet water removes any poison or disease present in the food or beverage after 1 minute. It cannot remove poison or disease from food or drink that is already in a creature's system.

Tracking Dust

This fine dust is typically applied in areas where you are searching for existing tracks or where you want to detect a creature passing through at a later time. Thieves in areas where tracking dust is common often employ ossip wax to enter an area without leaving footprints.

Tracking Dust			Level 4+ Common
You spread the fine grains of this silver dust to reveal the subtlest tracks.			
Lvl 4	80 gp	Lvl 19	8,400 gp
Lvl 9	320 gp	Lvl 24	42,000 gp
Lvl 14	1,600 gp	Lvl 29	210,000 gp
Alchemical Item		Formula Cost: 160 gp	
Key Skill: Nature or Thievery		Time: 1 hour	
Utility Power (Zone) ✦ Consumable (Standard Action)			
Effect: The *tracking dust* creates a zone of 5 contiguous squares that lasts for 1 hour (you can arrange the squares however you like). When a creature makes a Perception check to track in the zone, the creature can make the check using either its normal Perception modifier or the +7 bonus provided by the dust.			
Level 9: +9 bonus.			
Level 14: +12 bonus.			
Level 19: +14 bonus.			
Level 24: +17 bonus.			
Level 29: +19 bonus.			
Special: Recognizing the zone requires a hard Perception check of the item's level.			

Twinned Flames

Twinned flames is the name given to pairs of inert magical flames that are commonly used to detonate alchemical traps, either at a safe distance or through the use of a *precarious crystal*. Alchemists create these items using a process that squeezes a candle flame down to its tiniest essence, then splits it into two flames, making their fire inert. When one half of the flame is magically reignited, its twin flares at the same moment.

Twinned Flames		Level 10+ Common
This tiny spark is almost invisible until it is fanned into life. When it is, its twin flame reignites as well.		
Lvl 10	200 gp	Lvl 30	125,000 gp
Lvl 20	5,000 gp		
Alchemical Item	Formula Cost: 120 gp	
Key Skill: Arcana or Nature	Time: 30 min.	
Property		
To use this item's power, you must first link the item to another alchemical item in hand or in an adjacent square as a standard action. The level of the linked item must be the same as or lower than the level of the *twinned flames*.		
Utility Power ✦ Consumable (Standard Action)		
Effect: You activate the power of the linked alchemical item. You do not need to have line of effect to the item, but you must be within 1 mile of it.		

Universal Solvent

The first alchemists to pursue an ultimate dissolving agent took great precautions against the possibility that the universal solvent would eat its way to the center of the earth and gradually unmake the foundations of the world. Although the final product proved not to be as effective as they feared, it is still considered a classic of alchemy.

Universal Solvent		Level 10 Common
This clear solution can dissolve almost any adhesive.		
Lvl 10	200 gp	
Alchemical Item	Formula Cost: 600 gp	
Key Skill: Arcana or Thievery	Time: 30 min.	
Utility Power ✦ Consumable (Standard Action)		
Effect: When you apply this substance to a creature or object in your square or an adjacent square, it destroys any type of mundane bonding agent affecting that creature or object (including sovereign glue).		
Universal solvent allows a creature immobilized by mundane agents such as a kobold slinger's gluepot or an aboleth slime mage's *slime burst* power to immediately succeed on a saving throw against the effect when it's applied. It does not affect the aftereffects of those substances (such as *slime burst*'s slowing effect), nor does it have any effect on creatures immobilized by other effects (for example, a ghoul's *claw* attack).		

RETURN TO SENDER

News of the discovery of the location of the Arkhosian Winter Palace reached two adventuring parties at the same time. As each excavated the rubble in search of an entrance to the buried ruin, a rivalry developed between the Spellblades and the Wildroot Wanderers. The Spellblades hired a salamander mercenary to set the Wanderers' dig site on fire.

Unfortunately for them, the Wanderers were able to subdue the salamander. They took two slabs of stone and used *sovereign glue* to hold them together, and then glued the salamander onto this impromptu platform. They then piled vials of *alchemist's fire* on top of the salamander, and smeared *ossip wax* on the bottom of the slab to enable it to float through the air. Finally, they stuck a *precarious crystal* onto the bottom of the slab, connected to a flask of *universal solvent*. Then they kicked the slab to send it floating over the Spellblades' camp.

When those adventurers scrambled out of their tents, their motion caused the *precarious crystal* to burn through the cork holding in the *universal solvent*, which dissolved the *sovereign glue* between the slabs and caused a freed and angry salamander to fall onto the heads of its former employers in a rain of fire.

APPENDIX 1: HIRELINGS AND HENCHMEN

Adventurers are a cut above the commoners inhabiting the world—they have talent, specialized training, and access to magic that makes them akin to gods among mortals. Well, maybe not that far, but heroes are something special. Who else can beard the dragon in its lair? Who else can survive a trap-laden gauntlet to root out the goblin bandits lurking in the cavern beyond? Who else can put down zombies by the dozens?

The thing is, for all that heroes can accomplish beyond most peoples' wildest imagining, adventurers need the common people. Non-adventuring men and women do the things that heroes are unable or unwilling to do. What good is a knight without the suit of armor someone else made? How is the paladin going to survive his or her quest without a sword in hand? Horses? Someone has to breed them and train them. And when the adventure is done, when the heroes return, burdened with their spoils, they're bound to be craving a hot meal and warm bed that only the sleepy little communities on the frontier can provide. The mundane tasks fall to the ordinary people to handle, and without those people, there's little point to squaring off against monsters and plundering their vaults.

Commoners are content to leave the adventuring business to the professionals. They happily take their coins and provide services in return. They listen to the tales of high adventure, danger, and daring, living through the stories the adventurers tell, but they are also relieved to go about their lives without having to follow in those people's steps or face those same challenges.

That said, with the right motivation, these common people might be coaxed from relative safety into a wider world of adventure, accompanying the heroes on their quests and lending aid, albeit in minor ways, to help the heroes accomplish their goals. These companions are the henchmen, the lackeys, the hirelings, and the servants. For the right price, they can lend their unique talents to an adventurer's cause.

Hirelings and henchmen have been part of the DUNGEONS & DRAGONS® game since the beginning. In older editions, henchmen gave adventuring parties a bit of extra muscle, took the brunt of enemy attacks, and gave the heroes the extra help they needed to achieve their objectives and survive their challenges. Thus far, 4th Edition has nibbled on the henchmen concept by offering different avenues for characters to acquire companions. Certain classes, such as the beastmaster ranger and the sentinel druid, have pets.

Dungeon Master's Guide 2 provides extensive rules for creating companion characters, either from scratch or by adapting an existing creature to fill this role. While these options are sufficient for most groups, there's something missing—an element of leadership that harkens back to the classic experiences of the game. This appendix provides an expansion to the existing options that cover hirelings and henchmen and puts in your hands the ability to gather and hire the nonplayer characters you need.

The optional rules in this section add a level of complexity that might not be suitable for every group. For large parties, hirelings and henchmen add to the challenges posed by having so many people around the table. Novices might find extra characters in the mix too difficult to manage, and adding several nonplayer characters can dilute other characters' roles in the party.

On the other hand, hirelings and henchmen can solve some of the problems that arise from having too few players in the group. They can step into missing roles, bolster characters having a tough time performing in their role, and act as special rewards for roleplaying or fulfilling a quest. They can serve as a development from the campaign's unfolding story. Before you put this material to use, check with your Dungeon Master to ensure that a companion is suitable for your group.

HIRELINGS

The young man who carries your torch lights the way down the dungeon corridor. The valet cleans and mends your clothes, ensuring that all the final preparations are made before you meet the king. The mercenary guard watches over the camp at night, letting you get your rest before you continue your hunt for the troll that made off with the merchant's daughter. These characters are all hirelings: men and women in your employ whose efforts make your travels and missions easier.

Hirelings are similar to companion characters in that they accompany you, but they differ in the capabilities they possess. Hirelings are minor characters and thus do not provide the same degree of support a companion character can provide. Where a companion character might work for a share of the treasure, a hireling is directly in your employ and works for a fee.

Gaining a Hireling

You don't have to hunt for hirelings. Go to just about any settlement, and you're bound to find some enterprising entrepreneur who has a talent you might find useful. Any number of mercenaries, porters, and similar kinds are ready and willing to work for a price. To gain a hireling, you have to find a willing servant and

Hirelings

meet the hireling's fee. At the DM's discretion, you might have to succeed on a skill check to convince the character to accompany you, with Bluff, Diplomacy, Intimidate, and Streetwise being the most common skills. Alternatively, you might find a hireling as part of treasure. As strange as this might sound, a monster might keep any number of potential hirelings as prisoners. It's no stretch to think a dragon might keep a minstrel on hand to entertain it, or an artist to paint its portrait, or a mercenary in the larder to gobble up when cows and sheep grow scarce.

FOR THE DM: ABUSE

Coin ensures a hireling's loyalty up to a point.

Just as an adventurer isn't likely to put up with abuse from his or her employer, a hireling isn't likely to stick around if mistreated. Other hirelings can grow wise to a callous master who carelessly sends servants to their doom.

You don't have to track attitudes or a list of offenses. Just think about the adventurer's personality and how well he or she treats the hireling. If you can't imagine someone putting up with that treatment, have the hireling make his or her exit at the first opportunity. As word gets out about the adventurer, you might increase the skill check DCs required to hire these followers.

Hireling Statistics

Regardless of a hireling's occupation, all have certain common statistics.

Level: Hirelings exist at every level. Heroic tier hirelings are the common kinds one expects to find pretty much anywhere people gather. Paragon tier hirelings are experts in their fields. Finding nonplayer characters at this level of accomplishment who are willing to work for someone else can be hard. Epic tier hirelings are tremendously rare; they are the greatest crafters and artists in their respective fields. Such characters have plans, ventures, and goals of their own to pursue, so they are never available for hire without the DM's consent.

Price: A hireling's price depends on his or her level. The price is generally per day of service. Long-term service can sometimes be gotten at a lower rate or in return for a share of any profit from the expedition or undertaking. Included in the price are the hireling's initial fee, salary, food, equipment, and the materials the hireling might need along the way. It's important to note the price is an abstraction intended to simplify the process of acquiring and maintaining hirelings.

Duration: A hireling remains in your service for as long as you keep paying him or her.

Hireling	Level Varies
Medium natural humanoid	—

HP 1; a missed attack never damages a hireling	Initiative —
	Perception +0

AC level + 14, **Other Defenses** level + 12
Speed 6

STANDARD ACTIONS

⊕ **Melee Attack** (weapon) ✦ **At-Will**
Attack: Melee 1 (one creature); level + 5 vs. AC
Hit: One-half the hireling's level + 3 damage.

⊛ **Ranged Attack** (weapon) ✦ **At-Will**
Attack: Ranged 10 (one creature); level + 5 vs. AC
Hit: One-half the hireling's level + 3 damage.

Occupation

When you employ a hireling, you do so to gain a particular service or benefit. These benefits are tied to the hireling's occupation. Choose one occupation and add its traits to the hireling's statistics block.

Hireling	Level Varies

A dutiful servant attends to the little complications that interfere with your adventures.

Lvl 1	15 gp	Lvl 11	350 gp	Lvl 21	9,000 gp
Lvl 2	20 gp	Lvl 12	520 gp	Lvl 22	13,000 gp
Lvl 3	25 gp	Lvl 13	680 gp	Lvl 23	17,000 gp
Lvl 4	35 gp	Lvl 14	840 gp	Lvl 24	21,000 gp
Lvl 5	40 gp	Lvl 15	1,000 gp	Lvl 25	25,000 gp
Lvl 6	70 gp	Lvl 16	1,800 gp	Lvl 26	45,000 gp
Lvl 7	100 gp	Lvl 17	2,600 gp	Lvl 27	65,000 gp
Lvl 8	135 gp	Lvl 18	3,400 gp	Lvl 28	85,000 gp
Lvl 9	170 gp	Lvl 19	4,200 gp	Lvl 29	105,000 gp
Lvl 10	200 gp	Lvl 20	5,000 gp	Lvl 30	125,000 gp

Minor Character

Property

You gain the service of a hireling. The creature is an ally to you and your allies. The hireling can perform one standard action and one move action each turn. It acts after you on your initiative count. The hireling has no healing surges.

Beast Handler

Cost: Standard

These grooms care for your beasts. They can keep your horse in excellent health, your dog fed, and your falcon ready to hunt.

TRAITS

✪ **Beast Handler** ✦ **Aura** 5
All allied beasts in the aura gain a +1 power bonus to Fortitude and Will.

Guide

Cost: Standard

Expeditions into the wilderness can only benefit from a well-trained guide. These hirelings blaze the trail to the heroes' destination. The cost doubles if the guide is leading you into dangerous territory.

TRAITS

✪ **Trailblazer** ✦ **Aura** 5
Allies in the aura gain a +2 power bonus to Dungeoneering checks and Nature checks.
Level 15: +3 power bonus.
Level 25: +4 power bonus.

Linkboy

Cost: Standard

Few fighters are willing to sacrifice a two-handed weapon or their shield to haul the party's torch. When no one is able or willing to attend to the group's light, a linkboy provides an extra pair of hands.

TRAITS

✪ **Torch** ✦ **Aura** 5
Squares in the aura are illuminated with bright light.

Mercenary

Cost: Standard × 3

Mercenaries are the perfect soldiers for hire, ready to lend their swords and shields provided the pay is right.

TRAITS

✪ **Veteran Warrior** ✦ **Aura** 1
Allies in the aura gain a +1 power bonus to AC and Reflex. In addition, the hireling gains a +2 power bonus to AC and Reflex.

STANDARD ACTIONS

⊕ **Melee Attack** (weapon) ✦ **At-Will**
Attack: Melee 1 (one creature); level + 5 vs. AC
Hit: The hireling's level + 3 damage.

⊛ **Ranged Attack** (weapon) ✦ **At-Will**
Attack: Ranged 10 (one creature); level + 5 vs. AC
Hit: The hireling's level + 3 damage.

Pilot

Cost: Standard × 2

Whether commanding the mariner's wheel on a greatship, driving a wagon team, or guiding an airship to dock, a seasoned pilot is an asset to any crew.

TRAITS

Seasoned Pilot
When used as a pilot, the hireling grants the vehicle a +1 bonus to the vehicle's speed.

Porter

Cost: Standard

Porters make their living hauling stuff. They are useful hirelings since they can heft considerable weight and still reach places a mule or horse could not.

TRAITS

Strong
The hireling's normal load is 75 pounds, heavy load is 150 pounds, and maximum drag load is 375 pounds.
Level 1-5: Base speed 5, travel 6 hours per day.
Level 6-10: Base speed 6, travel 8 hours per day.
Level 11-30: Base speed 7, travel 10 hours per day.

Sage

Cost: Standard × 3

Sages are experts in a particular field of knowledge. Few sages venture from their personal domains, though if you can convince one to accompany you, his or her knowledge is yours for the asking.

TRAITS

✧ Sage Knowledge ✦ Aura 5

Choose one knowledge skill for the sage: Arcana, Dungeoneering, History, Nature, or Religion. Allies in the aura gain a +2 power bonus to skill checks involving the chosen skill.
Level 15: +3 power bonus.
Level 25: +4 power bonus.

STANDARD ACTIONS

Lore Use ✦ Daily

Effect: One ally gains a +5 item bonus to the next skill check made involving the skill chosen for *sage knowledge*.

Scribe

Cost: Standard × 2

Limners and copyists, these trained individuals are adept at recording and copying whatever you put in front of them.

TRAITS

Scribe Document

During a short or an extended rest, the hireling copies one page of text or illustrations. It is a rough copy if performed during a short rest or a perfect copy if performed during an extended rest.

FOR THE DM: HIRELING TRAITS

Like companion characters, hirelings have traits to help them stand out as more than trap springers and door openers. You don't need extensive details; you need only enough information to give them a little life.

Race: A hireling's race does not affect his or her statistics, but it can reveal a lot about personality and appearance. Hirelings favor employers who are friendly to their people.

Physical Description: Come up with one or two distinguishing characteristics to make the hireling stand out. Height, weight, and coloring are good places to start, as are interesting elements such as a limp, a squint, boils, or a ruddy complexion.

Personality: Don't worry too much about motivations, secrets, or behaviors when it comes to hirelings. Instead, assign a word to the hireling to summarize his or her personality. Examples include serious, driven, craven, unhinged, reckless, or loyal.

Seasoned Crew Member

Cost: Standard

These able sailors can ensure that a ship reaches a distant port safe and sound.

TRAITS

Able Crew

If a vehicle's crew is entirely made up of seasoned crew member hirelings, the vehicle gains a +1 bonus to all defenses.

Spy

Cost: Standard × 3

Spies can keep you supplied with the information you need when you need it most.

TRAITS

Espionage

The controlling hero gains a +2 power bonus to Streetwise checks.
Level 15: +3 power bonus.
Level 25: +4 power bonus.

Valet

Cost: Standard

Skilled valets are indispensable to those moving through high society because these servants know how to make you look and act your best when you're dealing with the rich and powerful.

TRAITS

✧ Etiquette ✦ Aura 3

When dressed in suitable clothing, the controlling hero and all allies gain a +2 power bonus to Diplomacy checks while in the aura.
Level 15: +3 power bonus.
Level 25: +4 power bonus.

PETS

A pet can be an interesting way to develop your character's personality and appearance. A house cat, a small snake, a raven, or another animal adds color and can reveal something about the character's interests. If you're interested in acquiring a companion animal, consider the following options.

Class: As of this writing, two classes provide animal companions. The first is the beastmaster ranger introduced in *Martial Power*™ and the second is the sentinel druid from *Heroes of the Forgotten Kingdoms*™. In both cases, you get the benefit of a companion creature, with supporting powers to let you coordinate your efforts. If you're not inclined to play either class, you can use the hybrid rules from *Player's Handbook*® 3 to pick up the Beast Mastery class feature and add to the class you want to play.

Familiars: Another option, specifically for arcane characters, is to take the Arcane Familiar feat from

Arcane Power™. In addition to cats, falcons, and serpents, you can also pick up strange pets such as bound demons and book imps. Any arcane class can take the feat, so if you have a multiclass or hybrid class, this is a great option.

Companion Character: With your DM's permission, you can use the companion character rules from *Dungeon Master's Guide®* 2 to turn a monster into a companion character. This is a good solution if you have a smaller than normal party since the pet counts as a full member of the party.

Pet Background: Perhaps the easiest solution to acquiring a pet is to add it to your character sheet as a background element. A pet as a background element abstracts a creature with no significant statistics or ability to affect a combat's outcome in a meaningful way. A pet snake, a trained raven, a house cat, and a small dog are all suitable creatures for this option. Think about how you acquired the pet and how you feel about it. Come up with at least one way the pet helped you in the past. And don't forget to name it!

If you choose the pet as your major background benefit, work with your DM to find an appropriate skill. A raven trained to filch small objects might grant a +2 bonus to Thievery checks. A small, vicious dog might grant a +2 bonus to Intimidate checks or Perception checks. A chatty parrot or raven might grant a +2 bonus to Bluff checks.

HENCHMEN

Where hirelings are minor supporting characters, lending aid to an adventuring group in small ways, henchmen are nearly full-fledged characters in their own right, whose presence in the adventuring group gives the heroes an edge. These characters are counted as full members of the adventuring party. Henchmen have many of the same features, traits, and powers available to player characters, but simplified to allow a player to manage a henchman at the same time that he or she plays a primary character.

Henchmen, also known as companion characters, can take many forms. Some might be beasts and monsters, being creatures drawn from the *Monster Manual®* or *Monster Vault*™ books. Others are akin to characters, using the same kinds of powers available to heroes. A few might be unique, crafted by a DM or drawn from a published supplement such as the ones presented below.

Gaining a Henchman

Adding a henchman to your adventuring party can be as simple as posting a notice in a local tavern or as complicated as completing a minor quest, negotiating payment, or tracking down the companion in a city, a wilderness setting, or a dungeon.

Companion: Henchmen are best used to fill in missing roles or to take the place of absent players. If the group lacks a leader, you might recruit one to accompany you on your adventurers to improve your chances for success. A companion can be a constant presence in your group or a sporadic one, depending on the game's needs.

Employee: Sometimes you might want a little help in taking on a dangerous mission. An extra warrior or striker could make a difference, especially if your group is light in these roles. A henchman can serve an adventuring group in exchange for something, such as coin, but sometimes the henchman might join the party so that he or she can gain the party's help in completing a minor or major quest. Employees are not open-ended allies. Their contracts stipulate an end point for their services.

If a henchman's compensation is monetary, the fee equals one-fifth of the value of a magic item equal to the party's level.

Ally: During your hero's adventures, he or she is bound to encounter friendly and helpful characters. You might make a short-term alliance against a common enemy, join forces with a rival adventuring group, or rescue an important character who chooses to fight at your side until you reach safety.

Creating a Henchman

Unlike hirelings, creating a henchman is the DM's job. *Dungeon Master's Guide 2* includes the rules the DM needs to turn a monster into a companion character or to create a unique companion.

Running a Henchman

Although the DM creates the henchman, it falls to you to use the character in combat and skill challenges. Outside combat, the DM controls the character, playing the character in accordance with his or her personality, motives, and secrets. In combat, the DM might hand off the character to a player to run.

Henchmen in Play

Remember a couple of things when using henchmen in your group. First, henchmen don't need magic items and thus should never be included in magic item distribution. Second, henchmen earn experience points just as you do and thus earn a full share of XP. Finally, henchmen gain levels and advance at the same rate as other characters in the group.

Sample Henchmen

If you need a henchman in a pinch, you can use any of the following characters.

Anaxana
Reckless Battle Mage

Anaxana is an eladrin magician—a reckless battle mage hungry for vengeance against her people's enemies.

She has a spare frame to the point of being gaunt. Her features are severe, with a long nose that gives her a hawkish appearance. She prefers simple gray robes and keeps a longsword in a scabbard on her weapon belt.

Missions involving hunting down and killing orcs or drow are the easiest ways to recruit Anaxana to the group. She hasn't a kind word for these monsters and delights in fighting them. She might linger with a party for missions that don't involve hunting her enemies but moves on if her bloodlust isn't sated.

Anaxana	Level 2 Controller
Medium fey humanoid, eladrin	—
HP 27; Bloodied 13;	Initiative +4
Healing Surges 7; Surge Value 6	
AC 15, Fortitude 15, Reflex 17, Will 14	Perception +0
Speed 6	Low-light vision
Saving Throws +5 against charm effects	

STANDARD ACTIONS

⊕ Longsword (weapon) ✦ At-Will
  Attack: Melee 1 (one creature); +9 vs. AC
  Hit: 1d8 + 1 damage.

⊗ Magic Missile (force, implement) ✦ At-Will
  Effect: Ranged 20 (one creature). The target takes 7 force damage.

↙ Burning Hands (fire, implement) ✦ Encounter
  Attack: Close blast 5 (creatures in the blast); +6 vs. Reflex
  Hit: 2d6 + 5 fire damage.
  Miss: Half damage.

✳ Freezing Burst (cold, implement) ✦ At-Will
  Attack: Area burst 1 within 10 (creatures in the burst); +6 vs. Reflex
  Hit: 1d6 + 5 cold damage, and Anaxana can slide the target 1 square.

MOVE ACTIONS

Fey Step (teleportation) ✦ Encounter
  Effect: Anaxana teleports up to 5 squares.

TRIGGERED ACTIONS

Shield ✦ Encounter
  Trigger: An enemy hits Anaxana.
  Effect (Immediate Interrupt): Anaxana gains a +4 power bonus to AC and Reflex until the end of her next turn.

Wand of Accuracy ✦ Encounter
  Trigger: Anaxana starts her turn.
  Effect (Free Action): Anaxana gains a +3 bonus to a single attack roll using a wand as an implement made before the end of her turn.

Skills Arcana +10, History +10, Insight +5
Str 10 (+1)   Dex 17 (+4)   Wis 8 (+0)
Con 13 (+2)   Int 19 (+5)   Cha 10 (+1)
Alignment unaligned   Languages Common, Elven
Equipment robes, longsword, wand, adventurer's kit

Sir Michael Everdawn
Disgraced Knight

Once a promising knight, renowned for his skill at arms and his fine pedigree, Michael fell from grace and is now a pariah in his own lands. He never speaks of how he reached his present state, though his overindulgence in spirits suggests a predilection for drunkenness that might have played a part in his fall.

Michael is a heavyset man with a paunch, red nose, and rheumy eyes. Despite his haggard appearance, he remains strong, powerful, and ferocious in battle. His battered armor shows signs of previous contests, and the faded heraldry, a rampant boar, hints at the better life he once lived.

The disgraced knight craves redemption. He eagerly joins any adventuring group that can promise him a chance to restore his name. While involved in a noble pursuit, he stays clear of the drink until idleness and frustration overcome him.

Sir Michael Everdawn	Level 2 Defender
Medium natural humanoid, human	—
HP 35; Bloodied 17;	Initiative +1
Healing Surges 11; Surge Value 8	
AC 21, Fortitude 18, Reflex 14, Will 16	Perception +2
Speed 5	

STANDARD ACTIONS

⊕ Longsword (weapon) ✦ At-Will
  Attack: Melee 1 (one creature); +9 vs. AC
  Hit: 1d8 + 5 damage, and Michael marks the target until the end of his next turn.

↓ Tide of Iron (weapon) ✦ At-Will
  Requirement: Michael must be using a shield.
  Attack: Melee 1 (one creature); +9 vs. AC
  Hit: 1d8 + 5 damage, and Michael can push the target 1 square, and then shift 1 square into the space the target last occupied.

MINOR ACTIONS

↙ Glowering Threat ✦ Encounter
  Effect: Close burst 2 (enemies in the burst). Until the end of Michael's next turn, each target takes a -5 penalty to attack rolls against any creature other than Michael.

TRIGGERED ACTIONS

Heroic Effort ✦ Encounter
  Trigger: Michael misses with an attack or fails a saving throw.
  Effect (No Action): Michael gains a +4 bonus to the attack roll or saving throw.

Power Strike ✦ Encounter
  Trigger: Michael hits an enemy with *longsword*.
  Effect (No Action): The triggering attack deals 1d8 extra damage.

Skills Athletics +10, Endurance +8, Intimidate +8
Str 18 (+5)   Dex 11 (+1)   Wis 12 (+2)
Con 14 (+3)   Int 8 (+0)   Cha 14 (+3)
Alignment good   Languages Common, Giant
Equipment plate armor, heavy shield, longsword, adventurer's kit

Cadra Forgesworn

Zealous Priestess

Cadra Forgesworn is a devout follower of Moradin. She's so zealous she comes off as a fanatic. She left her clan, not to seek fortune or glory, but to champion her patron in the world.

As with most dwarves, Cadra is short and stocky. Her determination makes up for any shortcomings in physical might, and when committed to a cause, she is as tenacious as a troll with a fresh carcass in its maw. She shaved her head and inked her scalp with battle scenes described in the *Book of Spite,* a holy tome favored by Moradin's more militant priests.

More than anything, Cadra hopes to leave a mark on the world, as Moradin commands. How she will do so has not yet revealed itself. She believes the adventurer's life is the surest way to achieve this end. She has worked with other groups before, and each association ended badly. Her abrasive personality could be to blame.

Ghesh

Mercenary Captain

A veteran officer from a disbanded mercenary company, Ghesh is now a sword-for-hire, selling his services to anyone who pays him the highest price.

Ghesh cuts an impressive figure. He's tall, muscled, and covered in glittering bronze scales. He keeps his equipment in impeccable condition, cleaning and oiling his mail and spear every night before bedding down.

Command comes easy to Ghesh, and he's not one to keep his opinions to himself. He believes his

Cadra Forgesworn	Level 2 Leader
Medium natural humanoid, dwarf	—
HP 34; Bloodied 17;	Initiative +2
Healing Surges 10; Surge Value 8	
AC 17, Fortitude 15, Reflex 13, Will 17	Perception +5
Speed 5	Low-light vision
Saving Throws +5 against poison effects	

TRAITS

Stand Your Ground
Cadra can move 1 square less than the effect specifies when subjected to a pull, a push, or a slide. In addition, when an effect would cause Cadra to fall prone, she can make a saving throw to avoid falling prone.

STANDARD ACTIONS

⊕ **Warhammer** (weapon) ✦ **At-Will**
Attack: Melee 1 (one creature); +8 vs. AC
Hit: 1d10 + 1 damage.

⊛ **Throwing Hammer** (weapon) ✦ **At-Will**
Attack: Ranged 5/10 (one creature); +8 vs. AC
Hit: 1d6 + 2 damage.

↯ **Blessing of Wrath** (weapon) ✦ **At-Will**
Attack: Melee 1 (one creature); +8 vs. AC
Hit: 1d10 + 5 damage.
Effect: Cadra or one ally within 5 squares of her gains a +3 power bonus to his or her next damage roll against the target before the end of his or her next turn.

⟿ **Sanctuary** ✦ **Encounter**
Effect: Ranged 10 (Cadra or one creature). The target gains a +5 bonus to all defenses until the target attacks or until the end of Cadra's next turn.

⬅ **Divine Glow** (implement, radiant) ✦ **Encounter**
Attack: Close blast 3 (enemies in the blast); +6 vs. Reflex
Hit: 1d8 + 5 radiant damage.
Effect: Allies in the blast gain a +2 power bonus to attack rolls until the end of Cadra's next turn.

MINOR ACTIONS

⬅ **Healing Word** (healing) ✦ **2/Encounter**
Effect: Close burst 5 (Cadra or one ally in the burst). The target spends a healing surge.

Dwarven Resilience ✦ **Encounter**
Effect: Cadra uses her second wind.

Skills Dungeoneering +10, Endurance +11, Heal +10
| Str 11 (+1) | Dex 12 (+2) | Wis 19 (+5) |
| Con 17 (+4) | Int 8 (+0) | Cha 10 (+1) |

Alignment lawful good **Languages** Common, Dwarven
Equipment scale armor, warhammer, 2 throwing hammers, holy symbol, adventurer's kit

Ghesh	Level 2 Leader
Medium natural humanoid, dragonborn	—
HP 30; Bloodied 15;	Initiative +2
Healing Surges 8; Surge Value 8	
AC 17, Fortitude 17, Reflex 13, Will 15	Perception +4
Speed 5	

TRAITS

Dragonborn Fury
Ghesh gains a +1 bonus to attack rolls while he is bloodied

STANDARD ACTIONS

⊕ **Longspear** (weapon) ✦ **At-Will**
Attack: Melee 2 (one creature); +8 vs. AC
Hit: 1d10 + 5 damage.

↯ **Viper's Strike** (weapon) ✦ **At-Will**
Attack: Melee 2 (one creature); +8 vs. AC
Hit: 1d10 + 5 damage.
Effect: If the target shifts before the start of Ghesh's next turn, it provokes an opportunity attack from an ally of Ghesh's choice.

↯ **Hammer and Anvil** (weapon) ✦ **Encounter**
Attack: Melee 2 (one creature); +8 vs. Reflex
Hit: 1d10 + 5 damage. One ally adjacent to the target uses a free action to make a melee basic attack against the target. The ally gains a +3 bonus to his or her damage roll.

MOVE ACTIONS

⟿ **Knight's Move** ✦ **Encounter**
Effect: Ranged 10 (one ally). The target takes a move action.

MINOR ACTIONS

⬅ **Healing Word** (healing) ✦ **2/Encounter**
Effect: Close burst 5 (Ghesh or one ally in the burst). The target spends a healing surge.

⬅ **Dragon Breath** (fire) ✦ **Encounter**
Attack: Close blast 3 (creatures in the blast); +6 vs. Reflex
Hit: 1d6 + 2 fire damage.

Skills History +6, Intimidate +9
| Str 19 (+5) | Dex 12 (+2) | Wis 8 (+0) |
| Con 13 (+2) | Int 10 (+1) | Cha 16 (+4) |

Alignment lawful good **Languages** Common, Draconic
Equipment chainmail, longspear, adventurer's kit

Rook
Shadowy Killer

Rook is the quintessential product of the drow city Erelhei-Cinlu. On its treacherous streets, Rook learned to survive by any means he had, cultivating his natural talents and his knack for knifework to carve a path to freedom. With the city years behind him, Rook has become an assassin who asks no questions and does the job with a professional detachment.

Not especially tall and rather spare of frame, Rook conceals himself with a hooded gray cloak and dark clothing. He fights with blades and crossbow from hidden positions to take his enemies by surprise. He regards every situation as a potentially violent one, so he keeps to himself when not on a mission.

Rook makes no apologies for who he is and what he does. He is a pragmatist and never hesitates to do what it takes to get the job done. Rook does not make friends. Instead, he takes clients. Every arrangement is a business agreement, and he expects payment for the work he does.

battlefield experience gives him the wisdom to advise his comrades in all things, from the way they grip their weapons to the tactics they use in combat. Some people find Ghesh domineering, though none deny his expertise.

FOR THE DM: USING THE SAMPLE HENCHMEN

The henchmen included here are set at 2nd level. Use the rules in *Dungeon Master's Guide 2* to increase the level as needed. The descriptive elements give you enough to get started with these characters, but don't feel bound by them. Alter them as needed. Finally, be sure to give the character a secret to help ground the character in the campaign.

Rook	Level 2 Striker
Medium fey humanoid, drow	—
HP 29; **Bloodied** 14;	**Initiative** +5
Healing Surges 7; **Surge Value** 7	
AC 17, **Fortitude** 13, **Reflex** 17, **Will** 15	**Perception** +1
Speed 5	Darkvision

STANDARD ACTIONS

⊕ **Dagger** (weapon) ✦ **At-Will**
Attack: Melee 1 (one creature); +9 vs. AC
Hit: 1d4 + 5 damage.

⊙ **Hand Crossbow** (weapon) ✦ **At-Will**
Attack: Ranged 15/30 (one creature); +8 vs. AC
Hit: 1d6 + 5 damage.

↓ ⟳ **Sly Flourish** ✦ **At-Will**
Effect: Rook uses *dagger* or *hand crossbow*, and gains a +3 bonus to the damage roll.

⟳ **Impact Shot** (weapon) ✦ **Encounter**
Attack: Ranged 15/30 (one creature); +8 vs. AC
Hit: 2d6 + 5 damage, and Rook can push the target 1 square.

MOVE ACTIONS

Tumble ✦ **Encounter**
Effect: Rook shifts up to his speed.

MINOR ACTIONS

⟲ **Cloud of Darkness** ✦ **Encounter**
Effect: Close burst 1. The burst creates a cloud of darkness that remains in place until the end of Rook's next turn. The cloud blocks line of sight, squares within it are totally obscured, and creatures entirely within it are blinded until they exit. Rook is immune to these effects.

TRIGGERED ACTIONS

Striker's Edge ✦ **At-Will** (1/turn)
Trigger: Rook hits an enemy granting combat advantage to him.
Effect (No Action): The triggering attack deals 1d6 extra damage.

Skills Acrobatics +10, Intimidate +9, Stealth +10		
Str 10 (+1)	**Dex** 19 (+5)	**Wis** 11 (+1)
Con 12 (+2)	**Int** 10 (+1)	**Cha** 16 (+4)

Alignment unaligned   **Languages** Common, Elven
Equipment leather armor, 2 daggers, hand crossbow, 20 bolts, adventurer's kit

APPENDIX 2: MAGIC ITEM STORIES

In fantasy fiction, the protagonists often acquire enchanted objects that move the story forward. In some campaigns, however, magic items are often irrelevant to the plot, tending only to improve characters' mechanical abilities.

Yet even the lowliest magic items are created for a purpose. Artisans do not labor to craft an item of exceptional quality without intending for it to accomplish something extraordinary. Every magic item, even a *+1 magic dagger*, has a story, whether or not the party ever learns it.

Although it's certainly not necessary to define the history of all the items the characters obtain, every story created for an item adds color to the campaign world and the shared experience of the DM and the players. Using the rules for adding item levels as treasure (see the sidebar), the same *+1 magic dagger* a character acquires at the beginning of his or her career can become the world-renowned weapon he or she wields as part of his or her epic destiny. Such an item deserves a story.

The following lists present some sample story hooks and details that you can add to standard magic items to provide adventure ideas or to inspire a quest. You can also create your own hooks customized to your campaign setting.

SAMPLE STORY HOOKS

The item was or is . . .
1. Stolen from a king's treasury
2. Owned by a priest who sold his soul to devils
3. Found in the severed hand of its former owner
4. Inherited from a friend or a stranger
5. Once the property of a mighty war chief
6. Created to prevent a war; started one instead
7. A gift between lovers—a token of affection
8. The triumphant life's work of an amateur crafter
9. Sought after by powerful evil creatures
10. Created by a god
11. The container for a soul
12. One of a pair that seek to be reunited
13. Extraordinarily lucky or unlucky for its bearer
14. Made on another plane of existence
15. Once used to defeat a supremely powerful foe
16. Under constant surveillance by otherworldly beings
17. Occasionally wet with blood or tears
18. Part of a rare series of items crafted by a fabled smith
19. Owned by someone who is now a jealous ghost
20. Prophesied to cause either disaster or peace

SAMPLE ITEM DETAILS

The item (is) . . .
1. Covered in runes viewable only by starlight
2. Completely transparent
3. Etched with the symbol of a devil or demon
4. Inscribed with a date in the future
5. Topped with a gemlike eye that watches the bearer
6. Heavier than it should be
7. Well used; nicks and scratches score its surface
8. Well made; has been passed down over generations
9. Festooned with totemic feathers or tokens
10. Resonates continuously with low, unpleasant sound
11. Barbed and sharp-edged
12. Always looks dirty
13. Seems exceptionally fragile or delicate
14. Wholly or partially constructed from bone or flesh
15. Gives off a faint glow that cannot be dimmed
16. Exudes a fragrant or pungent odor when it is used
17. Permanently bloodstained
18. Inscribed with a famous name
19. Recites a verse or riddle when used
20. Always looks clean

APPENDIX 3: ITEM LEVELS AS TREASURE

Sometimes a magic item enters the campaign at the correct level, but a player wants her character to hold onto that item at higher levels rather than replacing it with a newer, higher-level item. You can allow the character to invest monetary treasure in Enchant Magic Item rituals to increase the item's power. Or, alternatively, item level increases can be given out as treasure.

Item levels granted as treasure follow the same guidelines as normal magic item placement. An increase in an item's enhancement bonus should be given out only when the characters have attained an appropriate level to earn magic items with the improved bonus.

MAGIC ITEM SCALING

Item Level	Enhancement Bonus
1-5	+1
6-10	+2
11-15	+3
16-20	+4
21-25	+5
26-30	+6

The value of an item's enhancement bonus increase equals the difference in cost between the item's lower-level form and its higher-level form. This value should be primarily subtracted from the magic items given out in an adventure, with only a small portion coming from gold or other monetary treasure.

For example, a character who has +1 *delver's armor* wants to increase the effectiveness of that armor rather than seek another set of more powerful armor. According to the table, that character should be of a level suitable for using 6th-level items before such an increase can occur. The difference in cost between +1 *delver's armor* and +2 *delver's armor* in the *Player's Handbook* is 2,720 gp—roughly the cost of a 7th-level magic item (2,600 gp). The item level can thus replace a 7th-level item normally placed as treasure, with the additional 120 gp taken out of monetary treasure. Likewise, the increase in the armor's enhancement bonus could partially take the place of an 8th-level treasure (worth 3,400 gp), with the difference (680 gp) made up by a 3rd-level magic item of use to the party.

This system can even be used to turn mundane items into magic items. A character's nonmagical heirloom longsword might be empowered by exposure to magic or a heroic deed to become a signature magic weapon.

APPENDIX 4: ITEM LISTS

The following section contains master lists for all the magic items in *Mordenkainen's Magnificent Emporium*. Items are sorted by level, by rarity (common, uncommon, or rare), and by type. Each level header indicates the price of items of that level. Each entry includes the page number on which the item can be found. Weapons and armor entries include information about the category of each item. Common items sell for 20 percent of their purchase value, while uncommon items sell for 50 percent of their purchase value. Rare items are highly prized, and sell for their full purchase value.

Level 1   360 gp

COMMON TOME

Magic tome +1		52

COMMON WONDROUS ITEMS

Eternal chalk		83
Restful bedroll		88

UNCOMMON WONDROUS ITEM

Mountebank's deck		87

UNCOMMON CONSUMABLE (20 gp each)

Potion of cure light wounds		96

Level 2   520 gp

UNCOMMON ROD

Rod of revenge +1		48

COMMON ARMOR

Armor of escape +1	Any	12
Robe of useful items +1	Cloth	17

COMMON WEAPONS

Lesser cloaked weapon +1	Any	29
Weapon of long range +1	Any ranged, any thrown	35

COMMON ROD

Rod of smiting +1		49

COMMON TOTEM

Totem of trailblazing +1		54

COMMON WAND

Apprentice's wand +1		54

COMMON ARMS SLOT ITEM

Tusk shield		62

COMMON HEAD SLOT ITEM

Reading spectacles		70

COMMON NECK SLOT ITEMS

Amulet of life protection +1		71
Lesser badge of the berserker +1		74

COMMON WONDROUS ITEMS

Backpack of concealment		80
Hunter's flint		86

COMMON CONSUMABLE (25 gp each)

Oil of lasting flame		99

Level 3   680 gp

UNCOMMON ARMOR

Ebon armor +1	Chain, scale, plate	14

UNCOMMON WEAPONS

Seeker weapon +1	Any ranged, any thrown	31
Shock spear +1	Spear	31
Weapon of accuracy +1	Any ranged, any thrown	35
Weapon of surrounding +1	Any melee	35

UNCOMMON STAFF

Staff of withering +1		51

UNCOMMON WAND

Wand of fear +1		55

COMMON ORB

Orb of forceful magic +1		45

COMMON WAND

Wand of inevitability +1		56

COMMON ARMS SLOT ITEM

Vanguard's shield	62

COMMON NECK SLOT ITEM

Periapt of health +1	75

COMMON WONDROUS ITEM

Floating lantern	84

Level 4   840 gp

RARE ROD

Rod of absorption +1	47

RARE WAND

Wand of frost +1	56

RARE HEAD SLOT ITEM

Exceptional factotum helm	67

UNCOMMON ARMOR

Wintersnap armor +1	Any	17

UNCOMMON WEAPONS

Lifestealer weapon +1	Any melee	29
Warning weapon +1	Any	33
Way-leader weapon +1	Spear	33
Weapon of defense +1	Any melee	34
Weapon of submission +1	Any melee	34

UNCOMMON KI FOCUS

Body of fire ki focus +1	44

UNCOMMON ORB

Orb of relentless sympathy +1	46

UNCOMMON STAFFS

Staff of command +1	50
Staff of striking +1	50

UNCOMMON ARMS SLOT ITEM

Ranging defender shield	61

UNCOMMON WONDROUS ITEM

Guardian's whistle	85

COMMON HOLY SYMBOL

Symbol of the sun +1	43

Level 5   1,000 gp

RARE ARMOR

Gloaming armor +1	Cloth, leather, hide	15

RARE WEAPON

Weapon of speed +1	Any ranged, any thrown	35

RARE TOTEM

Totem of the woodlands +1	54

RARE HEAD SLOT ITEM

Helm of seven deaths	69

UNCOMMON ARMOR

Armor of the charging wind +1	Cloth, leather, hide	13
Doppelganger armor +1	Any	14

UNCOMMON AMMUNITION (50 gp each)

Shadowshaft ammunition +1	37
Shiver-strike ammunition +1	37

UNCOMMON TOTEM

Totem of thorns +1	53

UNCOMMON WONDROUS ITEM

Chime of opening	81

UNCOMMON CONSUMABLES (50 gp each)

Elixir of clairvoyance	91
Elixir of protection from evil	94
Elixir of treasure finding	94
Potion of clarity	95
Scroll of protection	101
Vial of darkness	101

COMMON WONDROUS ITEMS

Enchanted reins	82
Instant campsite	86

COMMON CONSUMABLES (50 gp each)

Cryptspawn potion	90
Elixir of aptitude	90
Unreadable ink	101

Level 6   1,800 gp

RARE HANDS SLOT ITEM

Life-draining gauntlets	66

RARE HEAD SLOT ITEM

Eyes of charming	67

UNCOMMON WONDROUS ITEM

Nolzur's inkwell	88

UNCOMMON CONSUMABLE (75 gp each)

Elixir of invisibility	93

COMMON TOME

Magic tome +2	52

COMMON FEET SLOT ITEM

Shoes of water walking	64

COMMON WAIST SLOT ITEM

Baldric of time	78

COMMON WONDROUS ITEM

Climber's rope	81

COMMON CONSUMABLES (75 gp each)

Elixir of climbing	92
Lesser elixir of dragon breath	95
Trackless ashes	101

Level 7   2,600 gp

RARE WAND

Wand of wonder +2	57

RARE WAIST SLOT ITEM

Belt of dwarvenkind	79

RARE WONDROUS ITEM

Map of unseen lands	87

UNCOMMON ARMOR

Armor of dogged grit +2	Chain, scale, plate	12

UNCOMMON WEAPON

Giantslayer weapon +2	Any melee	27

UNCOMMON ORB

Orb of enduring magic +2	45

UNCOMMON ROD

Rod of revenge +2	48

UNCOMMON STAFF

Staff of the viper +2	50

UNCOMMON FEET SLOT ITEM

Boots of elvenkind	63

UNCOMMON WONDROUS ITEMS

Bottled smoke	80
Decanter of endless water	82
Pearl of power	88

UNCOMMON CONSUMABLE (100 gp each)

Nolzur's marvelous pigments	99

COMMON ARMOR

Armor of escape +2	Any	12
Robe of useful items +2	Cloth	17

COMMON WEAPONS

Lesser cloaked weapon +2	Any	29
Weapon of long range +2	Any ranged, any thrown	35

COMMON ROD

Rod of smiting +2	49

COMMON TOTEM

Totem of trailblazing +2	54

COMMON WAND

Apprentice's wand +2	54

COMMON HEAD SLOT ITEM

Crown of leaves	67

COMMON NECK SLOT ITEMS

Amulet of life protection +2	71
Lesser badge of the berserker +2	74

Level 8   3,400 gp

RARE WEAPON

Frost brand weapon +2	Any melee	26

RARE WANDS

Wand of conjuring +2	55
Wand of lightning +2	56

RARE WONDROUS ITEM

Crystal ball	81

UNCOMMON ARMOR

Ebon armor +2	Chain, scale, plate	14

UNCOMMON WEAPONS

Seeker weapon +2	Any ranged, any thrown	31
Shock spear +2	Spear	31
Weapon of accuracy +2	Any ranged, any thrown	35
Weapon of surrounding +2	Any melee	35

UNCOMMON AMMUNITION (125 gp each)

Reaving ammunition +2	37

UNCOMMON HOLY SYMBOL

Candle of invocation +2	42

UNCOMMON KI FOCUS

Tidal wave ki focus +2	45

UNCOMMON ROD

Rod of death +2	48

UNCOMMON STAFF

Staff of withering +2	51

UNCOMMON WAND

Wand of fear +2	55

UNCOMMON ARMS SLOT ITEM

Greater storm shield	60
Twilight shield	62

UNCOMMON CONSUMABLES (125 gp each)

Dust of disappearance	98
Elixir of chameleon power	91
Elixir of defense	92
Elixir of levitation	93
Oil of red flame	99

COMMON ARMOR

Fishscale armor +2	Hide, scale	15

COMMON WEAPON

Punishing weapon +2	Any	31

COMMON ORB

Orb of forceful magic +2	45

COMMON TOME

Tome of undeniable might +2	53

COMMON WAND

Wand of inevitability +2	56

COMMON FEET SLOT ITEM

Shoes of the tireless gait	64

COMMON NECK SLOT ITEM

Periapt of health +2	75

COMMON CONSUMABLES (125 gp each)

Elixir of accuracy	90
Elixir of water breathing	95
Powder of appearance	99

Level 9   4,200 gp

RARE WEAPON

True dragonslayer weapon +2	Any	32

RARE ROD

Rod of absorption +2	47

RARE TOME

Manual of puissant skill +2	52

RARE WAND

Wand of frost +2	56

RARE FEET SLOT ITEM

Boots of leaping	63

UNCOMMON ARMOR

Armor of scintillating colors +2	Cloth, leather, hide, chain	12
Blending armor +2	Any	13
Shallow grave armor +2	Any	17
Wintersnap armor +2	Any	17

UNCOMMON WEAPONS

Lifestealer weapon +2	Any melee	29
Stinging spear +2	Spear	32
Warning weapon +2	Any	33
Way-leader weapon +2	Spear	33
Weapon of defense +2	Any melee	34
Weapon of submission +2	Any melee	34

UNCOMMON KI FOCUS

Body of fire ki focus +2	44

UNCOMMON ORB

Orb of relentless sympathy +2	46

UNCOMMON STAFFS

Staff of command +2	50
Staff of striking +2	50

UNCOMMON ARMS SLOT ITEM

Gleaming diamond bracers	60

UNCOMMON FEET SLOT ITEMS

Boots of levitation	63
Halfling boots	64

UNCOMMON HANDS SLOT ITEM

Gauntlets of remote action	65

UNCOMMON NECK SLOT ITEM

Sneak's cloak +2	75

UNCOMMON WONDROUS ITEM

Elven chain shirt	82

UNCOMMON CONSUMABLES (160 gp each)

Elixir of giant strength	93
Potion of regeneration	97

COMMON HOLY SYMBOL

Symbol of the sun +2	43

COMMON KI FOCUS

Steadfast stone ki focus +2	44

COMMON NECK SLOT ITEM

Brooch of unerring defense +2	71

COMMON WONDROUS ITEMS

Endless quiver	83
Map of orienteering	87

Level 10   5,000 gp

RARE ARMOR

Gloaming armor +2	Cloth, leather, hide	15

RARE WEAPONS

Flame tongue weapon +2	Heavy blade, light blade	26
Mace of disruption +2	Mace	29
Weapon of speed +2	Any ranged, any thrown	35

RARE HOLY SYMBOL

Necklace of prayer beads +2	42

RARE ROD

Rod of beguiling +2	48

RARE TOME

Emerald tome of the devourer +2	51

RARE TOTEM

Totem of the woodlands +2	54

RARE CONSUMABLE (200 gp each)

Elixir of luck	93

UNCOMMON ARMOR

Armor of the charging wind +2	Cloth, leather, hide	13
Doppelganger armor +2	Any	14

UNCOMMON AMMUNITION (200 gp each)

Firesight ammunition +2	36
Shadowshaft ammunition +2	37
Shiver-strike ammunition +2	37

UNCOMMON TOTEM

| Totem of thorns +2 | 53 |

UNCOMMON NECK SLOT ITEMS

| Amulet of aranea +2 | 71 |
| Cloak of displacement +2 | 72 |

UNCOMMON WAIST SLOT ITEM

| Diamond cincture | 79 |

UNCOMMON WONDROUS ITEM

| Flask of the veiled horde | 83 |

UNCOMMON CONSUMABLES (200 gp each)

Potion of clarity	95
Potion of cure moderate wounds	96
Potion of lesser haste	97
Scroll of protection	101

COMMON HANDS SLOT ITEM

| Gauntlets of swimming and climbing | 65 |

COMMON HEAD SLOT ITEM

| Helm of languages | 68 |

COMMON WONDROUS ITEMS

| Lens of discernment | 86 |
| Spymaster's quill | 89 |

COMMON CONSUMABLES (200 gp each)

| Lesser elixir of speed | 95 |
| Potion of invulnerability | 97 |

Level 11   9,000 gp

UNCOMMON HEAD SLOT ITEM

| Eyes of the eagle | 67 |

UNCOMMON WAIST SLOT ITEM

| Healer's sash | 79 |

UNCOMMON WONDROUS ITEM

| Unfettered thieves' tools | 89 |

UNCOMMON CONSUMABLE (350 gp each)

| Elixir of flying | 92 |

COMMON TOME

| Magic tome +3 | 52 |

COMMON ARMS SLOT ITEM

| Bracers of infinite blades | 60 |

COMMON WAIST SLOT ITEM

| Survivor's belt | 80 |

Level 12   13,000 gp

RARE WAND

| Wand of wonder +3 | 57 |

UNCOMMON ARMOR

| Armor of dogged grit +3 | Chain, scale, plate | 12 |
| Hide of worms +3 | Leather, hide | 16 |

UNCOMMON WEAPONS

| Giantslayer weapon +3 | Any melee | 27 |
| Hammer of storms +3 | Hammer | 28 |

UNCOMMON AMMUNITION (500 gp each)

| Foe-seeker ammunition +3 | 36 |

UNCOMMON ORB

| Orb of enduring magic +3 | 45 |

UNCOMMON ROD

| Rod of revenge +3 | 48 |

UNCOMMON STAFF

| Staff of the viper +3 | 50 |

UNCOMMON WONDROUS ITEM

| Gem of seeing | 84 |

UNCOMMON CONSUMABLES (500 gp each)

Elixir of gaseous form	92
Quaal's feather anchor	100
Quaal's feather sail	100

COMMON ARMOR

| Armor of escape +3 | Any | 12 |
| Robe of useful items +3 | Cloth | 17 |

COMMON WEAPONS

| Lesser cloaked weapon +3 | Any | 29 |
| Weapon of long range +3 | Any ranged, any thrown | 35 |

COMMON ROD

| Rod of smiting +3 | 49 |

COMMON TOTEM

| Totem of trailblazing +3 | 54 |

COMMON WAND

| Apprentice's wand +3 | 54 |

COMMON NECK SLOT ITEMS

| Amulet of life protection +3 | 71 |
| Lesser badge of the berserker +3 | 74 |

COMMON RING

| Lesser ring of feather fall | 76 |

Level 13   17,000 gp

RARE WEAPONS

Captain's weapon +3	Any melee	25
Frost brand weapon +3	Any melee	26

RARE WANDS

Wand of conjuring +3	55
Wand of lightning +3	56
Wand of thunder +3	57

RARE ARMS SLOT ITEM

Greater stonewall shield	60

UNCOMMON ARMOR

Ebon armor +3	Chain, scale, plate	14

UNCOMMON WEAPONS

Seeker weapon +3	Any ranged, any thrown	31
Shock spear +3	Spear	31
Weapon of accuracy +3	Any ranged, any thrown	35
Weapon of surrounding +3	Any melee	35

UNCOMMON AMMUNITION (650 gp each)

Reaving ammunition +3	37

UNCOMMON HOLY SYMBOL

Candle of invocation +3	42

UNCOMMON KI FOCUS

Tidal wave ki focus +3	45

UNCOMMON ROD

Rod of death +3	48

UNCOMMON STAFF

Staff of withering +3	51

UNCOMMON WAND

Wand of fear +3	55

UNCOMMON ARMS SLOT ITEM

Searing shield	61

UNCOMMON FEET SLOT ITEM

Boots of the shadowed path	63

UNCOMMON NECK SLOT ITEM

Greater talisman of repulsion +3	74

UNCOMMON WONDROUS ITEM

Iron bands of Bilarro	86

UNCOMMON CONSUMABLE (650 gp each)

Elixir of defense	92

COMMON ARMOR

Fishscale armor +3	Hide, scale	15

COMMON WEAPON

Punishing weapon +3	Any	31

COMMON ORB

Orb of forceful magic +3	45

COMMON TOME

Tome of undeniable might +3	53

COMMON WAND

Wand of inevitability +3	56

COMMON NECK SLOT ITEM

Periapt of health +3	75

COMMON CONSUMABLE (650 gp each)

Elixir of accuracy	90

Level 14   21,000 gp

RARE ARMOR

Greater armor of eyes +3	Any	15

RARE WEAPONS

True dragonslayer weapon +3	Any	32
Wind weapon +3	Any melee	35

RARE HOLY SYMBOL

Phylactery of faithfulness +3	43

RARE ROD

Rod of absorption +3	47

RARE TOMES

Manual of expansive learning +3	52
Manual of puissant skill +3	52

RARE WAND

Wand of frost +3	56

RARE HEAD SLOT ITEM

Exceptional factotum helm	67

RARE RING

Incendiary ring of fireblazing	76

UNCOMMON ARMOR

Armor of scintillating colors +3	Cloth, leather, hide, chain	12
Blending armor +3	Any	13
Shallow grave armor +3	Any	17
Wintersnap armor +3	Any	17

UNCOMMON WEAPONS

Lifestealer weapon +3	Any melee	29
Stinging spear +3	Spear	32
Warning weapon +3	Any	33
Way-leader weapon +3	Spear	33
Weapon of defense +3	Any melee	34
Weapon of submission +3	Any melee	34

UNCOMMON AMMUNITION (800 gp each)

Stonehold ammunition +3	37

UNCOMMON KI FOCUS

Body of fire ki focus +3	44

UNCOMMON ORBS

Orb of relentless sympathy +3	46
Stone of good luck +3	47

UNCOMMON STAFFS

Staff of command +3	50
Staff of striking +3	50

UNCOMMON NECK SLOT ITEMS

Cloak of the shadowthief +3	73
Cloak of the stalking shadow +3	73
Sneak's cloak +3	75

COMMON HOLY SYMBOL

Symbol of the sun +3	43

COMMON KI FOCUS

Steadfast stone ki focus +3	44

COMMON NECK SLOT ITEM

Brooch of unerring defense +3	71

COMMON WAIST SLOT ITEM

Cincture of vivacity	79

Level 15   25,000 gp

RARE ARMOR

Gloaming armor +3	Cloth, leather, hide	15

RARE WEAPONS

Flame tongue weapon +3	Heavy blade, light blade	26
Greater dancing weapon +3	Any melee	27
Greater luckblade +3	Heavy blade, light blade	28
Mace of disruption +3	Mace	29
Mighty dwarven thrower +3	Hammer	30
Weapon of speed +3	Any ranged, any thrown	35

RARE HOLY SYMBOL

Necklace of prayer beads +3	42

RARE ORB

Prismatic orb +3	46

RARE ROD

Rod of beguiling +3	48

RARE TOME

Emerald tome of the devourer +3	51

RARE TOTEM

Totem of the woodlands +3	54

RARE WAND

Wand of fire +3	55

RARE HEAD SLOT ITEM

Helm of teleportation	69

RARE NECK SLOT ITEMS

Greater medallion of the mind +3	73
Greater necklace of fireballs +3	74

UNCOMMON ARMOR

Armor of the charging wind +3	Cloth, leather, hide	13
Doppelganger armor +3	Any	14

UNCOMMON AMMUNITION (1,000 gp each)

Firesight ammunition +3	36
Shadowshaft ammunition +3	37
Shiver-strike ammunition +3	37

UNCOMMON TOTEM

Totem of thorns +3	53

UNCOMMON ARMS SLOT ITEM

Shield of aversion	62

UNCOMMON HANDS SLOT ITEM

Gloves of missile snaring	65

UNCOMMON NECK SLOT ITEMS

Amulet of aranea +3	71
Cloak of displacement +3	72
Periapt of wound closure +3	75

UNCOMMON WONDROUS ITEMS

Broom of flying	80
Chime of opening	81
True portable hole	89

UNCOMMON CONSUMABLES (1,000 gp each)

Bead of force	98
Elixir of clairvoyance	91
Elixir of protection from evil	94
Elixir of treasure finding	94
Potion of clarity	95
Scroll of protection	101

COMMON WONDROUS ITEMS

Flying hook	84
Pouches of shared acquisition	88

COMMON CONSUMABLES (1,000 gp each)

Cryptspawn potion	90
Elixir of aptitude	90

Level 16   45,000 gp

RARE HANDS SLOT ITEM
Life-draining gauntlets	66

RARE HEAD SLOT ITEM
Eyes of charming	67

UNCOMMON CONSUMABLES (1,800 gp each)
Elixir of invisibility	93
Potion of heroism	96
Quaal's feather pigeon	100

COMMON TOME
Magic tome +4	52

COMMON ARMS SLOT ITEM
Bracers of infinite blades	60

COMMON WAIST SLOT ITEM
Baldric of time	78

COMMON WONDROUS ITEM
Gem of auditory recollection	84

COMMON CONSUMABLES (1,800 gp each)
Elixir of climbing	92
Lesser elixir of dragon breath	95

Level 17   65,000 gp

RARE WAND
Wand of wonder +4	57

RARE HANDS SLOT ITEM
True gauntlets of ogre power	66

RARE WONDROUS ITEM
Greater horn of blasting	85

UNCOMMON ARMOR
Armor of dogged grit +4	Chain, scale, plate	12
Hide of worms +4	Leather, hide	16
Plate mail of etherealness +4	Plate	16

UNCOMMON WEAPONS
Giantslayer weapon +4	Any melee	27
Hammer of storms +4	Hammer	28

UNCOMMON AMMUNITION (2,600 gp each)
Armor-sapping ammunition +4	36
Foe-seeker ammunition +4	36

UNCOMMON ORB
Orb of enduring magic +4	45

UNCOMMON ROD
Rod of revenge +4	48

UNCOMMON STAFF
Staff of the viper +4	50

UNCOMMON FEET SLOT ITEM
Boots of elvenkind	63

UNCOMMON NECK SLOT ITEM
Scarab of insanity +4	75

UNCOMMON RING
Ring of borrowed spells	76

UNCOMMON WONDROUS ITEMS
Bottled smoke	80
Pearl of power	88

UNCOMMON CONSUMABLES (2,600 gp each)
Elixir of phasing	94
Potion of shadow's essence	97

COMMON ARMOR
Armor of escape +4	Any	12
Robe of useful items +4	Cloth	17

COMMON WEAPONS
Lesser cloaked weapon +4	Any	29
Weapon of long range +4	Any ranged, any thrown	35

COMMON ROD
Rod of smiting +4	49

COMMON TOTEM
Totem of trailblazing +4	54

COMMON WAND
Apprentice's wand +4	54

COMMON HANDS SLOT ITEM
Hero's gauntlets	65

COMMON NECK SLOT ITEMS
Amulet of life protection +4	71
Lesser badge of the berserker +4	74

Level 18   85,000 gp

RARE ARMOR
Blessed armor of Kord +4	Chain, scale, plate	14

RARE WEAPONS
Captain's weapon +4	Any melee	25
Frost brand weapon +4	Any melee	26
Maul of the titans +4	Hammer	30

RARE WANDS
Wand of conjuring +4	55
Wand of lightning +4	56
Wand of thunder +4	57

RARE HEAD SLOT ITEM
Helm of brilliance	68

RARE NECK SLOT ITEM
Cloak of the manta ray +4	72

RARE WONDROUS ITEM
Crystal ball	81

UNCOMMON ARMOR

Ebon armor +4	Chain, scale, plate	14

UNCOMMON WEAPONS

Seeker weapon +4	Any ranged, any thrown	31
Shock spear +4	Spear	31
Weapon of accuracy +4	Any ranged, any thrown	35
Weapon of surrounding +4	Any melee	35

UNCOMMON AMMUNITION (3,400 gp each)

Reaving ammunition +4	37

UNCOMMON HOLY SYMBOL

Candle of invocation +4	42

UNCOMMON KI FOCUS

Tidal wave ki focus +4	45

UNCOMMON ROD

Rod of death +4	48

UNCOMMON STAFF

Staff of withering +4	51

UNCOMMON WAND

Wand of fear +4	55

UNCOMMON ARMS SLOT ITEM

Greater storm shield	60

UNCOMMON NECK SLOT ITEM

Greater talisman of repulsion +4	74

UNCOMMON WONDROUS ITEM

Iron bands of Bilarro	86

UNCOMMON CONSUMABLES (3,400 gp each)

Elixir of defense	92
Oil of red flame	99

COMMON ARMOR

Fishscale armor +4	Hide, scale	15

COMMON WEAPON

Punishing weapon +4	Any	31

COMMON ORB

Orb of forceful magic +4	45

COMMON TOME

Tome of undeniable might +4	53

COMMON WAND

Wand of inevitability +4	56

COMMON NECK SLOT ITEM

Periapt of health +4	75

COMMON CONSUMABLES (3,400 gp each)

Elixir of accuracy	90
Elixir of water breathing	95

Level 19   105,000 gp

RARE ARMOR

Greater armor of eyes +4	Any	15

RARE WEAPONS

True dragonslayer weapon +4	Any	32
Wind weapon +4	Any melee	35

RARE HOLY SYMBOL

Phylactery of faithfulness +4	43

RARE ROD

Rod of absorption +4	47

RARE TOMES

Manual of expansive learning +4	52
Manual of puissant skill +4	52

RARE WAND

Wand of frost +4	56

UNCOMMON ARMOR

Armor of scintillating colors +4	Cloth, leather, hide, chain	12
Blending armor +4	Any	13
Shallow grave armor +4	Any	17
Wintersnap armor +4	Any	17

UNCOMMON WEAPONS

Lifestealer weapon +4	Any melee	29
Stinging spear +4	Spear	32
Warning weapon +4	Any	33
Way-leader weapon +4	Spear	33
Weapon of defense +4	Any melee	34
Weapon of submission +4	Any melee	34

UNCOMMON AMMUNITION (4,200 gp each)

Stonehold ammunition +4	37

UNCOMMON KI FOCUS

Body of fire ki focus +4	44

UNCOMMON ORBS

Orb of relentless sympathy +4	46
Stone of good luck +4	47

UNCOMMON STAFFS

Staff of command +4	50
Staff of striking +4	50

UNCOMMON ARMS SLOT ITEM

Gleaming diamond bracers	60

UNCOMMON NECK SLOT ITEMS

Cloak of the shadowthief +4	73
Cloak of the stalking shadow +4	73
Sneak's cloak +4	75

UNCOMMON WONDROUS ITEM

Elven chain shirt	82

UNCOMMON CONSUMABLES (4,200 gp each)

Elixir of giant strength	93
Potion of regeneration	99

COMMON HOLY SYMBOL

Symbol of the sun +4	43

COMMON KI FOCUS

Steadfast stone ki focus +4	44

COMMON NECK SLOT ITEM

Brooch of unerring defense +4	71

Level 20   125,000 gp

RARE ARMOR

Gloaming armor +4	Cloth, leather, hide	15
Robe of the archmage +4	Cloth	16

RARE WEAPONS

Flame tongue weapon +4	Heavy blade, light blade	26
Greater dancing weapon +4	Any melee	27
Greater luckblade +4	Heavy blade, light blade	28
Mace of disruption +4	Mace	29
Mighty dwarven thrower +4	Hammer	30
Weapon of speed +4	Any ranged, any thrown	35

RARE HOLY SYMBOL

Necklace of prayer beads +4	42

RARE ORB

Prismatic orb +4	46

RARE ROD

Rod of beguiling +4	48

RARE TOME

Emerald tome of the devourer +4	51

RARE TOTEM

Totem of the woodlands +4	54

RARE WAND

Wand of fire +4	55

RARE NECK SLOT ITEMS

Greater medallion of the mind +4	73
Greater necklace of fireballs +4	74

RARE WONDROUS ITEM

Greater flying carpet	85

UNCOMMON ARMOR

Armor of the charging wind +4	Cloth, leather, hide	13
Doppelganger armor +4	Any	14

UNCOMMON AMMUNITION (5,000 gp each)

Firesight ammunition +4	36
Shadowshaft ammunition +4	37
Shiver-strike ammunition +4	37

UNCOMMON TOTEM

Totem of thorns +4	53

UNCOMMON NECK SLOT ITEMS

Amulet of aranea +4	71
Cloak of displacement +4	72
Cloak of the phoenix +4	72
Periapt of wound closure +4	75

UNCOMMON WAIST SLOT ITEM

Diamond cincture	79

UNCOMMON CONSUMABLES (5,000 gp each)

Bead of force	98
Potion of clarity	95
Potion of cure critical wounds	95
Scroll of protection	101

COMMON CONSUMABLE (5,000 gp each)

Potion of invulnerability	97

Level 21   225,000 gp

RARE HEAD SLOT ITEMS

Ioun stone of agility	70
Ioun stone of allure	70
Ioun stone of insight	70
Ioun stone of intellect	70
Ioun stone of might	70
Ioun stone of vigor	70

RARE RING

Ring of humanoid influence	77

UNCOMMON HEAD SLOT ITEM

Eyes of the eagle	67

UNCOMMON RING

Ring of resourceful wizardry	77

UNCOMMON WAIST SLOT ITEM

Healer's sash	79

UNCOMMON CONSUMABLE (9,000 gp each)

Elixir of flying	92

COMMON TOME

Magic tome +5	52

COMMON ARMS SLOT ITEM

Bracers of infinite blades	60

COMMON HEAD SLOT ITEM

Ioun stone of sustenance	70

COMMON WAIST SLOT ITEM

Baldric of valor	79

Level 22   325,000 gp

RARE WAND
Wand of wonder +5	57

RARE HEAD SLOT ITEM
Ioun stone of perfect language	70

RARE WONDROUS ITEMS
Daern's instant fortress	82
Greater horn of blasting	85

UNCOMMON ARMOR
Armor of dogged grit +5	Chain, scale, plate	12
Hide of worms +5	Leather, hide	16
Plate mail of etherealness +5	Plate	16

UNCOMMON WEAPONS
Giantslayer weapon +5	Any melee	27
Hammer of storms +5	Hammer	28

UNCOMMON AMMUNITION (13,000 gp each)
Armor-sapping ammunition +5	36
Foe-seeker ammunition +5	36

UNCOMMON ORB
Orb of enduring magic +5	45

UNCOMMON ROD
Rod of revenge +5	48

UNCOMMON STAFF
Staff of the viper +5	50

UNCOMMON NECK SLOT ITEM
Scarab of insanity +5	75

COMMON ARMOR
Armor of escape +5	Any	12
Robe of useful items +5	Cloth	17

COMMON WEAPONS
Lesser cloaked weapon +5	Any	29
Weapon of long range +5	Any ranged, any thrown	35

COMMON ROD
Rod of smiting +5	49

COMMON TOTEM
Totem of trailblazing +5	54

COMMON WAND
Apprentice's wand +5	54

COMMON NECK SLOT ITEMS
Amulet of life protection +5	71
Lesser badge of the berserker +5	74

Level 23   425,000 gp

RARE ARMOR
Blessed armor of Kord +5	Chain, scale, plate	14

RARE WEAPONS
Captain's weapon +5	Any melee	25
Frost brand weapon +5	Any melee	26
Maul of the titans +5	Hammer	30

RARE WANDS
Wand of conjuration +5	55
Wand of lightning +5	56
Wand of thunder +5	57

RARE ARMS SLOT ITEMS
Greater stonewall shield	60
Shield of the doomed	62

RARE HEAD SLOT ITEM
Helm of brilliance	68

RARE NECK SLOT ITEM
Cloak of the manta ray +5	72

UNCOMMON ARMOR
Ebon armor +5	Chain, scale, plate	14

UNCOMMON WEAPONS
Seeker weapon +5	Any ranged, any thrown	31
Shock spear +5	Spear	31
Weapon of accuracy +5	Any ranged, any thrown	35
Weapon of surrounding +5	Any melee	35

UNCOMMON AMMUNITION (17,000 gp each)
Reaving ammunition +5	37

UNCOMMON HOLY SYMBOL
Candle of invocation +5	42

UNCOMMON KI FOCUS
Tidal wave ki focus +5	45

UNCOMMON ROD
Rod of death +5	48

UNCOMMON STAFF
Staff of withering +5	51

UNCOMMON WAND
Wand of fear +5	55

UNCOMMON NECK SLOT ITEM
Greater talisman of repulsion +5	74

UNCOMMON WONDROUS ITEM
Iron bands of Bilarro	86

UNCOMMON CONSUMABLES (17,000 gp each)
Elixir of defense	92

COMMON ARMOR
Fishscale armor +5	Hide, scale	15

COMMON WEAPON

Punishing weapon +5	Any	31

COMMON ORB

Orb of forceful magic +5	45

COMMON TOME

Tome of undeniable might +5	53

COMMON WAND

Wand of inevitability +5	56

COMMON NECK SLOT ITEM

Periapt of health +5	75

COMMON CONSUMABLE (17,000 gp each)

Elixir of accuracy	90

Level 24   525,000 gp

RARE ARMOR

Greater armor of eyes +5	Any	15

RARE WEAPONS

True dragonslayer weapon +5	Any	32
Wind weapon +5	Any melee	35

RARE HOLY SYMBOL

Phylactery of faithfulness +5	43

RARE ROD

Rod of absorption +5	47

RARE TOMES

Manual of expansive learning +5	52
Manual of puissant skill +5	52

RARE WAND

Wand of frost +5	56

RARE HEAD SLOT ITEM

Exceptional factotum helm	67

UNCOMMON ARMOR

Armor of scintillating colors +5	Cloth, leather, hide, chain	12
Blending armor +5	Any	13
Shallow grave armor +5	Any	17
Wintersnap armor +5	Any	17

UNCOMMON WEAPONS

Lifestealer weapon +5	Any melee	29
Stinging spear +5	Spear	32
Warning weapon +5	Any	33
Way-leader weapon +5	Spear	33
Weapon of defense +5	Any melee	34
Weapon of submission +5	Any melee	34

UNCOMMON AMMUNITION (21,000 gp each)

Stonehold ammunition +5	37

UNCOMMON KI FOCUS

Body of fire ki focus +5	44

UNCOMMON ORBS

Orb of relentless sympathy +5	46
Stone of good luck +5	47

UNCOMMON STAFFS

Staff of command +5	50
Staff of striking +5	50

UNCOMMON ARMS SLOT ITEM

Ranging defender shield	61

UNCOMMON NECK SLOT ITEMS

Cloak of the shadowthief +5	73
Cloak of the stalking shadow +5	73
Sneak's cloak +5	75

COMMON HOLY SYMBOL

Symbol of the sun +5	43

COMMON KI FOCUS

Steadfast stone ki focus +5	44

COMMON NECK SLOT ITEM

Brooch of unerring defense +5	71

Level 25   625,000 gp

RARE ARMOR

Gloaming armor +5	Cloth, leather, hide	15
Robe of the archmage +5	Cloth	16

RARE WEAPONS

Flame tongue weapon +5	Heavy blade, light blade	26
Greater dancing weapon +5	Any melee	27
Greater luckblade +5	Heavy blade, light blade	28
Mace of disruption +5	Mace	29
Mighty dwarven thrower +5	Hammer	30
Weapon of speed +5	Any ranged, any thrown	35

RARE HOLY SYMBOL

Necklace of prayer beads +5	42

RARE ORB

Prismatic orb +5	46

RARE ROD

Rod of beguiling +5	48

RARE STAFF

Greater staff of power +5	49

RARE TOME

Emerald tome of the devourer +5	51

RARE TOTEM

Totem of the woodlands +5	54

RARE WAND

Wand of fire +5	55

RARE HEAD SLOT ITEM

Helm of teleportation	69

RARE NECK SLOT ITEMS

Greater medallion of the mind +5	73
Greater necklace of fireballs +5	74

RARE RING

Ring of X-ray vision	77

UNCOMMON ARMOR

Armor of the charging wind +5	Cloth, leather, hide	13
Doppelganger armor +5	Any	14

UNCOMMON AMMUNITION (25,000 gp each)

Firesight ammunition +5	36
Shadowshaft ammunition +5	37
Shiver-strike ammunition +5	37

UNCOMMON TOTEM

Totem of thorns +5	53

UNCOMMON NECK SLOT ITEMS

Amulet of aranea +5	71
Cloak of displacement +5	72
Cloak of the phoenix +5	72
Periapt of wound closure +5	75

UNCOMMON WONDROUS ITEM

Chime of opening	81

UNCOMMON CONSUMABLES (25,000 gp each)

Bead of force	98
Elixir of clairvoyance	91
Elixir of protection from evil	94
Elixir of treasure finding	94
Potion of clarity	95
Scroll of protection	101

COMMON CONSUMABLES (25,000 gp each)

Cryptspawn potion	90
Elixir of aptitude	90

Level 26   1,125,000 gp

RARE HANDS SLOT ITEM

Life-draining gauntlets	66

RARE HEAD SLOT ITEM

Eyes of charming	67

UNCOMMON CONSUMABLE (45,000 gp each)

Potion of heroism	96

COMMON TOME

Magic tome +6	52

COMMON ARMS SLOT ITEM

Bracers of infinite blades	60

COMMON CONSUMABLES (45,000 gp each)

Elixir of climbing	92
Lesser elixir of dragon breath	95

Level 27   1,625,000 gp

RARE WAND

Wand of wonder +6	57

RARE WONDROUS ITEM

Greater horn of blasting	85

UNCOMMON ARMOR

Armor of dogged grit +6	Chain, scale, plate	12
Hide of worms +6	Leather, hide	16
Plate mail of etherealness +6	Plate	16

UNCOMMON WEAPONS

Giantslayer weapon +6	Any melee	27
Hammer of storms +6	Hammer	28

UNCOMMON AMMUNITION (65,000 gp each)

Armor-sapping ammunition +6	36
Foe-seeker ammunition +6	36

UNCOMMON ORB

Orb of enduring magic +6	45

UNCOMMON ROD

Rod of revenge +6	48

UNCOMMON STAFF

Staff of the viper +6	50

UNCOMMON FEET SLOT ITEM

Boots of elvenkind	63

UNCOMMON NECK SLOT ITEM

Scarab of insanity +6	75

UNCOMMON WONDROUS ITEM

Pearl of power	88

COMMON ARMOR

Armor of escape +6	Any	12
Robe of useful items +6	Cloth	17

COMMON WEAPONS

Lesser cloaked weapon +6	Any	29
Weapon of long range +6	Any ranged, any thrown	35

COMMON ROD

Rod of smiting +6	49

COMMON TOTEM

Totem of trailblazing +6	54

COMMON WAND

Apprentice's wand +6	54

COMMON HANDS SLOT ITEM

Hero's gauntlets	65

COMMON NECK SLOT ITEMS

Amulet of life protection +6	71
Lesser badge of the berserker +6	74

Level 28   2,125,000 gp

RARE ARMOR

Blessed armor of Kord +6	Chain, scale, plate	14

RARE WEAPONS

Captain's weapon +6	Any melee	25
Frost brand weapon +6	Any melee	26
Maul of the titans +6	Hammer	30

RARE WANDS

Wand of conjuring +6	55
Wand of lightning +6	56
Wand of thunder +6	57

RARE HEAD SLOT ITEM

Helm of brilliance	68

RARE NECK SLOT ITEM

Cloak of the manta ray +6	72

RARE WONDROUS ITEM

Crystal ball	81

UNCOMMON ARMOR

Ebon armor +6	Chain, scale, plate	14

UNCOMMON WEAPONS

Seeker weapon +6	Any ranged, any thrown	31
Shock spear +6	Spear	31
Weapon of accuracy +6	Any ranged, any thrown	35
Weapon of surrounding +6	Any melee	35

UNCOMMON AMMUNITION (85,000 gp each)

Reaving ammunition +6	37

UNCOMMON HOLY SYMBOL

Candle of invocation +6	42

UNCOMMON KI FOCUS

Tidal wave ki focus +6	45

UNCOMMON ROD

Rod of death +6	48

UNCOMMON STAFF

Staff of withering +6	51

UNCOMMON WAND

Wand of fear +6	55

UNCOMMON ARMS SLOT ITEM

Greater storm shield	60

UNCOMMON NECK SLOT ITEM

Greater talisman of repulsion +6	74

UNCOMMON WONDROUS ITEM

Iron bands of Bilarro	86

UNCOMMON CONSUMABLES (85,000 gp each)

Elixir of defense	92
Oil of red flame	99

COMMON ARMOR

Fishscale armor +6	Hide, scale	15

COMMON WEAPON

Punishing weapon +6	Any	31

COMMON ORB

Orb of forceful magic +6	45

COMMON TOME

Tome of undeniable might +6	53

COMMON WAND

Wand of inevitability +6	56

COMMON NECK SLOT ITEM

Periapt of health +6	75

COMMON CONSUMABLE (85,000 gp each)

Elixir of accuracy	90

Level 29   2,625,000 gp

RARE ARMOR

Greater armor of eyes +6	Any	15

RARE WEAPONS

True dragonslayer weapon +6	Any	32
Wind weapon +6	Any melee	35

RARE HOLY SYMBOL

Phylactery of faithfulness +6	43

RARE ROD

Rod of absorption +6	47

RARE TOMES

Manual of expansive learning +6	52
Manual of puissant skill +6	52

RARE WAND

Wand of frost +6	56

UNCOMMON ARMOR

Armor of scintillating colors +6	Cloth, leather, hide, chain	12
Blending armor +6	Any	13
Shallow grave armor +6	Any	17
Wintersnap armor +6	Any	17

UNCOMMON WEAPONS

Lifestealer weapon +6	Any melee	29
Stinging spear +6	Spear	32
Warning weapon +6	Any	33
Way-leader weapon +6	Spear	33
Weapon of defense +6	Any melee	34
Weapon of submission +6	Any melee	34

UNCOMMON AMMUNITION (105,000 gp each)

Stonehold ammunition +6	37

UNCOMMON KI FOCUS

Body of fire ki focus +6	44

UNCOMMON ORBS

Orb of relentless sympathy +6	46
Stone of good luck +6	47

UNCOMMON STAFFS

Staff of command +6	50
Staff of striking +6	50

UNCOMMON ARMS SLOT ITEM

Gleaming diamond bracers	60

UNCOMMON NECK SLOT ITEMS

Cloak of the shadowthief +6	73
Cloak of the stalking shadow +6	73
Sneak's cloak +6	75

UNCOMMON WONDROUS ITEM

Elven chain shirt	82

UNCOMMON CONSUMABLES (105,000 gp each)

Elixir of giant strength	93
Potion of regeneration	99

COMMON HOLY SYMBOL

Symbol of the sun +6	43

COMMON KI FOCUS

Steadfast stone ki focus +6	44

COMMON NECK SLOT ITEM

Brooch of unerring defense +6	71

Level 30   3,125,000 gp

RARE ARMOR

Gloaming armor +6	Cloth, leather, hide	15
Robe of the archmage +6	Cloth	16

RARE WEAPONS

Flame tongue weapon +6	Heavy blade, light blade	26
Greater dancing weapon +6	Any melee	27
Greater luckblade +6	Heavy blade, light blade	28
Mace of disruption +6	Mace	29
Mighty dwarven thrower +6	Hammer	30
Weapon of speed +6	Any ranged, any thrown	35

RARE HOLY SYMBOL

Necklace of prayer beads +6	42

RARE ORB

Prismatic orb +6	46

RARE ROD

Rod of beguiling +6	48

RARE STAFF

Greater staff of power +6	49

RARE TOME

Emerald tome of the devourer +6	51

RARE TOTEM

Totem of the woodlands +6	54

RARE WAND

Wand of fire +6	55

RARE NECK SLOT ITEMS

Greater medallion of the mind +6	73
Greater necklace of fireballs +6	74

RARE WONDROUS ITEM

Greater flying carpet	85

UNCOMMON ARMOR

Armor of the charging wind +6	Cloth, leather, hide	13
Doppelganger armor +6	Any	14

UNCOMMON AMMUNITION (125,000 gp each)

Firesight ammunition +6	36
Shadowshaft ammunition +6	37
Shiver-strike ammunition +6	37

UNCOMMON TOTEM

Totem of thorns +6	53

UNCOMMON NECK SLOT ITEMS

Amulet of aranea +6	71
Cloak of displacement +6	72
Cloak of the phoenix +6	72
Periapt of wound closure +6	75

UNCOMMON WAIST SLOT ITEM

Diamond cincture	79

UNCOMMON CONSUMABLES (125,000 gp each)

Bead of force	98
Potion of clarity	95
Potion of heal	96
Scroll of protection	101

COMMON CONSUMABLE (125,000 gp each)

Potion of invulnerability	97

GEAR UP YOUR GROUP
AND GET READY TO FIGHT.

Be sure everyone is equipped for action—and improve every encounter—with D&D® accessories. Pick 'em up at the same place you got this book.

D&D® Dungeon Tiles
Define dungeons and add details to every encounter quickly and easily, and help your game come to life.

D&D® Premium Dice
Everyone needs dice. And some need more than others. Keep 'em all in a D&D logo-embroidered dicebag.

Deluxe Dungeon Master's Screen
Conceal your secrets behind this information-filled screen featuring imagination-inspiring artwork by Wayne Reynolds.

D&D Fortune Cards™
Add more excitement to every round and give your character an interesting edge with the challenge of D&D Fortune Cards.

DUNGEONSANDDRAGONS.COM